What men around America are saying about
Stu Weber's first book *Tender Warrior*

"Tender Warrior is a very meaningful and enlightening book for any man to read who is interested in seeking to become a man in the full sense of the word. Stu Weber certainly has captured the dilemma that many men find themselves in in today's society, and outlines strategies for becoming more fully human and also more fully Christ-centered in their lives."

TOM OSBORNE, HEAD FOOTBALL COACH-UNIVERSITY OF NEBRASKA

(NATIONAL CHAMPIONS 1995)

"Tender Warrior is a must read for every man seeking true masculinity, written in a style that is easy to understand and apply. From the viewpoint of a member of the profession of arms, Stu Weber is credible. He has been there and paid his dues. I recommend the book as a manual for a men's accountability group."

ROBERT L. VERNON, ASSISTANT CHIEF OF POLICE

LOS ANGELES, (RET.)

"These are the two most helpful books written for men in the last five years." (*Tender Warrior* and *Real Men Have Feelings Too* by Gary Oliver)

H. NORMAN WRIGHT, BEST SELLING AUTHOR AND NATIONAL SPEAKER

"When Stu Weber wrote *Tender Warrior,* he unintentionally wrote an autobiography. Never have I read a book which has more credibility in terms of the author's own life. In a day when our culture is at once confused and concerned over gender identity, men everywhere would do well to recalibrate their personal compasses by the Biblical benchmarks found in *Tender Warrior.* I highly recommend this book!"

DR. BRUCE H. WILKINSON, PRESIDENT AND FOUNDER

WALK THRU THE BIBLE MINISTRIES

"This is a book of encouragement. In a day where the meaning of the word loyalty has been lost, Stu Weber reminds us as men, especially in chapter four, to exercise staying power."

COACH BOBBY BOWDEN, FLORIDA STATE FOOTBALL

(NATIONAL CHAMPIONS-1994)

"Weber is particularly good at showing how times of tension are potential learning experiences that can either be grasped or unwittingly passed by. Weber demonstrates a keen ability to weave a tale and turn a phrase."

BOOKSTORE JOURNAL

"Just when we need it most, just when the battle for the hearts of men and their families is most intense, in God's perfect timing, comes Stu Weber's *Tender Warrior*. This is a book which both tiptoes into your consciousness and your conscience, and thunders in with powerful impact. It is a book that every man and all those who love men should read."

BOB BRINER, PROSERV TELEVISION-PRESIDENT
AUTHOR OF *ROARING LAMBS*

"I was handed this book by a friend and I found it so inspiring that I shared it with several of my closest friends. In professional football where emotion is a key ingredient to success I found this book to be a true source of inspiration. Stu Weber shows men how they can be strong individuals by standing together as warriors in God. His *Tender Warrior* shows how we can be men off the field as well as on."

KEN RUETTGERS, LEFT TACKLE-GREEN BAY PACKERS (#75)

"*Tender Warrior* provides hope for men by challenging their assumptions and shaping their convictions. Read it. Devour it. Then live it. This is the time for real men to emerge."

DENNIS RAINEY, FAMILY LIFE-NATIONAL DIRECTOR

"Stu Weber challenges us to be the men which God intended. For the sake of our wives, our children, and our nation, I hope that every American male will read and heed this memorable book."

DAN COATES, UNITED STATES SENATOR, INDIANA

LOCKING ARMS

LOCKING ARMS

God's Design for Masculine Friendships

Stu Weber

Multnomah Books

LOCKING ARMS
published by Multnomah Books
a part of the Questar publishing family

© 1995 by Stu Weber
International Standard Book Number: 0-88070-722-4

Edited by Larry R. Libby

Cover design by David Uttley and David Carlson

Printed in the United States of America.

For information:
QUESTAR PUBLISHERS, INC.
POST OFFICE BOX 1720
SISTERS, OREGON 97759

Library of Congress Cataloging-in-Publication Data
Weber, Stu.
    Locking arms: God's intention for masculine friendship/Stu Weber.
        p.   cm.
    ISBN 0-88070-722-4: $17.99
    1. Men--Religious life. 2. Friendship--Religious aspects--Christianity. I. Title.
BV4528.2.W43   94-42207
248.8'42--dc20   CIP

95 96 97 98 99 00 01 02 — 10 9 8 7 6 5 4 3 2

Dedication

To

OWEN RAYNOR
1942-1987
Gentle, Faithful, Strong

and

To my friend of many years,

JOHN HOLMLUND
who, like his namesake,
is being transformed
from a son of thunder
to a son of God...

and

to all those other good men out there
looking to join the fraternity of

TENDER WARRIORS.

CONTENTS

ACKNOWLEDGMENTS

Three families of friends have provided the impetus for this book—

> My own family of six—best friends for life
> thanks Linda, Kent, Ryan, Blake, and Jami Lyn

> My church family—soul-mates at Good Shepherd
> determined to be "learning together to live like Christ"

> My family at Questar—"partners" in the Kingdom Cause—
> too many names to note here, but bright faces every
> one. You define "team"!

And special thanks to three great man-friends on staff at Good Shepherd Community Church: Denny Deveny, Pastor of Counseling Ministries, fellow elder, and personal friend whose counsel shaped the heart of chapters 8 and 9 dealing with the milestones of friendship; Barry Arnold, Pastor of Global Outreach and Ministry to Men, whose insights and skills clearly strengthened key sections of this book; and Steve Tucker, Church Administrator, who stepped beside me to help meet the deadlines in timely fashion. Thanks, guys. I love being on the team with you and calling you my friends.

And extra special thanks to Larry Libby. You truly are the best editor/friend an author could have. I mean it! Thanks for locking arms with me.

Stu Weber
Portland, Oregon

What Old Men Remember

Together Is Better

"There was a man all alone; he had neither son nor brother.
There was no end to his toil."
ECCLESIASTES 4:8, NIV

ow far did we run that day? I'll never know. After so many hills, after so many miles, after so many turns through scrub brush and stands of scrawny pine, we became mindless running machines, lifting one foot after another after another after another.

All started well enough. The cadence was right. We were young. We were strong. We were soldiers. It was even exhilarating in a funny kind of way. The troops moved well. We found our rhythm. But the sun flamed ever higher in a brassy sky, the packs bit into our shoulders, our rifles grew heavier by the mile, and the dirt trail stretched endlessly on.

We'd been running every day, but this was something else. We'd been sweating from the time we rolled out of the rack before daybreak, but now moisture drained from every pore in our bodies. Sure, this was the physical training stage of U.S. Army Ranger school, and we expected exertion. Even exhaustion. But this was no morning PT rah-rah run in T-shirts.

This was something out of a nightmare.

We ran in full field uniform. Loaded packs. Helmets. Boots. Rifles. The works. As usual, the word was "You go out together, you stick together, you work as a unit, and you *come in together*. If you don't come in together, don't bother to come in!"

For a boy from the apple country of Washington state, the south Georgia heat felt like a soggy wool poncho draped over the top of my fatigues. The sun seared down on our helmets, burned into the metal on our nearly obsolete M-14s, drove hot needles in the exposed skin at the back of our necks. We ran through rolling country, kicking up clouds of powdery dust that stung our eyes and coated our throats.

Somewhere along the way, through a fog of pain, thirst, and fatigue, my brain registered something strange about our formation. Two rows ahead of me, I noticed one of the guys out of sync. A big, rawboned red-head named Sanderson. His legs were pumping, but he was out of step with the rest of us. Then his head began to loll from side to side. This guy was struggling. Close to losing it. Had anyone else noticed?

Yes, someone had.

Without missing a step, the Ranger on Sanderson's right reached over and took the distressed man's rifle. Now one of the Rangers was packing two weapons. His own and Sanderson's. The big redhead did better for awhile. The platoon kept moving, jaws slack, eyes glazed, legs pushing like pistons. But then the head began to sway again.

This time, the Ranger on the left reached over, removed Sanderson's helmet, tucked it under his own arm, and continued to run. All systems go. Our boots thudded along the dirt trail in heavy unison. Tromp-tromp-tromp-tromp-tromp-tromp.

Sanderson was hurting. Really hurting. He was buckling, going down. But no. Two soldiers behind him lifted the pack off his back, each taking a shoulder strap in his free hand. Sanderson gathered his remaining strength. Squared his shoulders. And the platoon continued to run. All the way to the finish line.

We left together. We returned together. And all of us were the stronger for it.

Together is better.

The fact is, there was no such thing as "lone rangers" in Ranger school. If we fell, we'd fall together. If we survived...it was because we locked arms.

Life gets heavy sometimes, doesn't it? The road stretches out there, on and on, and not all the surprises around each bend are good ones. It isn't easy being a man today. It isn't easy being the husband and dad God calls us to be in this rapidly unraveling culture. We give it a shot, and we find our rhythm for awhile, but sometimes the load of responsibility bites into our shoulders, and the race wears us down. Sometimes it all seems beyond endurance. We feel our knees begin to buckle and we fear falling short...a long, long way from the finish line.

Headship is a significant responsibility. Leadership is a weighty challenge. Masculinity is no small assignment. And that brings us to the point of this book. I am convinced in this day of confusion that the path to full-orbed masculinity winds through the doorway of friendship—man-to-man.

When God said, "It is not good that man should be alone," He wasn't kidding. And I think He had a lot more in mind than just marriage, good that it is. It was a comprehensive statement of principle. We men grow well in the company of men. Alone is hell, and men weren't made for it.

Yes, we would and should be willing to die for our wives and kids. They're our bone and flesh. But we long for someone to die *with*. A friend, a fellow soldier, a brother. A man can and must carry the weights of marriage and family responsibility. But he's a lot more effective at it when he walks beside at least one man friend with equally broad shoulders accustomed to bearing similar loads.

There is a richness to be savored in masculine friendships...like a hearty meal cooked over a red campfire in an iron skillet, and eaten by two hungry men as the stars come out. Friendship, man-to-man, is something special. Hard to describe, but golden to experience. Difficult to define, but as much a part of a man as fingers on the hand. The presence of friendship—or its absence—will mark our days until we make our exit from this planet.

What is it, after all, that old men remember? When old men sit on their front porches and reflect on a life sped by, what landmarks rise up out of memory to mark the passing of years? What events loom out of the misty blur of time run together? Many times, they are memories forged when men stood shoulder to shoulder and faced toil, hardship, long odds, and danger…together.

Not long ago, I officiated at the funeral of a well-known businessman in our area. He had founded and built an enormously successful construction company—one of the giants in the region. Hospitals and shopping centers bearing his signature dot the landscape. But unlike some who attain to this man's stature, business wasn't "everything." Family and country held title to vast tracts of his heart. After spending portions of several days with his family and friends prior to the service, I found myself wishing I'd known him. He'd impacted people. He'd left big tracks.

He was a doer, well known for his love of competition and salesmanship. Gifted with a photographic memory, his mind for engineering was brilliant. But he never lost his blue-collar heart…a love for physical labor, sweat, and working out in the weather. He had made his fortune the old fashioned way.

And how he loved the red, white, and blue! He had served in World War II, fighting off kamikaze pilots in the Pacific, and returned to the service a few years later for more fighting in Korea.

Most notably, the man had a tender center. He was generous to a fault. But, his friends told me, you never wanted to mistake that kindness for weakness. He simply would not tolerate negative words about his family or his flag.

The funeral home auditorium was packed. Six honorary pall bearers sat in the front row. They were senior men, heavy hitters, men of accomplishment in their own right. Two of them in particular caught my attention. One had eyes that reached out and grabbed you—deep pools that flashed beneath heavy brows. Another was a big man, 6'5" and 250 pounds, unusually powerful for his age. But for all his size and strength, his face was not hard. He was thinking about something.

In keeping with the spirit of the man remembered, the service had elements of both lightness and deep reflection. Remembered humor and a sobering sense of loss. Men like this come along only now and then. At the front and center was a gold metal plaque bearing his likeness and, beneath it, his country's flag—Old Glory—folded in a neat triangle.

At the conclusion of the service, the honorary pall bearers stood, removed their boutonnieres, and filed by the likeness of their friend. One by one they approached, turned, and departed out the side aisle before the gathered company. The third man was the one with the powerful eyes. Before the picture and flag, he stopped. Just for a second. Humbly, with an obvious desire not to attract attention, those eyes looked into the likeness of his friend. It seemed like time stopped. Slowly, altogether without fanfare, his right hand rose to his brow in a precise, military salute. My heart leapt inside my chest. I nearly came out of my chair! What a gesture to his friend! One old warrior to his fallen comrade. Neither had likely saluted in years. But it all came back...right to the surface. No one in the little auditorium that day will forget it.

The fifth pall bearer was the big man. He approached, hesitated, turned, took three steps...and there in front of hundreds of people, this giant of a man could hold back no longer. A sob exploded from his chest. It was not prolonged. Only a single contorted gasp. But it spoke loud and clear. *This was my friend. I will never be the same.*

What was running through each of those men's minds and hearts as they stood before the memory of their friend? Afterward, I worked my way across the room to the man with the steel eyes and sharp salute. Who was this intriguing man? I introduced myself and asked about their relationship. They were friends, to be sure...and more. They were partners. Fellow soldiers. They had stood shoulder to shoulder for half a lifetime.

His words were simple and few—but they packed a lot of freight.

"We were in business together for over thirty years," he told me. "Thick and thin!" His eyes seemed to lose focus for a moment. He was looking back on a long, winding road. He was seeing again the ups and downs…the good times and bad times…the lean days and the gravy days. No one had handed these men anything. They'd built it all together. Then the eyes focused again, and he said softly, "He ran the field. I ran the office."

It was a mouthful. Thirty years distilled into eight words. *What was it like? We partnered, we maximized one another's strengths, and we covered one another's weaknesses. He did his part, I did mine, and we pulled that old wagon together.*

I stood in the courtyard, following the service, at the edge of the circle of friends. Two of them lit cigarettes. I listened.

What do senior men, uncomfortable in old sport jackets and ties, talk about outside a funeral parlor? What do they remember when one of their own moves on?

What do old men recall, sitting on the park bench in the morning sun, or out on the front porch at twilight? What memories dance in the embers when old-timers lean forward and stir the fire? What stands out?

They remember laboring side by side. Rugged days on tough jobs. Crisis times when one friend inspired the other. Toiling in the fields together at harvest, racing against an early fall. Enduring cold rain and wet brush on the steep flanks of a mist-shrouded mountain. Coaxing a balky truck on a long, weary run across seven states. Chasing a man-killer deadline until four in the morning, then going out for ham and eggs at an all-night diner. Battling to the edge of physical endurance on a deadly fireline in a narrow, tinder-dry canyon. Clawing back to port in a frail fishing boat in the teeth of a sudden Nor'easter. Breaking through a difficult engineering puzzle in the design and construction of a towering new building. Throwing together an impromptu sales presentation for a tough client at the last possible minute—and closing the deal against all odds. Searching the hills and draws with flashlights and lanterns on a raw March night for little lambs dropped into a hard, unforgiving world.

They remember war, and fighting together. Memories of two men crouching in a fox-hole on a shell-torn jungle island. Or the "pom-pom-pom-pom" of deck guns warding off kamikazes. Or jumping into waist-deep water off Omaha Beach, not expecting to live out the hour. Or clinging to a thin line of sanity in the chaos and terror of an engine room below decks on a great carrier under attack.

Ask an old man what he remembers about a life gone by. What will he tell you? Catch him just right—in a strong moment of reality—and *he'll tell you of someone who stepped into his life in an hour of deep trial and pain.* He'll tell you about the time the moving van rolled up to the door, and only one man with a bad back and a wide, familiar grin showed up to help. And then he'll tell you about that man. He'll tell you about the day his dad had a heart attack, and a friend at work wrapped an arm around his shoulder and said, "You get outa here. Jump in your car and go. I'll write your reports." He'll tell about not finding work and being too ashamed to ask for help, and the friend who came along and said, "Here's a stake to see you through. Pay me back when you get situated." In his more candid moments, he might tell you about the time he'd failed so miserably he felt like no one could ever like him again—let alone love him—and one friend who did both.

What makes old men smile as they sift through yellowed snapshots of days gone by?

It's the crazy things they did together. When two men tried to haul a bull elk out of a deep canyon. When a dad and son rode their Harleys through a driving thundershower, laughing in the rain. When two buddies hopped a freight train and got booted off at two in the morning on the backside of nowhere. When two golf partners shot the absolute worst round of their lives—on the same day—and could still laugh about it in the old clubhouse.

Men who make it to old age with a battered carpet bag stuffed with memories are the fortunate ones. Pity the souls who shuffle into the twilight with no store of shared laughter, divided burdens, mutual dangers, and two-handled dreams.

It's friendship that plays the music, pours the coffee, and opens the windows on this bus ride through life. Sure, you could live without it but…why should you?

Listen…

"The soul of Jonathan was knit to the soul of David, and Jonathan loved him as himself."

Wow, we say. Wish I had a buddy like that. These two men relished the kind of lifelong friendship we all thirst for. Oh, we tease—somewhat awkwardly—about "male bonding," but down deep it isn't a joking matter. We all long for a buddy, a man-friend, who will go to the wall with us. Every soldier needs his Ranger buddy. Every fighter pilot his wing man. And every man needs his man-friend.

God gives us at least three growth-agents to get us through our three-score and ten in this old world: His Word, His Spirit, and His Body. And when we are most confused, when life presses in on us the hardest, it is often His Body—"God with skin on"—the touch of a friend—that is most effective in picking us up, dusting us off, and setting us back on course. Men need men in order to set masculinity back on its original and magnificent God-designed course.

Men learn to be men by standing close to men, by watching men, by enjoying brotherly *espirit*…by locking arms. Someone has said, "Passing the torch of manhood is a fragile task." I believe that task is best accomplished in the mysterious, sometimes awkward, but always soul-shaping throes of great friendships.

This is a book about that kind of friendship. It's not another finger-pointing, guilt-laden "you-need-a-friend" kind of message. Most of us know that all too well. It is more. This is a book about an unusual and powerful dynamic that takes place when two or three men lock arms and spirits in long-term friendship.

Masculine friendship is not just one more option to be added to an already impossible list of responsibilities. It is the *means* to accomplish

SNAPSHOTS:
MY FRIENDS TELL THEIR STORIES

I was a 25-year-old seminary student trying to sort through the meaning of ministry in a world without heroes. He was a 65-year-old construction superintendent, and former police chief, security chief, base commander, and decorated veteran of two wars. He was an army engineer who had built harbors and airstrips from Normandy to Berlin, roads and bridges across Korea, and survived multiple surgeries which had weakened his once powerful body. He was, to me, a tangible hero.

Every time we met, over every cup of java, I asked questions. And then just listened. Questions about men. About values. About judgment. As winter gave way to spring, he shared his stories and I worked hard to earn his respect. For he and his wife had been spurned by their small town church because of her alcoholism. And though he was the son and grandson of Baptist preachers, he had not been to church in many years.

One morning as we finished our coffee, he got quiet, lit his pipe, and just looked at me for a moment. "I've told my family I may not make it through this next surgery," he said. "And if I don't, I've told them I want you to do my funeral. You're an honorable young man and I'm proud to know you."

My friend survived. And because of our friendship I think some reconciliation took place in his family. I believe there is great value in listening to an older man tell his tale without hastening judgment on his life.

that list. Masculine friendship is not just a convenience like a warm sweater that could be "comfortable" on a day when you could probably get along without one. It's more than that. It promises an out-of-the-ordinary release of God's power.

Just imagine a large car stuck in the sand. When one man puts his back and leg strength against the rear end of the car, nothing happens. Two men might rock it forward a little. But three men pushing together feel the weight yield, and the tires claw out of the hole. Three men get the car out of the ditch and back on the road. Some of us have been straining against immovable problems and dug-in frustrations for a long time. Every day we push and shove, grit our teeth and dig in our heels, but the mass doesn't budge. Nothing seems to change. Could it be that our good God might be *allowing* these very kinds of situations in our lives to help us learn an elemental truth? Some loads need more than a lone man's strength. Some problems won't budge until two or three friends put their shoulders into it.

Together. God's way, every time.

How can a man learn to be a man, a husband, a father, a provider and protector—a full-orbed King, Warrior, Mentor, and Friend? By walking with other men who are doing it. You learn to play ball by playing ball. And masculinity is a team sport. You and I, as men living in a tragically disoriented culture, need to experience the life-building power of what Paul called a "brother, fellow-worker, fellow-soldier." It is time we heed the call of the High King to His High Communion. It is time God's men come to His table in the Round and, in the company of men, drink deeply of a fresh understanding of His Kingdom and just what it takes to enjoy a man's role in it.

Get ready to watch your biggest worries and most intractable problems finally roll out of the sand. Once you've locked arms with a brother or two, you'll never look at obstacles the same way again.

Stick with me, fellow soldier. You'll see what I mean.

1. Both the Old and New Testaments make it clear that we, as men, are accountable for more than just ourselves. God holds us accountable for our mates and children as well. Do you take that seriously? Do you lead? Do you lead with confidence and compassion—or more with noise and bluster? Does your family really *want* to follow you?

2. It's said that to have a friend, you must *be* a friend. Who is it out there who needs you as a friend right now? (We're seldom effective at something without putting any effort into it. Don't be surprised if you find you have to *think* for awhile about this business of finding and becoming a real friend.)

LOCKING ARMS

1. What is it that old men remember?

2. Are you building memories with friends who've locked arms with you? Do you have such buddies? What do you appreciate most about them?

3. When we consider the Hollywood image of virile American manhood, we generally think of the strong, silent, self-sufficient type who needs no friends or relationships—a real Lone Ranger. But in reality, most are more like lonely rangers. Do you feel lonely for a buddy you know you can always call on? When do you feel it most?

4. "Masculine friendship," this chapter tells us, "is not just one more option to be added to an already impossible list of responsibilities. It is the means to accomplish that list." What does that statement mean to you?

5. "Some loads need more than a lone man's strength." Excluding obvious life crises for the moment, what might those "loads" be? Are you aware of anyone in one of those "heavy" situations right now that you or your group might befriend?

6. Has someone shown true friendship to you recently? We men sometimes feel the appreciation, but struggle to express it. Do you need to express to this man-friend just how much he's meant to you? How could you do that? When will you do that?

CHAPTER TWO

A Tale of Three Amigos

A Bond Forged in Need

"A friend loves at all times, and a brother is born for adversity."
PROVERBS 17:17

I'm thinking right now about two of my closest friends.
The two of them met in high school; I came along a few years later. Here were two fast friends. They loved each other. Trusted each other. It was all for one and one for all. More than anything else, I wanted in that fraternity. And they admitted me.

I'm thinking right now about the last time the three of us were together.

After years of friendship, raising families, joint vacations, special holidays, hunting trips, dinners, and telephone conversations, we were together again. The three amigos.

It was on a hilltop in Eastern Oregon on the opening morning of deer season. As we had many times before, the three of us and our sons were hunting together. Like we *never* had before, that little band of fathers and sons stood in a silent circle among the pines and junipers, our hats in our hands, our hearts in our throats. As the sun crested the hills, we watched John working feverishly—desperately—to pump life back into Owen's body.

But CPR couldn't avail. Owen was already gone, struck down with a massive heart attack. Our friend died in our presence, still in his early forties. The fraternity was testing its metal—albeit in an unexpected and unwanted way—but the "knit" was taking on a new dimension. And now heaven holds an even richer anticipation for the two of us left behind.

How did such a priceless, lifelong bond begin? Simply enough. It wasn't always so deep. But it grew. From a momentary encounter to a full-blown friendship, out of all proportion to its humble beginning. Yet in another sense, it began just like it ended (for the time being, this side of heaven), in a moment of need, pain, and confusion.

A FRIENDSHIP BORN IN NEED

Friendships are born, enriched, and deepened in moments of need and vulnerability. When resources are depleted. When the fires of courage burn low. When the slats have been kicked out of a man's long-held dreams. Friendships that sprout from that sort of soil are the kind that endure through the years. Like a deep-rooted oak, weathering a thousand storms, growing stronger by the day.

John and Owen had met twenty-five years before as fuzzy-chinned high school boys. John had just scrimped, slaved, and saved to purchase that icon of masculinity, his first set of wheels. She was a '52 Ford with a flathead V-8. You can imagine—he'd had his eye on her for weeks, steeling himself to bargain with the dealer. He finally strolled onto the lot, trying so hard to look casual, the hard-won cash burning in his hip pocket. One look at John and the salesman would likely have felt smugly secure holding to the sticker price. Desire flamed in the boy's eyes. Made his hands tremble. There was no way this kid was going to walk.

And he didn't. He drove that classic beauty off the lot with an empty wallet and a heart bursting with pride. What he couldn't have known was that he'd just been set up by a crooked dealer. He hadn't had the car for twenty-four hours before it blew a rod.

Moments after it happened, John sat on the curb beside the road, head in hands, the picture of dejection. His beloved Ford's hood yawned wide, and the young man's spirit sagged into his shoes. John's prospects looked bleak indeed. He had no money, no mechanical skills, and didn't even know anybody with the inclination—let alone the expertise—to help him. He was humiliated, heartbroken, and angry, as only an adolescent boy can experience those emotions.

Then Owen came along, three years older and a whole lot wiser in the ways of these chariots. They really hadn't known one another at all before those moments by the disabled Ford.

"No problem, John," said Owen with a twinkle in his blue eyes. "We'll just *fix* it."

Owen had just rebuilt his own Ford, and knew what to do. He even had an extra crankshaft and pistons sitting in the garage at home. They towed the wounded '52 back to John's driveway, and that very day they pulled the engine. Together. A friendship had begun that would last a lifetime—and beyond. It was a friendship that would touch other lives (like mine), and eventually effect wives, children, churches, communities, and generations.

And where had it begun?

At a time of lowered defenses.

At a crossroads of need.

At a moment when one young man glanced through his window, made a quick decision, signaled a turn, applied his brakes, and willingly entered another young man's broken heart and world.

John and Owen. Evenings and weekends. Together for weeks. Crawling under that beast, busting knuckles, groaning and laughing, cranking up the radio, drinking Cokes, matching rods and pistons. Finally she was reassembled. They fired her up, *and the engine froze.*

Yes, but the friendship was warming up. The two boys looked at each other, shrugged their shoulders, and went at it again with fresh determination. They tore it apart and put it back together. Pan, oil, plugs. Ratchets and crescents. Then, when they had her sewed up, they held their breath, hit the ignition again, and—*Eureka!*

That friendship, springing from an hour of extremity, flowed through a lifetime of shared passions. John introduced Owen to motorcycles. Owen introduced John to airplanes. The two of them introduced me to both. It was grand.

John summed it all up in a brief word at Owen's funeral service.

"He was a servant," he said, "and he was my friend."

And that's how meaningful friendships start, don't they? Serving one another. Helping the other guy out. Taking an interest. Reaching out a hand. Getting down and dirty in the trenches where life sometimes "blows a rod." What would have happened if Owen had driven right by the dejected teenager sitting on the curb by his disabled car in his great moment of disappointment and grief? *Nothing* would have happened. No mutual dividing of pain. No comfort. No laughter. No joy. No companionable silences. No shared experiences down through the months and long years. No heightened anticipation of reunion beyond the limits of life itself.

But Owen didn't miss the moment. And that moment touched eternity.

The application, I suppose, is pretty simple. Reach out in your need! And reach to other men in theirs. Let the heat and pressure of your troubles drive you right into friendship.

Thinking about "heat" reminds me of someone who recently tried to get me enthusiastic about a process called "cold welding." It seems that there's a kind of goop you can smear on two pieces of metal, leave overnight, and it will produce a "weld" roughly equivalent to a true weld. My source told me you could beat it with a hammer and it won't fall apart.

Well, maybe. I guess it could come in handy if you wanted to patch a shovel or jury-rig a pair of hedge shears, but would you trust your life to an airplane welded by cold goop?

Not this boy. I want to see a weld where two pieces of metal are *fused* by the incredible blue-white heat of an electric arc or the searing flame of a gas torch. It takes heat to fuse metal. And the best friendships are fused by the heat and urgency of adversity.

You say, "Man, I wish I had a friendship like that." But down in your heart you think that maybe you don't have what it takes. Yes, you do. You do have what it takes. You have *need.* A hurt. A struggle. A

SNAPSHOTS:
MY FRIENDS TELL THEIR STORIES

I was already in a major depression. Then I got nailed with this intestinal stuff I'm predisposed towards, and just sat home staring at the walls. Feeling totally alone. Crying by the hour. Just numb.

I would get up at about 2:00 p.m. every day, eat a little, stay up until about 7:00 p.m., and then go back to bed and sleep until noon or later the next day. My wife was a great support, really strong, always there.

One day, out of the blue, my two friends called, and asked if they could come visit me. I was terrified at that point, couldn't talk, didn't want to see anybody but my wife. Any little thing set me off crying. Old tapes of "failure, no good, shame, abandoned, worthless, going to end up in the gutter just like your dad" kept running through my head, taking me further down.

My buddies showed up. They just sat down and said, "We care. We don't understand why this is happening, it doesn't make any sense to us, but we care." Then one of them said, "I've gone through something similar. The pain gets intense, doesn't it? No matter what happens, I value our friendship, and will help in any way I can. It's okay to cry! If I could take some of the pain, I would. We'll carry some of it for you, okay?"

pain. An empty place. A weight biting into your shoulders. And maybe—just maybe—you have the guts to take the risk and be vulnerable to someone else. A gritty determination to follow that need of yours right into a friendship.

Stay at it, man. There's another guy out there. And he's looking for you. But you have to take your heart in your hand…and reach out.

Just like Jonathan reached out to David. The young prince of Israel admired the son of Jesse in the shepherd boy's shining moment of conquest and glory. But their hearts were welded through the long days of shared danger, risk, and pain, when, as David put it, "There is hardly a step between me and death" (1 Samuel 20:3).

Ponder David's words to Jonathan after his friend's death on the bloody slopes of Mount Gilboa. They are words from deep down inside one soul struggling to project themselves through the very wall of death to link with the soul brother.

> How have the mighty fallen in the midst of battle!
> Jonathan is slain on your high places.
> I am distressed for you, my brother Jonathan;
> You have been very pleasant to me.
> Your love to me was more wonderful than the love of women
> (2 Samuel 1:25-26).

There…David said it. Said it for us all. Yes, the love of a man for his lady is incredibly rich. There is nothing on earth like it. Still…there is a quality in masculine friendship that is reserved for fraternity. Man to man. Brother to brother. Shoulder to shoulder. There is something there that defies description. Some kind of bond, some kind of soul-knit, some magnificent element that is "sensed," read more in the white spaces than the words themselves. Only those who have sat at the round table, among equals, committed to the cause at any cost, can taste it.

C. S. Lewis did.

In a perfect Friendship—when the whole group is together, each bringing out all that is best, wisest, or funniest in all the others. Those are the golden sessions; when four or five of us after a hard day's walking have come to our inn; when our feet are spread out toward the blaze and our drinks are at our elbows; when the whole world, and something beyond the world, opens itself to our minds as we talk; and no one has any claim on…another, but all are freemen and equals as if we had first met an hour ago, while at the same time an Affection mellowed by the years enfolds us. Life—natural life—has no better gift to give. Who could have deserved it?[1]

Does that make you hunger for that kind of friendship? You were *made* for that kind of friendship. It's just that we so rarely experience it in this broken world. Friendship is natural life's best gift. Warm, committed, down in the bedrock, I'll-go-to-the-wall-with-you friendship.

Remember "Lonesome Dove," television's blockbuster miniseries? It was the saga of two men, Woodrow Call and Gus McCray. Both strong. Stronger together. Men with a rock solid commitment to each other. To be sure, both were stubborn eccentrics. They called each other into question regularly, but they never questioned the friendship. They knew, at the soul level, the one would gladly die for the other. They'd ride through any storm for each other. Come hell or high water. "Ah giv' him mah word," became the bottom line of the relationship. And a big chunk of America watched—fascinated, tainted perhaps with cynical disbelief, but touched with unspoken longing—as Woodrow Call dragged the body of Gus McCray three thousand miles to bury him "'neath the pecan trees at the picnic place 'cause…Ah giv' him mah word." Period.

America may have questioned it. Jacob wouldn't have. Seems to me I recall the old patriarch asking his son to swear he'd carry his bones back over the long miles to bury him at home "with my fathers." And

Joseph did it without flinching. Even though it took an act of Congress (okay, Pharaoh) to do it (see Genesis 47:29-31, 50:1-14). There's something to it, isn't there? There was something between two men who understood each other. And others stood around in awe, watching one man move a whole community, "a very great company," just to fill out a relationship.

Joseph might have been heard to declare in Western Hebrew, "Ah giv' him mah word."

I find myself longing for that kind of commitment in a friendship. To give it and receive it. Don't you?

AS THE WILD GOOSE FLIES

As I write these words I'm seated at the table of a cozy cabin at the edge of the Eagle Cap Wilderness in Northeastern Oregon. Moments ago, some Canadian geese flew by the window. Majestic, graceful, powerful "honkers" making their way up Bear Creek Canyon, on their way to…somewhere. The Creator outdid Himself in this neck of the woods. And here, as in every place that His image is clear, together is better.

I love the seasons here. Spring, summer, fall, winter. Each paints its mural with colors and fragrance and textures from its own distinctive palette. But I have to plead favoritism when it comes to fall. Each fall the weather shifts. You can smell it in the air. The wind picks up. The temperature drops. And the wild goose answers some compelling call to take to the skies.

Goose hunting has a special anticipation all its own. So every October a father, a friend, and a couple of our sons head for the Deschutes River to meet that goose. Actually, *geese*. Hundreds, even thousands of geese moving south down the Pacific flyway as they have for centuries.

Half the fun is in the ritual preparing for the hunt. And the other half of the fun is in the friendship and fellowship—to the point that the hunt becomes almost incidental. Up at 3:15 A.M. (Ouch!) Man this is crazy. Or is it? Headlights pull into the driveway at 3:45. Toss in decoys, shotguns, and lunch. Keep Ol' Zipper, the black Labrador retriever, off the lunches. Sleepy-eyed to the highway. Breakfast down the road at Jake's Diner (do they ever change the oil on that grill?). And to the mouth of the Deschutes well before daylight. Stars twinkle in a crisp, black sky. Cold chills the bones, but hearts are warm and the mile-and-a-half hike will keep the frost at bay. Decoys in the water. Bodies crouching in the blinds. Light breaks. *And here they come…*

It's plenty exciting to watch those big guys settle in for a water landing. But it's an even greater thrill to watch them high, high in the autumn sky, flying in formation. They know what they're doing on these long, transcontinental hauls. How do they fly those kind of distances? In a word, *together.*

Together. It's one of the most powerful words in the English language. And geese know how to use it to full advantage. They seem to know instinctively that life is a team sport.

Wildlife biologists tell us that a flock of geese, by flying in a "V" formation, actually adds at least 71 percent more flying range than if each bird were flying on its own. As each bird flaps its wings, it actually creates an updraft for the bird immediately following. Left to itself, the lone goose experiences a drag and resistance that causes it to long for the flock. When the lead bird in the formation tires, it simply rotates back in the wing and another flies the point.

Draft horses experience a similar, if earthbound, dynamic. Draft horses were made for pulling. Some years ago at a midwestern county fair the champion animal pulled a sled weighted at 4,500 pounds. The second-place animal dragged 4,000 pounds. Then someone proposed harnessing the two big fellas together, to see what they could do as a team. Together, they pulled 12,000 pounds!

So let me ask the obvious. If our feathered friends know it, and the four-footed beasts experience it, why should we be so slow to learn it? Together is better. Especially when hardship presses in. And there's a tough pull ahead.

Some men have caught it. They've reached out toward other men in moments of need and vulnerability. They've taken the risk and grabbed a few friends. And they've changed their world! The power of friendship, the strength of two or more, can make you fly higher and longer, pull bigger loads, and be more of the man you were meant to be.

Men, together, can change our world.

Take Paul the apostle, for example. We think of him as a singular giant of sorts. Indeed, he was a giant. But he was not singular. The man seemed never to go anywhere alone. Paul always walked with a friend. Paul played team ball. If it wasn't Timothy, it was Silas. If not Epaphroditus, then Acquilla and Pricilla. Or Stephanas, Luke, Fortunatus, Achaicus, Epaphras, or John Mark.

These guys loved each other. Paul regarded them as *brothers* who marched beside each other, fought through life together, took risks together, even "came close to death for the work of Christ" together. They held one another in highest regard (see Philippians 2:25-30). And they really *knew* one another, intimately.

Again, C. S. Lewis writes:

One knows nobody so well as one's "fellow." Every step of the common journey tests his metal; and the tests are fully understood because we are undergoing them ourselves...You will not find the warrior, the poet, the philosopher, or the Christian by staring in his eyes—better fight beside him, read with him, argue with him, pray with him...[2]

And that's where you discover true friendship. Right in the push, pull, and stress of life's battles. That's why we all need a man-friend, walking the common journey—marriage, family, profession, character, values. A friend who tests our metal and strengthens us in our callings.

THEY REFUSE TO WALK ALONE

Back to the apostle from Tarsus for a moment. Yes, Paul hated to walk alone. In fact, if I'm reading my Bible right, on one occasion the powerful missionary even backed right out of a highly promising ministry opportunity because he didn't want to go it alone.

It wasn't like the veteran missionary to pass up a wide-open door of ministry, was it? This guy *lived* to bring men and women to Jesus. But he punted the opportunity, because he couldn't find his friend.

What was it, Paul? Loneliness? Discouragement? Exhaustion? Needed a lift? Needed a listening ear? Needed a brother's prayers?

Whatever it was, the mighty apostle backed away. He dropped out of the point like a tired lead goose. He packed his bags and left town. He just couldn't do it. Couldn't handle it. Not just then. Not alone.

You can hear it in his words. And what you can't see in print you can read between the lines.

> Now when I came to Troas for the gospel of Christ and when a door was opened for me in the Lord, I had no rest for my spirit, not finding Titus my brother; but taking my leave of them, I went on to Macedonia (2 Corinthians 2:12-13).

He couldn't find his buddy, so the deal was off. Together is better.

And Jesus was no different, unique as He was, giant that He was. He chose not to walk alone. The Lord insisted on sticking with a group. He started His ministry with a team. "And He appointed twelve, *that they might be with Him*" (Mark 3:14).

Jesus started with a fellowship. A small fraternity. He wanted those guys to learn to live together. Before they could preach, they had to "be with" Him and one another. And when He did finally send them out, He insisted they go at least "two by two." You don't need a bag, He told them. You don't need luggage, or an American Express Card, or an extra pair of socks. But you *do* need a companion. Don't go unless you go with someone else. You go out together and you come in together.

Jesus started that way, and finished that way, too. When the God-man concluded His earthly ministry, it was with the fraternity. On His last night with the guys, I think it nearly broke His heart that they were struggling to hang in there with Him. These were big moments. He was going to the wall. And He wanted His friends to go with Him. When the pressure's on, a guy wants his soulmates standing beside him. At the start. At the finish. And at the sometimes heartbreaking in-betweens.

Jesus didn't want to go it alone. I often wonder—maybe the reason angels came to minister to Him in some of the tough spots was because none of His men were there.

The Lord wanted His friends, especially the big fisherman, there at the end. And He said so. Straight forward. To Peter, "Simon, are you asleep? Couldn't you keep watch for just an hour?" *Couldn't you hang in there with Me, Peter, on this night above all nights? Couldn't you give Me a shoulder to lean on a little? Couldn't you be with Me, My friend? Just to know you're hard at it with me would mean alot.*

Just a few hours prior to those dark moments in the garden, He had called His fellowship of rusty knights together around the table. In words freighted with emotion, He said, "I have earnestly desired to eat this Passover [meal] with you before I suffer" (Luke 22:15).

Imagine it. Glancing around the table at His men-friends, He let His eyes meet theirs, one at a time "with an Affection mellowed by the years." Then He went a step further, saying, "And I will never eat it again until it is fulfilled in the kingdom."

You guys mean the world to me. So much so, I'm not going to do this again until we're together again. In the Real World. In My Father's house.

Jesus' relationship with His friends meant so much to Him that He determined to deny Himself history's most meaningful meal-celebration (intended to be "celebrated unto all generations") until they could all be there together again. Significant! Jesus knew together is better. Jesus was a man, a man's man, and He didn't like "alone."

In fact, the worst moments of His life were those alone moments. While He hung on the cross, even His Father left Him alone for a time. It was hell.

To walk alone is hell. Men weren't made for it.

THE NAME OF THE GAME

With three boys at home, Linda and I have spent most of our adult lives either buying groceries or attending sporting events. Some time ago Lindy, just for fun, added up the number of the boys' actual organized athletic games we've watched over the years. She came up with at least 1,800. They've played them all—T-ball, soccer, tennis, football, basketball. (No wonder I'm tired!)

Our favorite team sport has been basketball. It's such a comprehensive game. The variety of its demands on the athlete are incredible—speed, hand-eye coordination, strength, quickness, finesse, power, touch, and intense mental concentration—it's all there. But most important to basketball is *teamwork.*

Teamwork is the name of the game. All five athletes, all totally involved, all the time. No coasting while another carries the ball. No relaxing while another decides what to do next. Never a dull moment. Up—all the time. Intensity, intensity, intensity. Adrenaline is the dominant body fluid. Move with the ball. Move without the ball. Fill the lanes. Clear the boards. Move, move, move, all the time. Keep anticipating. Keep the rhythm. Stay alert. *Stay together.* TOGETHER. Basketball is the consummate team sport.

So is life. So is masculinity. It's not wise to fly solo...nor is it much fun. And playing together takes practice. A lot of practice.

How about you? Could you name your teammates? Who is the man beside you? Who's filling the lane next to yours? Do you have a friend? One who knows how to play to your strengths and cover your blind spots? One who knows your weaknesses, habits, and tendencies? One who cares for your soul? One who would go to the wall with you?

Let's get on with it. Let's learn just how we can find some friends, lock arms, and rediscover the power of masculine friendship. We can do it. Right here. Right now. Even in a culture turned inside out and upside down in its confusion and despair. Sure, we're a bit out of practice. We men have sort of been "benched" for the last twenty-five years or so. But with some practice, we can knock the rust off our armor and get back in the battle stronger than ever.

Yes, seeking solid friendship is risky. Most everything in life of any value is risky. You never know what might happen when you reach out. You might be hurt. You might be ignored, rebuffed, or rejected. Then again, you might find that the guy sitting on the curb by a stalled Ford will someday be fighting for *your* life on a distant hilltop in the first light of dawn.

Once linked by risk and adversity, brothers tend to be there when it really counts.

1. Jot down the names of your boyhood best friends. Now, next to that list, write down the names of your adult best friends. Which list is longer? Which list was easier to complete? Try to put your finger on why that might be.

2. The best friendships are not those based on competition or sameness—nor those that are consistently "one-sided." The best friendships are often ones where men share common values and where they allow the strengths of one to complement the strengths of the other—providing what the other lacks. What kind of a friend do you need?

LOCKING ARMS

1. The best friendships are often born when someone steps forward to help another in need. Did someone ever step forward to help you bear a load too heavy? If it hadn't been for that individual's willingness to "be there" for you, how might your life have been different?

2. In this chapter we're told to "reach out in your need" and "reach out to others in theirs." Are you doing that? If not, what is it that really holds you back?

3. "Together is better. Especially when hardship presses in. That's why we need a man-friend, walking the common journey—marriage, family, profession, character, values." Why another man? Why not your wife?

4. In Mark 6, Jesus sent out His disciples telling them not to take anything for the journey—no bread, no bag, no money, not even an extra tunic. But He did tell them to go out in pairs. Why? In what sense have many of us reversed that order of priority in our own lives?

5. "To walk alone is hell. Men weren't made for it." When it comes right down to it, day to day, are you trying to walk alone? Why?

CHAPTER THREE

Rusty Knights in a Hostile Land

It's Not Easy Being a Man Today

"Harness the horses, mount the steeds! Take your positions with helmets on!
Polish your spears, put on your armor!"
JEREMIAH 46:4, NIV

He came riding out of the west, a red and setting sun at his back.

For a moment, his form merged with the stream of crimson light flowing into a small clearing through a gap in the dense forest. As horse and rider took shape in the gathering twilight, the man in the clearing saw that the horseman was a knight, covered head to toe with armor.

And the armor was red with rust.

There was a day he had been at his best. Strong. Capable. Energetic. Focused. Ready for battle. No longer. Something had happened to him. Something had robbed him of his heart. Something had left him less than a knight. Less than a man.

No longer confident, no longer purposeful, he simply wandered among the trees. Head down. Shoulders drooped. Feet out of the stirrups. Reins slack in his hands. Just a shadow of his intended glory.

I'm reminded of many of my brothers today. Modern man. Emasculated man. Just a shadow of God's intention for masculinity. Something has happened to manhood. Something has attacked its heart, so that manhood is somehow less masculine. Do you sense it? Yes, you can feel it all across this land. It is nearly palpable.

Garrison Keillor spoke it well when he said, "Manhood, once an opportunity for achievement, now seems like a problem to be overcome."[1] How true. How tragic. How unnecessary. He continues:

> What you find is terrible gender anxiety, guys trying to be Mr. Right, the man who can bake a cherry pie, go shoot skeet, come back, toss a salad, converse easily about intimate matters, cry if need be, laugh, hug, be vulnerable, perform passionately that night and the next day go off and lift them bales onto that barge and tote it. Being perfect is a terrible way to spend your life, and guys aren't equipped for it anyway.[2]

Because we live in a culture utterly confused in the area of gender issues, it is important we take stock. It's time to climb a tree and take a look around. Time to gather some bearings.

The other evening I was reading through a book treating the Vietnam era. *We Were Soldiers Once...and Young* had captured my heart. I was reflective. My wife, Lindy, had noticed a pattern. It wasn't the first time she'd seen a far-away look in my eyes. It seems, of late, I've been doing more thinking about that thin, traumatic slice of America's life than at any other point in the intervening years since the fall of Saigon. Lindy's question roused me from a mental visit to a world far away. She said (as only a wife can), "What's happening to you lately? You seem more contemplative than usual." I realized she was right. And I think it's something more than "mid-life."

I've been thinking a great deal about the course of our culture over the last quarter century. Like a wounded plane in a deadly spin, we're headed for a disaster—unless we can get a solid grip on the controls. Few dispute that. But we're ignoring some of the fundamentals of societal flight. Basic elements like, "what is man" and "what is a woman" are at stake.

I think a lot of men today—regardless of their ages (twenties, forties, sixties—you name it) are asking some healthy questions. We're rethinking what it means to be a man. And we're realizing that the last few decades have robbed men of confidence in their masculinity.

I said to Lindy, "You know, Hon, when you think about it—I was a soldier when it wasn't cool to be a soldier. I'm a pastor about a hundred years late in terms of community respect. And I'm a man in a day when it's politically incorrect to be masculine."

Revolting state of affairs, isn't it? I don't like it. And I don't expect you do, either. The last three decades have been one big accelerating downward spiral. A writer for *US News and World Report* recently phrased it like this:

> The fraying of America's social fabric is fast becoming a national obsession. Three out of four Americans think we are in moral and spiritual decline. Two out of three think the country is seriously off track. Doubts about the President's character have driven his standing in the polls down... Social dysfunction haunts the land: crime and drug abuse, the breakup of the family, the slump in academic performance, the disfigurement of public places by druggies, thugs, and exhibitionists...[3]

And that assessment is from the mainline news media, not some red-necked preacher.

What's going on? What's the bottom-line? I honestly believe that somewhere near the vortex of this negative siphon is the question, *What does it mean to be a man?*

You and I know that when you're talking about the "fraying of social fabric" you're talking about how people learn to live together. You're talking about men and women and boys and girls and families and homes. That's basic social fabric stuff. What we're experiencing is the deliberate unraveling of divinely intended gender function. And the result is serious *dys*function. Chuck Colson summarizes:

The fundamental pillar of our society, the family, has been under assault for years, and its crumbling has long been of vital concern to Christians. But do not miss the progression. *The artillery salvos are escalating against something even more fundamental: the very notion of what it means to be a man, what it means to be a woman...*[4]

In other words, if we're going to be healthy again, men are going to have to become healthy men again (and women healthy women). It's time for men to stand up, get a grip on biblical manhood, and quit apologizing for being men. What this culture desperately needs are men who are confident in their God-given masculinity and His intentions for it.

When you get right down to it, you'd just like to enjoy being a man, wouldn't you? We'd just like to be and do what men were *made* to be and do. Something down deep inside us just wants to be a man. Remember when men were men? And women women? And the differences were obvious? Remember when you didn't have to wonder? And weren't criticized for being a man? Can you remember when little boys couldn't wait to grow up and become men? When young men wore masculinity like their home team's colors? Maturing into manhood was like earning a varsity letter. It was a glad, grand thing to be a man. It was good to be part of the fraternity.

But now, in a culture that wants to elevate a higher standard of so-called diversity, we're destroying diversity in its most beautiful and elemental form.

Chuck Swindoll speaks for all of us when he asks:

Remember when men knew who they were, liked how they were, and didn't want to be anything but what they were? Remember when it was the men who boxed and wrestled and bragged about how much they could bench press? Remember when it was the women who wore the makeup, the earrings, and the bikinis? Remember when it was the men who initiated the contact and took the lead in a relationship, made lifelong commitments, treated a woman like a lady, and modeled a masculinity that displayed security and stability?[5]

Yes! Those were the days. But listen—we don't need to turn the clock back. We just need to bring genuine God-designed masculinity *forward.* For too long now we men have been out of focus. Lost our vision. Let our feet slip from the stirrups, our hands from the reins, and our hearts from the cause. And the noble armor of masculinity has rusted. Gordon Dalbey bemoans the loss of an entire generation—his own:

> Today in my mid-forties I span a history which has challenged painfully my sense of manhood. I grew up playing sandlot soldier in my white suburban neighborhood with boys whose mothers were all "housewives." After graduating from a private university in the 60s, I went to Africa as a Peace Corps volunteer and later taught at a junior high school in the Hispanic barrio of San Jose, California. By the 70s, I had become an enthusiastic supporter of civil rights, women's liberation, and the antiwar movement. In effect, I had become part of a generation of men who actively rejected our childhood macho image of manhood—which seemed to us the cornerstone of racism, sexism, and militarism.
>
> The 70s, however, offered us no model of authentic manhood sufficiently inspiring to supplant the boyhood image in our hearts. Lacking that, we could only reject our manhood itself as we rejected the macho image.
>
> By the 80s, alienated from our masculine heritage and intimidated by a growing host of strong women, we have become fearfully lost and vulnerable in the very culture we struggled to foster years ago. We realize that in rejecting the

macho image, we have gained a deeper sensitivity to other persons. But as we enter the 90s, we wonder what we have lost.[6]

We know we've lost something. We know we've lost our masculine souls. We don't know all that means, but we do know men are confused, hurting, and angry. It is no wonder that six times more men than women are arrested for drug abuse, that 88 percent of drunk drivers are men, and that 75 percent of all suicides in the United States are men.

An article in *Psychology Today* summarizes:

> Buffeted by the women's movement, constrained by a traditional and internalized definition of masculinity, men literally don't know who they are...what women want from them, or even what they want from themselves.[7]

Well, men, we've endured twenty-five years of dismantling confusion. It's time to restore our masculinity. It's time to learn to be men again. And there is no better place to learn to be a man than in the company of men. We learn to be masculine by standing close to men. And that is what this book is about—rediscovering our manhood by restoring the camaraderie of masculine friendship.

Let's drop back to that sunset meadow, when the lone rider came out of the west. The man in the clearing, you'll remember, saw that the horseman was a knight in armor, and the armor was red with rust.

Anodos, the man who stood in the pooled light of the westering sun and watched the approach of the dejected rider, wondered how a once proud and radiant knight could have found himself in such a state. Even the knight's great warhorse seemed dispirited and walked with a drooping head.

The knight explained to Anodos that somewhere, early in his journeys, he had in some way been shamed. He had turned aside from his noble quest and lost his way in a vast and dreary forest. As a result, a film of rust tarnished his once bright armor. The enchantment was such that the rust could not be removed except by the clash and impact of combat.

"Never," quoth the sad warrior, "shall this armor be furbished, but by the blows of knightly encounter, until the last speck has disappeared from every spot where the battle-ax and the sword of evil doers, or noble foes, might fall; when I shall lift my head again and say to my squire, 'Do thy duty once more, and make this armor shine.'"

Sir Percival, it seems, was doomed to wander the weary forest trails for untold years, ever looking for opportunity to knock the rust from his tainted armor through some valiant effort or clash of arms.

George MacDonald, of course, was a master storyteller, beloved of C. S. Lewis, J. R. R. Tolkein, and generations of readers on both sides of the Atlantic. But with due respect to the grand old gentleman, I think he had this story, part of his Phantastes all wrong.

Sir Percival didn't need a lot of slashing swords and bruising battle-axes and jarring jousts to restore his knightly splendor and put the sparkle back in his steely eyes. He didn't need solo encounters with hot-breathed dragons or a lonely search for the holy grail to lift his drooping head.

What the man needed was a friend. A fellow soldier to lock arms with.

Let's face it, to one degree or another, we're all rusty knights. Most of us grew up wanting to be knights in shining armor riding white horses and doing noble deeds. But somewhere between Camelot and Reality, we got off the trail. We've been banged up a little. The armor fits a little tighter around the middle than it used to, the joints squeak when we move, and we can't quite remember the sun-bright aspirations of our wide-eyed youth. And then there's that pesky rust. It starts with a spot or two in places you can't easily reach, and just spreads from there.

In the twilight of our disillusionment, we resign ourselves, like Sir Percival, to a life of endless battles and tedious struggle. In short, we surrender to the rust.

Where does the rust come from?

Given the day and culture in which we live, there are some of us who feel a little like Sir Percival. We were created to be knights, yet somehow we feel we ought to apologize for our knighthood. It's a bit embarrassing to own up to full-hearted masculinity in the 1990s. It's not politically correct to glory in one's manhood.

Barry Arnold, my fellow pastor at Good Shepherd Church, was recently writing some study questions about what it means to be a man. After he'd finished banging out the project on his computer, he thought he'd try out his built-in grammar-check program. What he got however, was more than scrutiny of run-on sentences and dangling modifiers.

The computer objected to his view on masculinity. He had typed the word "manliness." When the grammar check got to it, the alarms went off. Up onto the screen popped the words, "Try to describe the specific qualities associated with this word without reference to gender." Good grief! Give me a break. Use "manliness" without reference to gender? If you ask me, my friend's computer has contracted some kind of insidious feminist virus. I would have loved to have heard the conversations as the software was designed.

The term *manliness,* it seems, was too "gender specific."

In other words, there is no proper place for a discussion of masculine traits or virtues. It's poor grammar. It's bad taste. It's sexist. It's a cultural no-no. It's some kind of archaic anachronism that needs to be expunged from our speech, writing, and thoughts.

While speaking at a recent Promise Keepers gathering in Portland, Oregon, I came across the same cultural virus. Over thirty thousand men had gathered in one of America's most unchurched cities to celebrate their masculinity and learn to be men who keep their promises to their wives, their children, and their God. Barely a few minutes before I was to address the massive crowd overflowing Civic Stadium, I was hustled into a press conference to meet Portland's media.

One of the first questions from the reporters was a blunt, three-word slap:

"Why just men?"

The question said it all for any cynical members of the press crew. What's the point of a gathering for *men?* What's the point of a conference on manhood? Why invite men together to talk about the responsibilities and privileges and ideals of men? Wasn't that an antiquated sort of notion? Or worse—wasn't it a sinister attempt to reassert the discredited notions of a male-dominated culture?

(Can you imagine the press asking Patricia Ireland, president of the National Organization of Women, "Why NOW for *just women?*")

The next day a one-column headline buried in Section C of Portland's *Sunday Oregonian* coolly dismissed the largest paying crowd in the city's memory with these words: "Men Get Religion." It seems that a record-breaking multitude of men seeking to give their word and keep their promises must somehow be trivialized by associating it with some kind of "religion"…as though a gathering of men is, by definition, "far out."

Thanks to many years of feminist cultural reprogramming, manhood has fallen from public favor. The subject is slightly embarrassing. Something not to be discussed or considered in polite, correct circles.

Proud masculine suits of armor, once kept shined, oiled, and happily worn by generations of men, have been relegated to garages, attics, and basements. Men feel bewildered and confused by a nation that has turned hostile toward masculine distinctives. As *New York Times* columnist Natalie Angier recently expressed it:

> Women may not find this surprising, but one of the most persistent and frustrating problems in evolutionary biology is the male. Specifically, where did he come from, and why doesn't he just go away?[8]

During the last quarter century, men have quietly slipped off their once-gleaming armor and left it standing in a forgotten corner of some musty storage shed. It collects dust along with old bowling trophies and Uncle Harold's mounted moose head.

Robert Bly observes something of this emasculating trend:

The warriors inside American men have become weak in recent years...a grown man six feet tall will allow another person to cross his boundaries, enter his psychic house, verbally abuse him, carry away his treasure and slam the door behind; the invaded man will stand there with an ingratiating, confused smile on his face....[9]

If a man doesn't know what a man is, if he doesn't wear his masculinity and remember what it's for, he begins to rust.

It's time for men to come back. It's time for those old warriors who never let their armor rust beyond repair to take the point again and lead us back to God's intentions for our masculinity.

We need to come back, yes, but we must be careful just *how* we come back. For more than a quarter century now men have been mocked, criticized, and belittled. We're still the only group in America that it is politically correct to bash. But you don't motivate a man by swinging at him. Oh, he'll absorb the blows for awhile, but eventually he'll likely drop into a crouch and start swinging back! That kind of backlash no one needs.

If all we can muster is something of a backlash to the feminist movement, we will of all creatures be most miserable. Frankly, I fear such a backlash. I fear thoughtless over-reaction to some of the shrill rhetoric and absurd logic of the feminists. The backlash could be severe. People could be hurt.

Let me explain. Feminists insist that equality demands sameness. That men and women are the same, with no appreciable differences other than the obvious plumbing designs. Of course, nothing is further from the truth. And my fear is that some big lug will attempt to set the record straight on his own terms. That's precisely where people could be hurt.

A friend of my wife's who is a fine athlete shared a story with Linda the other day. Seems she was playing first base in a co-ed softball game. One of the blue-collared "good ol' boys" had quaffed a beer or two, stepped up to the plate, drove a grounder down the third base line and headed for first. The peg from the third baseman beat him to first where Linda's friend waited with the ball. Now, of course, I can't say for sure what was running through his mind, but it's not much of a stretch for me to imagine...

Oh, so you want to play with the men, sweetheart? Level field, right? Everything equal, eh? Well, let's see if you can take it. Rule says you've got to hold onto the ball in order to put me out. Let's see if we're equal.

Now, I don't know if he was thinking that way or not. But I do know what happened. The big 250 pounder smashed into Barbara, knocked her off her feet and across the gravel, leaving her unconscious. Hours later in a doctor's office, as the physician was surgically removing bits of gravel driven into Barbara's face, she must have wondered—was it the beer, or was it the gender wars? I hope the man was ashamed of himself. He was no warrior. He was only a brute. Not even half a man.

Yes, it's time for men to come back. But *real* men. Not overgrown caricatures. Warriors, yes. But not brutes. Tender Warriors. It's time for God's good men to lock arms and walk together toward the high ground of His noble intentions. And it's God's good men who have the answers. The secular men's movement faded because they could never get to the headwaters. It is believing men who may drink deep from the Genesis spring, refresh and renew the Creator's original designs, and seize the day.

It's time for such men to come back, to reclaim their armor from the pawn shops and garage sales and the back corners of the basement.

It's time, because the High King is calling out His knights. His Spirit is moving among His men like seldom in history. The High King is at work.

In the days before the Arthur of history and legend, the sharp axes of the Saxons were chopping at Britain from every side. Cruel and merciless, Saxon raiding parties devastated British villages, raping and pillaging and murdering. The beleaguered early Britons longed for a high king, and Arthur Pendragon answered the call, uniting his nation and driving the northern invaders back into the sea.

It's the same today. In a time of crumbling traditions and values, in a day of dangerous streets and collapsing homes, people long for stability and hope. They need to catch a glimpse of the powerful High King who loves them. And the King wants His knight-companions at His side.

In the movie *Glory*, one scene portrays a Union regiment of freed slaves, the 54th Massachusetts, sitting around a campfire on the night before the big battle. The fire crackles, the cicadas chirp, and several of the men hum a spiritual in unison as they clean their rifles. They know that on the morrow their lives will be on the line, and they must seize the day.

One soldier looks up from the fire at his fellows, willing them to give him eye contact.

He says, "We men, ain't we?"

That says it all, doesn't it? We're men. *Men.* We'll face the danger. We'll take the risks. We'll absorb the pain. We'll square our shoulders and—for the sake of heaven—we'll look death and hell square in the eyes.

And it will be this generation that gets it done. You and me. To paraphrase Churchill, when masculinity has endured a thousand more years, may they say that this day was among its finest hours.

Listen to the apostle's battle cry: "The night is almost gone, and the day is at hand. Let us therefore lay aside the deeds of darkness and put on the armor of light" (Romans 13:12).

Let's advance! Paul shouts, "in purity, in knowledge, in patience, in kindness, in the Holy Spirit, in genuine love, in the word of truth, in the power of God; by the weapons of righteousness for the right hand and the left" (2 Corinthians 6:6-7).

There's a battle surging around us. There are deeds to do and enemies to conquer and hearts to win and great quests to pursue. These are the days when the forces of light must marshal their strength against the encroaching armies of darkness and death. This is no time to plod along in disappointment and defeat.

No, we're not the shining knights we want to be; our armor isn't as bright, our vision isn't as keen, and our swords aren't as sharp as we wish they were. *That's why we need friends.* That's why we need soul brothers, Ranger buddies, and comrades-at-arms. Solomon wrote that as "iron sharpens iron, so one man sharpens another" (Proverbs 27:17).

Of course! How else do you get rid of the rust? One man sharpens another. One man puts the shine to another man's armor. One man readies another man for combat. One man breathes courage and wisdom and fire and endurance back into the heart of his brother.

Sir Percival didn't need to spend his life riding around by himself, doing solo combat with dragons, and trying to live down his bad résumé. What he needed was a fellow knight who could put an arm around his shoulder, help him put the past behind, lift his gaze, and point him toward glory in the service of the great King.

Come to think of it, that's what I need, too. Life's too short to wander the back trails and beat the brush alone. You and I may be a little rusty at this thing called masculine friendship, but that's okay. We'll work on the rust together, in the fine light of a new morning or by the light of a comradely fire. Shoulder to shoulder, we'll make this masculine armor shine again. By God's grace, we'll have the kind of armor that catches the very light of heaven.

1. Sir Percival rode through life head down, soul downcast, armor stained with rust, because of some event in his past when he hadn't acted in a knightly manner. And because of that, he wasted his days, not even seeking to make an impact. Is there some area of life where you've become a stoop-shouldered, rusty knight, not even trying to make an impact? Is it time for your head to come up, your sword to be lifted, and for you to become alert? Think about sharing that with someone who can encourage you.

2. Is there a "Sir Percival" where you work, living next door, or in your church who needs a friend? What kind of encouragement might you give to this individual?

LOCKING ARMS

1. "Manhood, once an opportunity for achievement, now seems like a problem to be overcome." There are expectations placed on you from every direction—what to be, what *not* to be. What's hardest for you about being a man today?

2. "Three out of four Americans think we are in moral and spiritual decline." What are you going to do about it? No, really. What are you going to do right where you live—in the God-given strength of your masculinity—to make some positive difference for the sake of your family, friends, church, and community?

3. "We learn to be masculine by standing close to men." What comes to your mind when you think of "standing close to men"? If that statement speaks strongly to you, explain why.

4. Name a few aspects of life that tend to make rusty knights of men—areas where they're not fighting the good fight. In discussing them, do you see some places where you need to take a stand?

5. "Iron sharpens iron, so one man sharpens another" (Proverbs 27:17). Sounds good; often quoted, assumed true. But how does it work?

6. Beaten, downcast, confused, paralyzed, rust-stained, lonely—a pretty good description of men today, don't you agree? Becoming healthy again, finding a friend, lifting your sword, standing close—don't those encouragements feel good? What are you thinking about this whole matter of masculine friendships right now?

CHAPTER FOUR

Of Tree Forts and True Friends

Breaking the Ice and Getting Started

*"An army can march anywhere and at any time of the year wherever
two men can place their feet."*
NAPOLEON

ver since I was a kid in a tree fort, I've loved trees. Strong. Tall. Freeing. Shade in the summer. Shelter in the winter. Some of the most fun, warm memories of my life involve trees…usually swinging in them or sitting under them.

One of my favorites was the big old weeping willow at my boyhood home. Its roots stretched across the backyard like huge underground snakes. Its trunk was enormous for a willow, several feet in diameter. The main branches were as big as neighboring tree trunks. And there, high in the wind and leaves, Tommy Harrison and I built our tree fort.

It was a glorious thing (in our eyes at least, our parents thought it something of a monstrosity). There, from the secure ramparts of that tree fortress, we fought off all kinds of imaginary enemies. We were absolutely invincible high in that tree, away from all that might threaten. Tommy and I spent whole days there, playing, reading comic books, plunking the BB gun, and even sneaking our first "smokes." (Mom caught us, too. Ouch! We paid for it.) Both that willow tree and that friendship were great places of refuge to me in my growing up years.

Then there were the two mature, fruit-bearing, hammock-holding apple trees. They grew west of town out on Route 7, behind Linda's childhood home. It was under those grand, wide-limbed old trees that Linda and I sat through lazy summer afternoons…and began to form a relationship that would blossom into marriage and last a lifetime. There, in the apple-sweet warmth under those languidly rustling leaves, we initiated our first serious commitments. Those interlaced apple boughs provided a place of warmth and security. So did that friendship…that became the love of my life.

And I remember an old scarred pine tree in Northeast Oregon. I had become a father by then. With great anticipation my then eight-year-old son, Blake, and I loaded the car and "headed for the wilds" for some quality adventure. But the weather—gray, overcast, and raining—disappointed us. Little did we know at the outset that such miserable weather would provide us with some indelible memories. Neither of us will ever forget snuggling up under a big pine tree near Bennett Peak. Blake was tucked under my arm. And we just sat…entranced…together…sheltered from the constant misting rain…for hours…utterly fascinated by a large herd of majestic Rocky Mountain elk grazing, completely at ease in the mist on the hillside opposite. That tree became a doorway to another world. There was a haven there under that tree for the two of us. And that friendship is still a great haven for both of us.

And you can't leave out the fir trees. I remember a towering, monster fir in the Eagle Cap Wilderness under which my brother and I took shelter while bow hunting. Its lower branches were so large and knit, nothing could penetrate that refuge. We had been covering country, hiking in the lee of an enormous ridgeline at the bottom of the Minam River canyon. With no warning whatsoever massive clouds carried along at the head of a front had cleared the ridge. In a flash, they were dumping huge amounts of rain. Eric and I literally ran for cover from the summer mountain downpour. There…sheltered…we waited out the storm. The quiet settled in. We did, too. And we reminisced, under the fir tree, as friends and brothers. ("Eric, do you remember the time when you planted the maple tree seed in the coffee can and put it in your bedroom? You were really convinced you were going to harvest maple bars off that thing.")

Juniper trees are one of my favorites. They're tough, hardy old rascals. And their scent is invigorating. After a rain, the cool, mingled fragrances of juniper and sage exceed that of any pampered, hot-house flower. Right now I'm visualizing one special juniper, a gnarly, ancient tree in Central Oregon not far from Grizzly Mountain. It holds special memories for me and a dear friend. The two of us and our sons had just cleared the rise and come to the old tree. We had unknowingly spooked several deer on the other side. There beside that sweet-smelling old sentinel, as the mule deer bounced away in typical bounding flight, the two of us chuckled as one of the boys shouted in innocent delight, "Look, Dad, dancing deer!" There in the midst of such natural splendor, child-like charm, and warm friendship, we just exulted. What joy. Beside the tree. And each other.

Let me tell you one more. There's a grove of shore pine in our present home's backyard. There, a couple of summers ago, under those pines and beneath our boys' now abandoned tree house, Lindy and I and two of the boys buried faithful "old Zac." An intelligent and loving black Lab-Elk Hound mix, Zac had been a member of the family for fourteen years. Fourteen years of playing ball, chasing Frisbees, and sleeping on the back deck with three growing boys. She was bright and fun-loving, practically raised the boys herself, and was probably our youngest son's best friend. (Why a female named "Zac"? That's another story for some other time.) There beneath the trees, with sweat rolling down our backs in the summer heat, two of the boys and I swung the pick and heaved the shovel as together we dug her grave in the hard clay. We wrapped her in a sheet and filled in the site. Then, with arms around each other, one of the boys suggested we "say a few words over her." (I think they may have been watching too many westerns that summer.) But we did. And we thanked God for His creative genius in giving us the pleasure of the company of a simple animal. We reflected under those trees. And in one another's arms.

FRIENDS ARE LIKE TREES

Now that I think about it, so many of the great moments of my life have taken place under trees. And as different as those trees were—willows, pines, firs, junipers, and apple, they all had, from my perspective, a couple things in common:

First, I drew shelter from them
    and protection
        and quiet
            and reflection
                and pleasure.

A haven. And second, I shared them all, every one of them, with a friend.

Trees and friends are a lot alike. They both provide shelter. Protection. Tranquillity. Peace. And a place for reflection. In actuality (as you know from your own experience), it was the relationship, the friendship—far more than the tree—that provided the more significant shelter and refuge.

Friendships are like trees—sending roots deep for stability, growing branches strong for shelter, tossing leaves here and there just for fun. And offering shade from the heat, peace from the pace, and haven from the hurry.

That's true today. And it's always been true.

Have you ever noticed that a lot of significant moments in Scripture took place under trees? (That Middle East sun could kill you.)

- Genesis 2:9—"And out of the ground the LORD God caused to grow every tree that is pleasing to the sight..."
- Genesis 18:1-4, 8—"Now the LORD appeared to him by the oaks of Mamre, while he was sitting at the tent door in the heat of the day. And when he lifted up his eyes and looked, behold, three men were standing opposite him...and [Abraham]

said,…'Please let a little water be brought and wash your feet, and rest yourselves under the tree;'…and he was standing by them under the tree as they ate."

• 1 Kings 19:4-5—Elijah, fleeing from Ahab and Jezebel, "went a day's journey into the wilderness, and came and sat down under a juniper tree; and he requested for himself that he might die, and said, 'It is enough; now, O LORD, take my life'…and he lay down and slept under a juniper tree; and behold, there was an angel touching him, and he said to him, 'Arise, eat.'"

• Jeremiah 17:7-8—The Lord Himself compared a man who trusts in Him with a tree planted by the water…

> That extends its roots by a stream
> And will not fear when the heat comes;
> But its leaves will be green,
> And it will not be anxious in a year of drought
> Nor cease to yield fruit.

And to top the trees theme off, when ultimate peace (and tranquillity, and perspective, and refuge) comes to this earth, when "the fullness of the whole earth" actually is His glory, when the Living One has His way on this planet, the trees themselves will participate in a powerfully expressive picture:

Isaiah 55:12 says, "All the trees of the field will clap their hands."

TREES ARE LIKE FRIENDS

Trees are like friends.

Trees…willows, apple, pine, fir, juniper.

Friends…boyhood buddies, growing sweethearts, fathers and sons, brothers.

Trees and friends have a lot in common. Both provide welcome shelter from the inevitable storms that sweep over the horizon.

In his landmark book, *Growing Strong in the Seasons of Life*, Chuck

Swindoll noted a poem by Samuel Taylor Coleridge. It was titled, "Friendship Is a Sheltering Tree."

That's right, isn't it? You need a few friends when the heat rises and the winds begin to blow. And you need them, just as well, when there is neither heat nor wind. Friends are the rich stuff of life. The cool, refreshing oases in the sometimes barren landscape of our years. Without meaningful friendships we will miss a great deal of the abundant life God intends for us.

Swindoll's reflective questions are appropriate: "Beneath whose branches are you refreshed? And who rests beneath yours?" Just who are your friends? Who do you count close and trusted? Who owns a piece of your heart's real estate? Not many, eh? Tough to name them when you get right down to it, huh? Maybe we really do need to start planting a few seedlings.

MAKING THE CONNECTION

Just how do you grow such trees? How do you gain such strong-limbed, sheltering friendships? How do you plant a few sentinel friends along the sidewalks of your life? Just how do you make the connection?

Listen up! It really isn't all that complicated. You *attract* them. You *win* them. You *make* them. You *befriend* them.

The King James Bible says it simply and clearly: *"A man that hath friends must show himself friendly"* (Proverbs 18:24).

I like that. Do you want to have a friend? Fine. *Be one.* Do you want people to reach out to you? *Reach out to them.* Do you want people to like you? *Show that you like them.* To have a friend you must befriend!

"Befriend" is a verb—and one of life's more powerful verbs at that. Webster's offers only one definition. Just six monosyllabic words, sixteen little letters—"to act as a friend to." To have a friend you must act as a friend to someone.

SNAPSHOTS:
MY FRIENDS TELL THEIR STORIES

The three of us needed each other and we knew it. We needed the support. We needed to connect. We needed someone who knew exactly why we were tired and even lonely.

I don't remember who admitted it first. But someone did. And from the admitting of feelings at some ball game or dinner table flowed a waterfall of emotion from the other two. We did it—we had actually connected.

We never missed a meeting. Every Sunday evening there was one thing on the calendar and nothing separated our newly established triangle of the heart. I can't tell you what those times did to my heart. How strong my bond was to these two MEN. I really think we *became* men that first Sunday night when the three of us gathered in His name.

SIX STEPS TO CONNECTING WITH A FRIEND

What does it mean to "act like a friend"? Let's walk through some simple, effective "how to's" to practice when working at being and gaining a friend.

1. Know yourself.

Stay with me here. Yes, this is a crucial first step. You need to take a good, unhurried time of self-evaluation. Acknowledge your weaknesses. Accept your strengths. Gain an accurate picture of yourself.

Paul writes: "I say to every man among you not to think more highly of himself than he ought to think [nor, by implication, too lowly]; but to think so as to have sound judgment" (Romans 12:3).

Ask yourself a few tough questions, and don't let yourself squirm away from the answers. Am I positive and winsome? Or am I complaining and pessimistic? Would I like *myself* for a friend? Am I defensive? Do I let my past failures hold me down or am I ready to get on with life? And, very importantly, am I honest? Can I be counted on?

Jesus said the heart of the Bible and the Christian life is loving God with all your heart, mind, and soul and "your neighbor as yourself." That phrase implies a form of healthy self regard, doesn't it? And it's very much a part of making friends.

Develop an *encouraging presence* and the vocabulary that goes with it. Stop the pity parties, shed the pessimism, and get rid of self-disparaging attitudes and comments. ("Well, I'm just not very…") Never withhold an encouraging word, never hesitate to perform a kind act. Smile. Wear a "yes face."

2. Identify your vision.

Identifying your vision is part of knowing yourself, but it is so crucial it's worthy of separate mention. What drives you? For what were you made? Recall that "sense of purpose" was what drove Jesus. Even when He was only twelve, He was flabbergasted when His parents didn't realize there was really only one place to look for Him—doing "My Father's business." It was His sense of vision that drew so many friends to Him. His friends so wanted to be with Him, they passed up promotions, careers, and personal time just to walk beside Him. His sense of purpose was at the heart of His magnetic ability to attract and hold friends. And then He took them beyond the vision into the relationship. Jesus not only had disciples. He had intimate friends. Too often we in the church today tend to view the disciples as merely a part of His organization, not friends He laughed and cried with, guys He walked, worked, and sweated with. Our Lord's vision for His church was a circle of friends. Really good friends.

It was the sharing of His personal vision that cemented His friendships. He opened His heart and mind to His companions. They knew what was going on "on the inside." He was graciously open, transparent, and vulnerable with His friends. He told them everything that mattered to Him.

> No longer do I call you slaves, for the slave does not know what his master is doing; but I have called you friends, for all things that I have heard from My Father I have made known to you (John 15:15).

Jesus was such a great friend and served His friends so well because He understood who He was.

> Jesus knowing that His hour had come...knowing that the Father had put all things in His hands, [knowing] that He had come forth from God, and [knowing He] was going back to God, rose from supper, and laid aside His garments; and taking a towel, He girded Himself about...and began to wash the disciples' feet (John 13:1, 3-4, 5).

He was unthreatened to perform the lowliest act of servanthood, because He knew very well who He was, where He had been, and where He was going. Jesus had a vision. And that made Him unfailingly attractive. And friendly.

Vision is the stuff of which friendships are made. Friends stand side by side looking at the mountain, contemplating the task, measuring what matters. And it is that common vision that *drives* the friendship.

Last fall, while archery hunting, I was sitting around the campfire with two of my great friends. I had had the privilege of introducing them to each other. Neither of them knew the other as well as I. But it was fascinating for me to watch these two strong men enjoy the budding of a new friendship. Because I knew each of their strengths I could have predicted where the conversation would go. Each of these men is going somewhere. Each understands himself. And each has a vision larger than himself. It was inevitable they would become good friends in short order.

Sure enough. There beneath the stars, beside the stream, at the foot of the north slope, they got to the heart of the matter almost immediately. One of them asked the other, "What is there in your life (and it's not fair to say 'family' or 'faith'), for which you would be willing die?" We had been together for just a couple of days at that point. But already we were getting to the things that mattered. C. S. Lewis said it best:

> The Companionship was between people who were doing something together—hunting, studying, painting or what you will. The Friends will still be doing something together, but something more inward, less widely shared and less easily defined; still hunters, but of some immaterial quarry; still collaborating, but in some work the world does not, or not yet, take account of; still traveling companions, but on a different kind of journey. Hence we picture lovers face to face, but friends side by side; their eyes look ahead.
>
> That is why those...people who simply "want friends" never have any. The very condition of having Friends is that we

should want something else besides Friends. Where the truthful answer to the question "Do you see the same truth?" would be "I see nothing and I don't care about the truth; I only want a friend" no friendship can arise...there would be nothing for the friendship to be about; and friendship must be about something, even if it were only an enthusiasm for dominoes or white mice. Those who have nothing can share nothing; those who are going nowhere can have no fellow-travelers.[1]

How do you sum up such grand words? Maybe as simply as this: Identify your vision, live for it, let it show, and then let your friendships be drawn to and around it.

3. Take the initiative.

When the Ultimate Friend determined to befriend us, guess who made the first move? Wherever you choose to see the starting point—creation, incarnation, conception, redemption—it was His move. Every time. He took the initiative. He took the risk. He extended Himself—all the way from heaven's royal avenues to a smelly stable south of the tracks in Bethlehem. That's quite a reach. That's a great friend.

Remember those grand words? "For the Son of Man has come to seek and to save that which was lost" (Luke 19:10).

He came looking for us, didn't He? He came with His hands outstretched.

Can you remember a time when you were "new on the block" and no one stretched out toward you? It was uncomfortable, embarrassingly awkward, and frustrating. Don't let it happen. Beat that awkward moment to the punch. *You* be the one to reach out. *You* be the one to start the conversation. And don't worry about rejection. In this life nothing works perfectly. Keep at it. Look people in the eye, learn names, study hearts. And reach out.

Nathanael was pleasantly shocked and warmed when the Stranger from Nazareth said to him: "Before Philip called you, when you were under the fig tree [there's that tree again], I saw you." The verb "saw" here is a word that emphasizes the direction of thought to the object seen. It emphasizes the discernment part of the seeing. It has to do with "perceiving." Jesus had, quite literally, "studied" the man. He even made extremely affirming comments about him, very early on—"no guile" in this man. Talk about accepting and affirming, right from the get go! (More on this later.)

4. Focus on the friend.

Jesus focused on Nathanael. He focused on Peter. He focused on blind Bartimaeus. He focused on little Zaccheus up in that tree. And He continued to focus on old friends and new friends right up to the end. Now, if ever there was a time when a man has a license to think of himself, it's at the zenith of life-crisis. Jesus sweat drops of blood in the garden as He faced death. Still, in the throes of His final days, He was focusing on His friends. He said, in essence, to Peter: "These next few days are going to be real bears. It's going to be tough for both of us. I want you to know I've prayed for you" (see Luke 22:31-32).

Part of what made Jesus such a great friend was His self-free focus upon the other person. He did the little things in a big way. From noticing a little child while in the midst of teaching (Luke 18:15-17) to recruiting help for His mother while He was enduring searing torture on the cross (John 19:26-27), Jesus focused on others.

The valet of President Teddy Roosevelt tells the story of a similar quality in that great man:

> My wife one time asked the President about a bobwhite. She had never seen one and he described it to her fully. Sometime later, the phone rang at our cottage (on the Roosevelt estate). My wife answered it and it was Mr. Roosevelt himself. He had called her, he said, to tell her that there was a bobwhite outside her window and if she would look out she might see it. Little things like that were so characteristic of him.[2]

A good friend is interested, genuinely interested, in others—their interests, passions, work, homes, and families. A good friend rejoices when his friend wins. He grieves when his friend hurts. He never dwells on his own aches, pains, and disappointments. Someone once said it so well: "Be kind. Everyone you meet today is fighting a hard battle."

Self focus never helped *anyone*. Focusing on others is not only helpful to them, it is healthy for you. The American Medical Association says it pretty clearly:

> Exercise regularly, eat a well-balanced diet and do something nice for someone. That's the advice you're apt to get from your doctor in the near future. There's more evidence than ever that helping others has definite health benefits for those who lend a helping hand. In an explosion of new research, the benefits of altruism [a seventy-five cent word for "unselfish regard for others"]—long praised by moralists—are being proven by psychologists, epidemiologists, and neuroscientists.[3]

5. Keep both your promises and confidences.

Say what you mean. Mean what you say. And keep it between you.

The use of your tongue is a key to your friendships. Scripture tells us explicitly that "death and life are in the power of the tongue" (Proverbs 18:21). If that's the case, if watching your tongue is really a life-and-death issue, think what an impact it can have in the making of lifelong friends…and lifelong enemies. "A word aptly spoken is like apples of gold in settings of silver" (Proverbs 25:11, NIV). Such a word, from a trustworthy source, gives genuine hope.

Our Ultimate Friend takes great and proper pride in His making and keeping promises. It is the quality He often chooses to associate most directly with His own name and character: "Know therefore that the LORD your God, He is God, the faithful God, who keeps His covenant and His lovingkindness to a thousandth generation" (Deuteronomy 7:9).

Someone has said, quite accurately, "Friendship cannot survive in an environment of broken dates, forgotten promises, unpaid loans, unreturned phone calls, weak excuses, and bald-faced lies."

On the other hand, friendship absolutely *soars* in an environment of acceptance, transparency, trust, and promises made and kept.

Nothing will destroy a friendship quicker than a broken confidence. According to Solomon, it's worse than a jaw-grinding toothache: "Like a bad tooth and an unsteady foot is confidence in a faithless man" (Proverbs 25:19). Again, "He who goes about as a talebearer reveals secrets, but he who is trustworthy conceals a matter" (Proverbs 11:13).

6. Stay steady, strong, and faithful—no matter what.

Remember, friends are like trees. There is refuge beneath their branches. There is safety. There is a haven to come to, no matter what. No matter the time (day or night), the weather (fair or foul), or the circumstances (pleasant or painful), trees and friends stay steady, strong, and faithful. Like a deep-rooted oak, friends weather the storms, hang on through the droughts, and grow stronger through the years.

Robert Fulghum captures the parallel between trees and friends. Listen to him tell the tale of a tree and a friendship:

> There is a tree…at the downhill edge of a long narrow field in the western foothills of the La Sal Mountains…a particular tree. A juniper. Large for its species—maybe twenty feet tall and two feet in diameter. For perhaps three hundred years this tree has stood its ground. Flourishing in good seasons, and holding on in bad times. "Beautiful" is not a word that comes to mind when one first sees it. No naturalist would photograph it as exemplary of its kind. Twisted by wind, split and charred by lightning, scarred by brushfires, chewed on by insects, and pecked by birds. Human beings have stripped…bark from its trunk, stapled barbed wire to it in using it as a corner post for a fence line, and nailed signs on it on three sides: NO HUNT-

ING; NO TRESPASSING; PLEASE CLOSE THE GATE. In commandeering this tree as a corner stake for claims of rights and property, miners and ranchers have hacked signs and symbols in its bark, and left Day-Glo orange survey tape tied to its branches. Now it serves as one side of a gate between an alfalfa field and open range. No matter what, in drought, flood, heat, and cold it has continued…at the greening tips of its upper branches and in its berrylike seed cones, there is yet the outreach of life.

I respect this old juniper tree. For its age, yes. And for its steadfastness in taking whatsoever is thrown at it.... Most of all I admire its capacity for…healing beyond all accidents and assaults. There is a will in it—toward continuing to be, come what may.

Last night, I went for a walk in the darkness of early autumn to check and see if someone had remembered to turn the Milky Way on and the wind off. Drawn back to the cabin by the yellow glow of a reading lamp in the living room, I stood outside the window for a long time and looked in at my wife curled up on the couch sewing a hem in a new pair of wool trousers for me.

For seventeen years she has been my companion, my friend, my co-conspirator.

Yesterday, we were outraged at one another over something that seems trivial now, but the fire of anger is not quite cooled beneath the surface ashes. Yesterday, I made her cry in frustration. Yesterday, she was mad at me. I know I drive her crazy sometimes. She's not always easy to live with either. Yesterday, old grievances were flung off the shelf where they are somewhat shakily stored.

Yet today we walked up the road to pick sweet corn from a neighbor's patch and walked back down the road hand in hand in our usual way. We're good at forgiving. We have to be. The weather of love [and friendship] comes and goes, and we must let it. It is a required condition of loving [and befriending] and being loved back.

And now, tonight, as I watch her through the window, I see her smile as she carefully fixes my trousers, perhaps thinking to make one leg slightly longer than the other in revenge.

The gate we passed through to pick corn was the one attached to the old juniper. And that tree comes to mind this night as I look in on her. I long for the love [friendship] we have to always be like that tree. With a steadfast ability to take it—a capacity for…healing and growing on, scars and all, come what may. [4]

Friends are like trees. It's time to plant, cultivate, and grow a few.

But they'll never germinate while you're reclining in your Lazy-Boy looking out the window. You have to make some tracks, cover some ground, and do some digging.

So let's get on with it. Life can get pretty dry without shade, and storms can be cold and wet when the long winds blow. Don't look for *me* out in that kind of weather.

I'll be under a tree.

"Beneath whose branches are you refreshed? And who rests beneath yours?" List them. Give thanks for them. *Pray for them.* Think of some small way to encourage each one, and get it done before the good intention fades.

LOCKING ARMS

1. "Trees are like friends." How? List some characteristics common to both strong trees and strong friendships.

2. Six steps were listed for connecting with a friend. Try to recall them. Explain what each one means:
   a. Know _____.
   b. Identify _____ _____.
   c. Take ____ _____.
   d. Focus ____ _____ _____.
   e. Keep both your _____ and _____.
   f. Stay _____, _____, and _____.

3. "We picture lovers face to face, but friends side by side; their eyes look ahead.... Friendships must be about something." What does this C. S. Lewis quote tell you about identifying a special friend.

4. The gnarled old juniper was said to be like friendship. "I long for the [friendship] we have to always be like that tree" with a "capacity for...healing and growing on, scars and all, come what may." Are you reminded of an old friendship out there wounded by some past assault? Are you encouraged to go back and lock arms again somehow? How could others encourage you and pray for you in that?

CHAPTER FIVE

Heading toward the High Country

When Friendship Overrules Logic

"My brother and fellow worker and fellow soldier..."

PHILIPPIANS 2:25

High country.

You can see it from the lowlands. It's up there above the pollution and haze. Up where the winds blow chill and clean, where wild flowers paint the upland meadows, where mountain peaks catch the first light of morning, cling to the last light of day, and loft their proud spires into the sky.

True friendship is the high country of life. And the highest peak of the high country might be called "Fellow-soldier Mountain."

At least Paul seemed to feel that way. When the great apostle described one friend in particular there seemed to be an increasingly rising crescendo in his voice as he related what they had been through together. Much like the announcer at a major public event, the introduction gathered momentum—"Ladies and Gentlemen, I give you the former governor of our state, the former congressman from New York, *the President of the United States."*

In similar and even more regal fashion Paul introduced his friend. This is "my brother" he said. This is my "fellow-worker." No...more yet...this is my "fellow-soldier!"

Fellow-soldiers are friends who've been through it together. As Louis L'Amour might have said, they've been over the mountain and ridden the river together. Side by side, they've walked into the long winds. They've weathered perils and storms and tight passages. They've faced ultimates together—like life and death.

When you face ultimates together, your souls tend to knit. Fellow-soldiering is the highest peak of friendship's high country. It's where we all long to go. It's the mountain we all wish to climb. The pure air we all yearn to breathe. The clear water that satisfies a soul-thirst deeper than a man can put words to.

Have you ever noticed that when you're headed for the high country, it's usually the roughest and rockiest roads that take you to the most beautiful places? It is in the throes of soldiering—facing life-and-death kinds of rough places together—that souls are welded.

Yes, the apostle Paul had a way of describing his friends. In a few words he captured the essence of their camaraderie. In a context of "kindred spirit" the old veteran looked up toward the ceiling, let his eyes gain that far-off glazed appearance, dipped his quill pen, and instructed all of us following in his train to "hold men like this (friend) in highest regard" (Philippians 2:25-30). The two of them had been through some battles together. They took similar risks, bore similar weights, and wore similar scars. Paul called Epaphroditus his "brother and fellow-worker and fellow-soldier." Their friendship reached its zenith in soldier terms. I know something about that kind of camaraderie from my own soldiering days.

FELLOW-SOLDIERING IN THE SIXTIES

A long time ago in what seems now like a galaxy far, far away, this nation was at war in the Republic of Vietnam. In the fall of 1967, freshly graduated from college, and at the heart of the season when the war was building to its peak, I found myself at Ft. Benning, Georgia. For junior officers bound for the Republic of Vietnam, Ft. Benning— home of the U.S. Army Infantry School—was a common stop. In those days virtually every young Regular Army lieutenant had orders to the U.S. Army Ranger School there.

I was no exception. With my head shaved, my body fit, and my mind alert, I stood in formation with 287 other men equally tense, proud, brave, and fearful all at the same time. A grizzled old Ranger cadre noncom stepped boldly in front of us, ordered us to "Stand at ease and listen up!" and began to speak.

Actually, he was shouting.

His head moved back and forth across the formation. It seemed as though his eyes met each of ours in turn. He was formidable. The guy had been around the block. He'd been to "Nam and back." And he had something to say.

Other training situations had been just that. Training situations. Somehow this was different. The man who swept his flinty gaze across our ranks had a presence about him. Everything about him—his appearance, voice, eyes, experience—demanded attention. Besides that, we were men who knew something of our destiny: We were in the pipeline to Vietnam. Lyndon Johnson had opened the spigot, and the current was flowing. You could feel it. This was for real.

The old Ranger's speech was as lean and tough as his body. Every punctuated word of it seemed to come from his gut: "We are here to save your lives. To do so we are going to do two things with you over the course of the next nine weeks. First, we are going to see to it that you overcome all your natural fears—especially height and water. And, second, we are going to show you just how much incredible stress the human mind and body can endure. Many of you will not complete the nine weeks. It is simply too tough. But for those who do, when we are finished with you, you *will be* the U.S. Army's best. America's best. You *will* be confident. You *will* survive, even in combat. And you *will* accomplish your mission!"

After his remarks designed both to inspire and intimidate, the man gave us our first assignment. "Step one in your training is the assignment of your 'Ranger Buddy.'"

It was an amazing statement when you think about it. He had just told us that we faced an unbelievably daunting task. He had just told us it would prove to be too demanding for many of us. (He was right. Of the 287 candidates, less than half finished the nine weeks, and only ninety or so were awarded the coveted "Ranger tab" to be worn proudly on the soldier's left shoulder.) But he had also made a highly insightful statement about the nature of a man's soul.

When you walk a rough road, it's best to walk beside a friend. Together is better!

By making step one the assignment of a Ranger Buddy, the intent of the old soldier's next words were burned into our minds:

"Difficult assignments require a friend. The two of you will stick together. You will never leave each other. You will walk together, run together, eat together, sleep together. You will help each other. You will encourage each other. And, as necessary, you will carry each other."

We got the point. It was the Army's way of saying, "Never go into the water alone. Never go into battle alone. Never, ever walk alone. Stay together, Rangers! Live together...and if necessary, die together."

It is a theme that rings strong and clear from the pages of the New Testament. Life is difficult on this broken, soon-to-be-judged world. Believers need one another. God's soldiers need fellow soldiers. God's man needs a Ranger Buddy.

FELLOW-SOLDIERING, NEW TESTAMENT STYLE

What the U.S. Army Ranger school "discovered" was really just the military version of Jesus' commission to His followers:

> After this the Lord appointed seventy-two others and sent them two by two ahead of him to every town and place where he was about to go. He told them,..."Do not take a purse or bag or sandals" (Luke 10:1-2, 4, NIV).

Jesus Christ, Commanding General of history's greatest and ultimately most victorious army, was emphatic. You don't need a bunch of money. You don't need the best of equipment. You don't need the latest of anything. But you do need a friend. Take no purse, no bag, no shoes...but always take a friend.

Is it any wonder therefore that Promise Keepers, the most obvious instrument of the Spirit's movement among Christian men in our day, would insist that Promise Number Two state precisely the same commitment: "A Promise Keeper is committed to pursue vital relationships with a few other men, understanding that he needs brothers to help him keep his promises."

It's an unshakable life principle. Stick with your friends. Stand together. Lock arms. And face the enemy together. There is no greater love than that a man lay down his life for friends. The bottom line is that *there are times among true fellow-soldiers that friendship overrules logic.* And those who have never been there will never understand. It is reserved for friends of fellow-soldier stripe.

That's why I was so stung and angered by an article that appeared in *The Oregonian* newspaper in the fall of 1993, describing events in Somalia. You will likely remember the episode in which eighteen U.S. Army Rangers died in a firefight with rebel elements there. The headlines stated it in bold letters: **"Rangers' Raid: A Valorous Failure."**

It seemed to me the headline was clearly written by one who had never been in combat and had certainly never been a part of any team or unit, such as the Rangers, where men depend upon one another in an ultimate sense. Listen to the article:

> At the time, the October 3 raid into south Mogadishu by Army Rangers seemed like just another security sweep to round up troublemakers.
>
> But judging from its early political impact, the firefight in which 18 Americans were killed and 75 wounded might well be one of those searing battlefield experiences whose memory shapes public opinion and defines what the United States will and will not do in the world for years after...
>
> But a reconstruction of the raid, based on interviews with

many of the commanders, officers, and diplomats, shed new light on the action and shows that it reached the brink of success.

But the mission collapsed when an Army helicopter was shot down—a setback the Rangers had no effective plan to deal with. In a display of valor, they refused to retreat until they had recovered the body of the dead pilot, prolonging the ordeal.

"We definitely achieved surprise," McKnight said. "We were right on track and in good shape."

But some 35 minutes into the operation, disaster struck: The lead Blackhawk helicopter was shot down by a rocket-propelled grenade.... A group of about 100 soldiers formed a perimeter around the downed helicopter. Their decision to stay changed the entire character of the operation.[1]

Off to the side, in a shaded column, the newspaper printed the following summary under the headline "The Ranger Credo."

The Problem: As the bullets and grenades whizzed through the streets of south Mogadishu on the night of October 3, the Rangers made a fateful decision: After they retrieved the wounded soldiers from a downed Blackhawk helicopter, they stayed to guard the body of a dead pilot caught in the wreckage. [Are you *certain* he was dead?]

The Policy: There is no Army requirement to retrieve the dead if lives are in jeopardy. But the elite Army Rangers go by their own ethic.

The Code: In conversation with the Rangers, this is how they describe the code: in a world where, at any moment, they could be dropped into a country to fight [in nearly impossible situations], their loyalty to those fighting beside them is as intense as their loyalty to their country. "The Ranger Creed," the code drilled into new volunteers, instructs each soldier to "complete the mission, though I be the lone survivor" and never to "leave a fallen comrade to fall into the hands of the enemy."[2]

Now then—was that raid a "valorous failure"? Hardly! There are matters of character that make and mark a man. And even apart from the watershed issues of the evangelical faith and salvation, some see them as worth dying for. I wish that reporter had not cheapened what those men did. There *are* a few things even more important than life itself.

Things such as keeping your word.

Things such as holding to your promise.

Things such as standing beside your brother.

Things such as proving your friendship.

Things such as staying and staying and staying...until you've given your all.

Things such as being a loyal fellow-soldier—no matter what—even to the point of death.

Now admittedly, some today—having the advantage of twenty-twenty hindsight and the somewhat silly job of pontificating about things they know little about—would have us read the fine print, reexamine the meaning of "fallen," and debate in the antiseptic, clinical world of the classroom what happens in the heat and dirt of life-and-death. I wonder how much those reporters in their safe newsroom really know about heat and dirt and selfless loyalty that offers a down payment in blood.

True, there are some who would have us believe "there is nothing worth dying for." But they are the ones who live only for this life. And only for this life's lower shelf, at that.

Now I ask you, which kind of a friend would you want? One that cuts and runs at the first sign of real trouble? Or one that will stay with you no matter what? In the heat of the intense, hectic, chaos of combat who has the time to fully and instantaneously measure the difference between a seriously wounded, unconscious body and one from which life has departed? And if there is *any* doubt whatsoever (and you were that body) what would you want your friends to do? There is no doubt in my mind. There is no greater love than that a man lay down his life for his friends.

But our "friendly reporter" reflected the values of an eroded America. An America where the loftiest value is SELF. Self orientation. Self improvement. Self preservation. Self assertion. Self-Self-Self. Our culture's highest value seems to be "being true to self." That is the Credo of the Cult of the Individual—the most destructive and insidious false religion in this country. And its venomous toxin is eating away at the fabric of our entire society.

In a culture that ironically lives for self but is committing suicide by degrees, there is little room for the heroic. In fact, it is politically correct today to trivialize heroism.

In the heart of every budding King, Warrior, Mentor, and Friend, there resides an ancient call to the heroic. Heroism finds its apex in sacrifice. But because our culture chides masculinity, it mocks the heroic. Listen to John Leo's fitting commentary:

> Fighter pilots must not be regarded as heroes, according to a current show on World War I at the Smithsonian's National Air and Space Museum. But why not? Many were indeed heroes, performing gallantly and selflessly in moments of great danger.... [We see here] the Smithsonian's unswerving commitment to political correctness... To the PC believers, heroism of any kind is likely to seem crude, primitive, macho and perhaps even sexist...
>
> PC people will grudgingly accept some heroism among the nonwhite and nonmale, but their hearts aren't in it. The idea of saving and protecting people, as many heroes do, seems alien, intrusive and macho.

The idea is penetrating society at large, mostly as a feeling that heroism is embarrassingly out of sync with a self-absorbed culture greatly interested in rights and not very interested in duty and sacrifice.

When terrorists boarded the *Achille Lauro* and murdered Leon Klinghoffer, John O'Sullivan...assigned a reporter to phone various philosophers, historians and sociologists for comment. An elderly, crippled man in a wheel chair defied the terrorists and paid the price. Had he acted rightly, and is such heroism a moral ideal today? Only one of those phoned took a positive view of Klinghoffer's stance. Most of those questioned condemned both Klinghoffer and the ideal of heroism itself...

The reporter, a young woman who admired Klinghoffer's action, was "somewhat shaken" by the cold self-calculation among the professors. Though Klinghoffer's defiance was certainly debatable, the rejection of self-sacrifice and heroism was clear. O'Sullivan says of the reporter: "What she had blundered up against was hostility to one element of traditional morality." [3]

That Somali raid was no "valorous failure." It was valorous all right. But it was no failure in the eyes of those Rangers. Maybe, just maybe, they were the ones thinking accurately. Maybe, just maybe, they were the ones who understood true success. Maybe, just maybe, they realized we are all going to die someday some way anyway, and that their commitment to each other was worth the price. Maybe they believed there was something higher than living out seventy years of workaday stuff. Maybe they believed there are some things worth dying for. And maybe Americans like our friendly reporter are the real failures—having failed to perceive the deepest of values.

FELLOW-SOLDIERS ARE "BROTHERS"

Yes, friendship, true soul-knitting, spirit-expanding friendship is so desirous, so valuable that sometimes it simply overrules logic. I think that principle may be some of what Paul was trying to communicate when he described Epaphroditus as his "brother."

Brotherliness is another word for biblical and masculine friendship. It is a wonderful thing—a gift to the soul. The word means, literally, "from the same womb." And we all know what that means: there is here a kindred spirit, a level of commitment, a blood-is-thicker-than-water element, that takes the bond to a higher level.

I have a physical and spiritual brother named Eric. Eric is my friend. We live in different cities separated by miles, we pursue different professional fields, and we certainly don't see one another as often as we would like. But we are brothers. And we both know there is no limit to our commitment to one another. I would do anything for him. He would do anything for me. That's what brothers are for!

Sometime back when my oldest son was a senior in high school and his younger brother a sophomore, an incident took place that was to mark their friendship. Blake, the younger of the two, was adjusting to high school. Still somewhat naive of "acceptable" sophomore deportment, he had unwittingly drawn the ire of an older student in some way that to this day he can't figure out.

On the day in question, he was bent over reaching into the lower level of his locker. Without warning and with force enough to rip his shirt, an older, bigger, and stronger kid grabbed him at the chest, stood him up, and ripped him around to face off. The kid squared off, mouthed some angry expletives, and prepared to beat the daylights out of the smaller Blake. A crowd gathered and tension shot down the hallway like an electric current. The spectacle was about to begin.

Later Blake told me, "Dad, I didn't know what to do. Run? Duck? Swing first? Stand and take it?" He went on to say, "But in the split second that I was trying to decide, something from the side caught my eye. It was big. And it was coming *fast!*"

It turned out that the something big and fast was Kent, Blake's six-foot-five older brother. Blake described Kent picking the other kid up, hauling him out of the hallway and into the school's courtyard, shoving him back against the wall, and announcing, "Don't you *ever* fight that kid in there. He's my brother. I don't even care if he starts it. Don't fight him. Because he's my brother and *I'll finish it for him.*"

Years later at Blake's wedding, he asked that Kent and Ryan (his younger brother), and his Dad all serve as his "best man." The four of us walked down the aisle together. I felt like a platoon leader again for the first time in years. As the four of us good friends stood there, the words Blake had written to Kent in the wedding program came back to me: "Kent—you are my older brother, and to those who have one— that says it all. You have shown me what the word 'loyalty' means and have been my example of unconditional love. Since the day you fought old 'so and so' off my back, I have held you on a shelf all its own. Thanks for always watching out for me and seeing to it that your younger brothers prosper. I love you, bro!... My oldest brother and friend—thanks for being a model I could follow. Your protection and love will always be deep in my heart." Brothers are born for adversity.

When I consider these things, I'm reminded of the old Boys Town USA poster. Remember the caption?

"He ain't heavy. He's my brother!"

The poster represented one of the oldest and most famous orphan-ages in this country. Father Flanagan had captured the heart of the orphanage and the hearts of America in that well-known poster. In the background are the wide-open, storm-wracked skies of the American Midwest. An ominous storm brews in the direction from which two young urchins have just come. The younger boy clings to the back of the older boy. The two have evidently just knocked on the door of a farm house seeking shelter. A rather matronly figure has answered the door and apparently quizzed the boys a bit and made comment about the fact that one is carrying the other.

The poster's caption is the words of the older boy's response.

He says simply, "He ain't heavy. He's my brother."

Now I don't know all that was meant by the author of that statement and poster, but I have an idea. I have the notion he may have meant something like this...

"Ma'am, I know it looks silly or difficult for me to be carrying him. But we're all we've got in this world. Each other is it. And this world is not all that friendly. With the two of us it's 'all for one and one for all.' Period. We're barely outrunning the storms. And he was struggling. So I carried him. If I didn't carry him, he wouldn't have made it. So I just don't let his weight effect me. He's my brother. As far as I'm concerned, the law of gravity just doesn't apply to us. We'll do anything for each other. Our love governs our attitudes. Our friendship overrules logic."

That's the way it is with friends, whether they face a storm sweeping across the prairies, a bully in a high school corridor, or a murderous mob in Mogadishu. The deepest of friendships will often overrule logic. The things that would normally come between people don't apply because we're friends. The points of irritation are governed by the relationship. And the steep prices sometimes demanded are simply worth the friendship.

IN THE TRENCHES

You've probably heard the powerful story coming out of World War I of the deep friendship of two soldiers in the trenches. Two buddies were serving together in the mud and misery of that wretched European stalemate (one version even identifies them as actual brothers). Month after long month they lived out their lives in the trenches, in the cold and the mud, under fire and under orders.

From time to time one side or the other would rise up out of the trenches, fling their bodies against the opposing line and slink back to lick their wounds, bury their dead, and wait to do it all over again. In the process, friendships were forged in the misery. Two soldiers became particularly close. Day after day, night after night, terror after terror, they talked of life, of families, of hopes, of what they would do when (and if) they returned from this horror.

SNAPSHOTS:
MY FRIENDS TELL THEIR STORIES

Bill is one of my very few "soul mates" in life. That's not to say that we have very much in common or that we share any of the same interests or skills or hobbies. We are soul mates because we connect at the level of life values. We are passionate about building the same kingdom and that cause is larger than the petty issues of our lives.

Several years ago I betrayed Bill. In my immaturity, I said some things that hurt him and would have provided any lesser man with reason to abandon the relationship. God used that confrontation to wake me up, to cause me to see my error and to confess my sin. It was a hard moment for both of us, but perhaps the most significant in defining our current relationship.

Bill never allowed my failure to damage our relationship. He forgave me fully, accepting my sincere apology and never mentioning the issue again. We are brothers in the battle of life.

On one more fruitless charge, "Jim" fell, severely wounded. His friend, "Bill" made it back to the relative safety of the trenches. Meanwhile Jim lay suffering beneath the night flares. Between the trenches. Alone.

The shelling continued. The danger was at its peak. Between the trenches was no place to be. Still, Bill wished to reach his friend, to comfort him, to offer what encouragement only friends can offer. The officer in charge refused to let Bill leave the trench. It was simply too dangerous. As he turned his back, however, Bill went over the top. Ignoring the smell of cordite in the air, the concussion of incoming rounds, and the pounding in his chest, Bill made it to Jim.

Sometime later he managed to get Jim back to the safety of the trenches. Too late. His friend was gone. The somewhat self-righteous officer, seeing Jim's body, cynically asked Bill if it had been "worth the risk." Bill's response was without hesitation.

"Yes, sir, it was," he said. "My friend's last words made it more than worth it. He looked up at me and said, 'I knew you'd come.'"

BORN FOR ADVERSITY

Proverbs 17:17 says, "A friend loves at all times, [but] a brother is born for adversity." That statement is three thousand years old and still rings true.

A brother is a friend for *all* times, but particularly for the *hard* times. For it is in the hard times when we are most needy, and therefore most real, most authentic, and—frankly—most unlovable. And that is the point of the old Proverb—a friend loves at all times and a brother shows up best in the very hardest of times. A brother sticks. A brother doesn't make excuses and slip out the back door. A brother wades into the mess and crud and stands with you. And that's when you can tell your real friends. You can't always tell who your friends are on the good days and in the easy-going times.

I have seen that same selfless spirit at work—defying all logic—many times in my life. And it draws me. I've seen it in the military. I've seen it in my own family. And I've seen it among members of an athletic team.

KEN RUETTGER'S STORY

It would take a good-sized hombre to carry Ken Ruettgers on his back and say, "He ain't heavy." Ken is the starting Left Offensive Tackle for the Green Bay Packers (first round out of USC, 1985). At 6'6", 290 pounds, and benching 450 pounds, Ken can hold his own in the battle of behemoths. But there was one big man willing to "carry" Ken. A man with the heart of a tender warrior beating under his gridiron armor. I recently asked Ken to put his story on paper for me, and this is an excerpt from what he sent:

In the spring of 1993 the Green Bay Packers signed a tackle named Tunch Ilkin via the new free agency system. I was personally interested in this signing activity, because I also earn my living playing offensive tackle for the Green Bay Packers. As the Packers' "transitional designee" I was expected to withhold services throughout training camp due to a contract dispute, or what is more commonly known to sports fans as a "hold out."

During a spring mini-camp that year Tunch and I met and had dinner, shared our mutual faith in Christ, and swapped stories about our families. I told Tunch about the accountability group I was part of back home in Bakersfield and how incredibly great it was being part of that group. We decided that we would start one in Green Bay during the season and add another lineman, Rich Moran.

The preseason was underway and I was still at home without a contract. I called Rich to hear what was going on in training camp. He said Tunch had been moved to my position and that an article about Tunch was in the paper. The article explained that Tunch had been born in Turkey and that his father brought his family over to America to find a better life for his wife and only child. In America the Ilkins lived in a one-room apartment and Tunch had to sleep on a cot in the kitchen every night. It was a meager existence for a new immigrant family in America. After playing for Indiana, Tunch had been signed as a free agent for the Steelers and was cut his first year and then brought back, barely making the team.

Later in his career with the Steelers he earned All-Pro honors, was the team's captain, and a two-time Pro Bowl selection. What an incredible competitor. He was destroying guys out on the field. And what a success story! Here I was holding out for millions and a former immigrant from Turkey with a great success story was taking my place. To say the least, I wasn't a real popular guy at that particular time around the Green Bay area.

Finally, after the last preseason game, one week before the opener, I signed a new four year contract and the next thing I knew I was in the hotel the night before the first game. I was pleasantly surprised to see that my new roommate was Tunch.

Later that night, after meetings and a snack, we were getting ready to hit the sack and I said, "Ya' know Tunch, even though I have been starting for eight years and feel honored to be doing so tomorrow, I feel unworthy to start in front of such a great player like you."

Tunch sighed deeply and then smiled.

"Rut, I've played thirteen wonderful years in the league and my role on this team is to be a backup to you and Tootie (the other tackle). I'm sure you'll have a great game tomorrow. Remember to use the 'punch' we've been working on all week."

Even in light of what Tunch had said that night I knew that it bothered him; going from team captain of the Pittsburgh Steelers, being an All-Pro and a Pro Bowler, and a man endeared to every Steeler fan, to the role of a back up in Green Bay where fans didn't know him. It would bother anyone. I later learned it was something he prayed about throughout the season.

Most players in a similar position might feel anger, jealousy, spitefulness, and that they'd been cheated and wronged along with a host of other emotions. Some players would want to take it out on the coaches and undermine the player starting in front of him at the expense of the team.

Not Tunch Ilkin. In fact, just the opposite was true.

Within the first week he was a close friend and a mentor. He worked with me and other lineman during and after practice refining our technique. Even though he wasn't starting, he was still a leader. He was still willing to give himself completely—all of his hard-won knowledge, secrets, and experience—for the benefit of his teammates. Still, it must have hurt, knowing he was sacrificing his edge as an older and wiser professional who had lost some of his physical talent after thirteen years.

Today's generation of football players would call Tunch's behavior stupid. Not too long ago most people would call it a virtue. A characteristic of sacrifice and leadership. Tunch was a true champion and his new teammates knew it and respected him because of it.

One of the techniques that he helped me refine was "the punch." It had always been a weakness in my game. In football, when an offensive lineman is pass blocking and focused on protecting the quarterback, one of the most effective weapons is the punch. A good puncher using both hands, explodes his fists, firing every muscle in his arms and back in a controlled violence, and plants them through the chest of the pass rusher, stopping his charge. That is a punch. Good footwork will get you in good position between the pass rusher and the quarterback, but the punch is what separates the men from the boys. It's the difference between a good block and a great block. The punch is a weapon used, like a boxer, to neutralize opponents. It stops the top pass rusher dead in his tracks. The punch penetrates the core of the defender and disarms him.

That's what Tunch so faithfully and patiently brought back to my game. Every week the film would reveal the improvement of my punching technique. Every week we would get together after practice and work extra on striking hand held punching bags and reviewing film to form strategy against that week's opponent. We would talk about it over breakfast. Besides talking about football and technique we enjoyed talking about politics, values, and tough decisions in life. We shared stories of great victories and painful defeats, of individual battles won and lost, of embarrassing moments and moments of pure conquering victory. It was more than great. We talked about biblical heroes and the good and bad characteristics of each, the temptations and how some overcame them and others fell, and the consequences of falling. Our families enjoyed meals together and our children played together.

The day after our eighth game I came into the locker room and Tunch was cleaning out his locker. He looked up at me and said, "They just cut me, Rut."

I couldn't believe it! *Tunch had just been fired.* My heart sank. I got a big lump in my throat and had to leave the locker room to regain my composure. The friendship that in just eight weeks was stronger than any other friendship I had ever experienced had just been cut short by the casualties of football.

I couldn't even believe I was feeling such strong emotions inside. After eight years of football I had seen friends come and go, get cut, or retire due to sudden injury. But I had never ever felt this way. I tried to rationalize Tunch's departure. After all, it was part of the game. It was expected. That's football. But not this. This wasn't suppose to happen. Not like this. Not in the middle of the season. Not in the middle of a great friendship.

I am thankful the following Sunday was a bye and we didn't have a game for two weeks. I don't think I could have prepared myself in time to rise to the occasion and compete at the level necessary that next Sunday. I could barely make it through a meeting that week. It was hard to watch film through teared up eyes. Practice became torturous. I was angry and had lost my desire to be part of such a pitiful occupation. Dinners at home were just as tough and I had lost my appetite. I had lost my companion, mentor, and friend. My partner was leaving. I felt alone in battle. Isolated.

It was only through Tunch revealing his contentment in respect to his long and blessed career and his desire to try to understand and follow God's new plan for his life that I found solace. I asked him how I could feel so strongly about him being fired when I was part of a game that regularly found players prematurely departing for various reasons. After all we really only had become close friends for eight weeks.

He explained that it was because of our strong friendship. A friendship based in the Lord Jesus. There is no friendship stronger than one based in God. Because the Holy Spirit was working in both our lives and our friendship, it allowed us to lay it on the line. We didn't hold back when it came to sharing thoughts, beliefs, and emotions with each other. We were willing to take a chance, a risk, and lay a friendship in the best base possible. We took a stand to stand strong for and with one another. That is why it hurt so badly and so deeply when Tunch was terminated.

The good news. Tunch was asked to come back five weeks later. He accepted the offer. We continued our friendship. And we went to the playoffs for the first time in twenty years as an organization.

During the off season following Tunch's time in Green Bay one of the coaches came up to me and told me that my punching technique had developed a funny cycle during the previous season. I was surprised to hear that a pattern was so evident. He said he could tell when Tunch had been cut and then returned. The power of friendship is amazing. The best ones punch through the surface and penetrate deep into the core of our souls stopping us in our tracks.

Well said, Ken.

Brothers. Fellow workers. Fellow soldiers. It doesn't matter if the friendship shows up on the football field, in the deadly heat of combat, or in the stress and pressure of today's workaday world. Once you've experienced logic-defying, fellow-soldier love, you'll never forget it.

Sometimes, it goes beyond logic. You don't fall on grenades because of "logic."

It wasn't "logic" that led Jesus to pack His cross on a lacerated shoulder and make that long climb up Mount Calvary.

It wasn't "logic" that caused Paul to walk away from ministry because he missed his friend Titus.

And it wasn't "logic" that motivated Jonathan to give up his sword, his robe, and his future because of his friendship with David.

Logic is fine for negotiating the swamps and haze of ordinary life in the lowlands.

But only love will take you to the high country.

A MAN FACES HIMSELF

1. Not all of us have been in the military, but most of us can identify facing "ultimates" in life—times that were life-threatening or life-changing. Do you remember anyone standing with you in one of those times? What is it you remember about that person?

2. There are a lot of times when we're out-classed or exhausted by the obstacles that oppose us. Young Blake was caught off guard and overwhelmed. He needed his big brother's intervention. The younger of the two waifs needed a brother to carry him. Do you know any "younger brothers" out there now who feel outclassed, outmanned, and overwhelmed by the obstacles they face? To whom could you be a brother in his time of adversity?

LOCKING ARMS

1. Once the young soldiers began to grasp the incredible demands they were facing in Ranger school, step one was to find "a Ranger Buddy," because "difficult assignments require a friend." When life hands you one of those difficult assignments, do you go looking for a friend—or find yourself isolating even more than ever?

2. Part of the Ranger Creed is to never "leave a fallen comrade to fall into the hands of the enemy." Name three or four times in a man's life when he might be susceptible to falling into the hands of "the enemy."

3. With his dying breath, the wounded soldier on the battlefield whispered gratefully to his friend, "I knew you'd come." What do you suppose it was about his friend that generated such trust? What would it take for a friend to have that much faith in you?

4. Tunch Ilkin…a former team captain, Pro Bowl veteran, the best of the best. Then he finds himself a back up player—before being cut from the team. That's a lot for a man to swallow. Some big disappointments and setbacks…perhaps similar to some of the things you've been facing. In what ways did Tunch model true manhood—and manly friendship?

Real Men Lock Arms

The Theology of Friendship (Part One)

"I pray...Father...that they may be one, just as we are one."
JESUS

T hey were cross-town high school rivals, looking back on generations of dog-eat-dog, in-your-face competition. It was their first face-off of the season—and by far the biggest game of the year. Both coaches had scouted their rivals, both teams were shot-through with adrenaline. It seemed like the whole town crammed into the gym to watch the combat. I was still in middle school at the time, cheering on the team I dreamed of playing for someday.

The first half lived up to its billing—and then some. A single point marked the difference in score as the sweat-drenched warriors strode into opposing locker rooms behind their respective generals.

During halftime, no one dared vacate their seat for a bag of popcorn. Only the direst of needs impelled fans to seek the hallways. This was the game of the year, and you didn't want to spend the second half craning your neck behind a standing-room-only crowd between the bleachers.

Rules at that time still required a center jump at the start of the second half. Ten players positioned themselves around the Cyclops at center court. The ball was up. Our guys controlled the tip, and ran their play...to absolute perfection. It was textbook all the way. If video tape had been in use in those days, it would have been highlight stuff for the eleven o'clock news.

The center made a sweet tip to the other big man at the circle. He wheeled in mid-air and—before his white Converse All-Stars touched down again on the hardwood—rifled a two-handed, over-the-head pass to one of our guards breaking down the sideline. That guard, in turn, ripped a one-handed cross-court "baseball" pass to the other guard breaking for the basket. He took the ball in mid-stride and soared for a lay-up. The ball kissed the little white square on the backboard and dropped nicely through the net.

Two points! Bedlam! The home crowd went nuts.

Then suddenly—like a plug jerked on a radio—the gym fell silent. Heads turned. Voices murmured. Faces wrinkled with perplexity.

Everyone in the gym—spectators, players, and referees—realized the same thing at the same moment. Wrong basket! Unbelievable. *How could that be?* It couldn't have happened. But it did. And two points went up in lights on the opponent's scoreboard to prove it.

The home team lost the game that night by one point. As it turned out, they had actually put the winning points in the other team's basket. Our heroes determined the final losing difference by their own great play. That spectacular fast break basket, flawlessly executed as it was, cost them the ball game.

Our team had done everything perfectly. Disciplined play…crisp passing…no wasted dribbling…every motion counting. But they lost.

If you aren't careful, life can be like that. You can do everything well, but if you forget where you're going, you will lose.

So what counts in life?

How do you add up the score?

What really matters?

What's the goal?

Passing and dribbling have to have a context. And so does friendship. Let's create a little context for friendship, so we don't run off in the wrong direction. The old German proverb says it so well: *The main thing is that the main thing always remain the main thing.* As you pursue life, as we pursue this thing called masculine friendship, what's the main thing? Let me remind us of the Creator's answer to that watershed question: "Whatever you do, do all to the glory of God" (1 Corinthians 10:31).

It doesn't get any more basic than that. "Hold on," you're saying, "here we go getting religious and I thought we were just trying to figure out friendship." We are. You watch. The main thing must remain the main thing. And if it doesn't, we all lose. So hang with me for a few pages here, put on your thinking cap, and let's have a little fun with some great theology. After all, theology is life. To know Him is to really *live.* There's a lot of food for thought coming up here, and it's in bite-size chunks. Some chapters are candy bars. This one is a power bar. But it's still sweet, and it's good for you.

FRIENDSHIP'S PURPOSE: THE GLORY OF GOD

What's God's glory have to do with friendship?

Just about everything.

The "glory of God," according to Scripture, is the foundational purpose for everything that exists. And, if you read it right, I think you'll find friendship at the very core—dead center, bull's eye, Ground Zero—of all God meant by His "glory."

Picture old Moses and the infant nation of Israel out in the Sinai desert. This is no Girl Scout picnic. What started out as a hilarious, soul-bursting, dream-making, nation-building trek to a new land of promise has quickly devolved into an epic nightmare.

Like weary children on a long hike, the people of God have become distracted and petulant. The vision of a glorious Promised Land that danced in their eyes in those first heady moments of exodus has long since faded. Now, they're preoccupied by their blisters, their stomachs, their petty discomforts, the length of the journey, and memories of their old lives back in "good ol' Egypt." Miriam's hit tune about crossing the Red Sea and drowning Pharaoh's armies has been replaced by whines of discontent.

When Moses descends from a summit meeting with God on Mount Sinai, he is greeted with the astounding picture of his people frolicking around a great idol—a calf molded from gold. Aaron offers the limpest of explanations. He says, in effect, "Well, we took our gold—you know, earrings and things—and I tossed 'em into the fire and—would you believe it?—out jumped this calf." (Read it for yourself, Exodus 32.)

Moses, the leader charged by God with getting these two million souls across the wilderness to Canaan, is beside himself. *A golden calf? A sexual orgy? My own brother leading the debauchery? This is insane.*

Yes, Moses is angry. But more than that, he's deeply discouraged. In the secret places of his own soul, the bright vision begins to flicker and fade. He's beginning to wonder if the desert is crossable, if the people are leadable, if the mission is really doable. Panic creeps up into the back of his throat like bitter bile. And in the pain of his own soul, he tells God he's not up to this task. The job is way over his head. He's fading, and he really can't go on.

If anyone ever needed a fresh glimpse of God, it's Moses. And he knows it. Unless he regains a vision of God's greatness and glory he might as well book return tickets to Egypt for the whole motley lot of them. He might as well reapply for his old job as Jethro's junior shepherd.

So what do *you* do when you're deeply discouraged and need a fresh vision of God? Maybe you do like Moses did. You up and ask for one.

He says essentially, "Lord, I don't know how else to say it. But somehow, I just have to *see* You. I'm not sure what I'm even asking for God, but if You want me to lead this unruly bunch, I need to lay eyes on You, just this once. I have to know You, Lord. Have to know what You're like. If I can't get some kind of grip on You, Lord, then You'd better just count me out. This thing's gotten way out of control."

SNAPSHOTS:
MY FRIENDS TELL THEIR STORIES

Here was a guy I was scared of approaching—he was a missionary kid, a Bible college student. He had to be so far beyond me spiritually. Why a guy like him wouldn't think twice about meeting with a spiritual weakling like me! What could we have in common?

I barely knew him, but something seemed to draw me to him. When I finally did get courageous enough to ask him, his immediate response was, "Sure, I would love to." He didn't even have to think twice!

What started out to be a weekly breakfast meeting to hold each other accountable for doing personal daily devotions, grew into many heartfelt personal conversations. What was shared together, never went any further than the man across the table. Then, after one year of meeting together, Tom took his family and left for the mission field.

I was overjoyed he was finally doing what he'd always dreamed of, but I also felt like my heart was being ripped out. I never knew I could grow to appreciate another man so much and not only value our friendship, but depend on it. We could talk about anything, anytime, anywhere, in total confidence and know the other guy was supportive in every way. I'd never known what fully open and trusting communication could be, and I thank him for showing me.

His actual words were "I pray Thee, show me Thy glory!" (Exodus 33:18).

So how does God respond to such a bold, impertinent request? Does He fry Moses right there in his dusty sandals? No. He answers His servant's prayer. It's easy to lose sight of the fact that God *wants* to be known by His people more than we'll ever want to know Him.

The Living One says in effect, "Okay, Moses, I'm going to show you who I am. I'm going to show you some things no human being has seen since Adam walked in the garden with Me. But we're going to have to make some special arrangements here. Because if you actually looked straight into My eyes, you'd sizzle like fat in the fire."

What happens next is so wrapped in mystery that it defies description. Moses himself, writing years later, recorded the Lord's special instructions:

> I Myself will make all My goodness pass before you, and will proclaim the name of the LORD before you; and I will be gracious to whom I am gracious, and will show compassion on whom I will show compassion.... You cannot see My face, for no man can see Me and live! (Exodus 33:19-20).

In some inconceivable kind of physical display, Almighty God places Moses in a protective place behind a rock and then—for good measure—covers him with His hand. Then, when it's safe, the strange encounter begins. He removes His hand for Moses to actually see with his own eyes the physical after-effects of God's passing—"My back" (NASB); "hindparts" (KJV).

Mind-boggling.

Now...screw that "thinking cap" down a little tighter.

Do you see what's actually happened here? God has taken some invisible kinds of things—goodness, grace, compassion, His "name"—and wrapped them in something physical and visible. His glory.

The Bible uses very physical terms to paint the picture of what happened here. These invisible character traits of the Lord took on physical capacities. They "passed by." They marked their presence in visible form. "My back parts" He had called them. You could say they were, quite literally, His "after glow." And God calls this physical, visible demonstration of His invisible, spiritual, character traits—His "glory."

Now let's drive for the friendship connection. On the one hand, His "glory is passing by." On the other, "I have passed by." He and His glory are inextricably linked. So we can say on good authority that the glory of God, our sole purpose for living, is the physical-visible demonstration of our God's great invisible character. I know that's a mouthful, but I don't want you to ever forget it. *The glory of God is a phenomenal, visible demonstration of His eternal invisible character.* (For those desiring extra credit—think through the meaning of the "cloud" by day and the "pillar of fire" by night.)

"Okay, you say, but I still don't see how *friendship* figures in this formula. What's this have to do with our task at hand?" Hang on. Let's get a grip on a little more theology. You'll love it. It'll knock your socks off. And you'll never look at your relationships the same way again.

THE PATTERN OF FRIENDSHIP: THE NATURE OF GOD

If the purpose of everything in general, and our friendships in particular, is the glory of God—a physical demonstration of God's invisible character—then it stands to reason that the next thing we need to know is what God is like.

What *is* God like? How would you answer such an enormous question?

How do you eat that proverbial elephant? One bite at a time. So let's take a quick mental jog through Scripture and see if we can't run by a few "bites" of what God is like. As a matter of fact, Scripture encourages us to "sample" Him in this way. As David put it: "O taste and see that the LORD is good; How blessed is the man who takes refuge in Him" (Psalm 34:8).

The Bible says a lot of things about Him. There are many adjectives that are appropriate for Him (however short of His actual Majesty they may fall). But there are really only a few things that the Bible says God IS.

Let's "bite" one off.

• **The Bible says "God IS love" (1 John 4:8).**

While it's beyond the scope of this book to deal with all this suggests, we can reduce it here to a key element or two. How about sacrifice? Sacrifice is at the heart of love. God is a sacrificer. He's always extending Himself, stretching himself out for the good of another. (Beginning to make the connection to the qualities of friendship?)

Time for another bite.

• **The Bible says "God IS light" (1 John 1:5).**

What does light imply? Honesty. Truth. Transparency. Openness. All wonderful qualities of friendship.

Let's grab another bite.

• **The Bible says "God IS spirit" (John 4:24).**

The spirit is that unseen core of one's personal identity. It is your spirit that makes you *you.* Your body is just the vehicle you're driving around. At another level, your soul (mind, will, emotions, etc.) is the unseen part acting as that vehicle's transmission. It takes the energy from the engine (the power plant) and transmits it to the wheels where the rubber meets the road. Within that analogy, your spirit is your engine, the power plant, the "genius" of the vehicle that makes a car a car and not just another wagon. Your spirit is the deepest level of personal identity. The irreducible minimum. You. It is at that intensely personal level of authenticity that God wishes to commune with you. And it is at that level that God wishes His kids to commune with each other—friend to friend—as a reflection of what He is like.

Ready for one more bite?

• **The Bible says "God IS one" (Deuteronomy 6:4).**

"Hear, O Israel! The LORD is our God, the LORD is one!"

Given Israel's confusion about what God expected of them and their attraction to the foolish polytheism around them, He determined to make it pretty plain. It's as if He was saying, "Israel, if you get nothing else, get this—your God IS ONE. Remember it. *Reflect it.* Learn to live together like your Triune God does."

Jesus developed the ramifications of that thought even more powerfully in His high priestly prayer in John 17. And you can see the implications for friendship. Get together. Like God does. Three in One. No one doing his own thing. (Consequently, private citizens in Israel weren't even permitted by God to harvest all their crops. They were to leave the corners of their fields for their less fortunate brothers. They were to look out for one another. Because, like their God who IS ONE, they were to live as one.) God wants His kids to live like He does, as best friends. God never goes anywhere without His two best Friends. And He would prefer you didn't either.

Wow, my head hurts! That's a lot to think about! But my heart is warmed by an incredible God, a God whose whole world is intended to reflect the beauty of relationships. There are no lone rangers in the Trinity. The Trinity always does it together. So get it together, friend. God doesn't want any lone rangers in His family, either. Because the kids are to reflect the Father. That's His glory.

As an aside, did you notice something? Those key passages that identify God's essence most clearly come primarily from just one biblical writer, one of Jesus' close friends. In fact, it can be argued that John, the beloved apostle, was Jesus' closest and best friend. He was the one who knew Him best, walked with Him closest, and connected with Him most intimately in spirit. John was the one man alive who was most able to get to the heart of the matter and answer the question, Who *is* this Man? Suggests something about friendship, doesn't it? Best friends can read one another like nobody else.

Well, let's try to get it together. When you put those four "bites" together, what do you have? God wants His kids to learn to live together like He does—in *loving, truthful, spiritual oneness.* Another way of saying that is SACRIFICIAL, TRANSPARENT, HEART-TO-HEART, UNITY.

That, my friends, is friendship.

It's also the church.

It is the communion of the Body. Don't you think Christ's Body ought to resemble the Triune God He is? Don't you think He ought to resemble Himself? Don't you think His Body should look like His Body? Of course! And I think that's precisely why Jesus, in His longest recorded prayer, prayed more for our *oneness* than any other thing. That's the point of the real "Lord's Prayer" in John 17. "Father, I pray they might be ONE just as [exactly as] we are ONE."

Do you want to please God? Get with His Body. Become a friend. Live like He does, man!

Let's take it a step further. If the purpose of friendship is God's glory, and if the pattern in friendship is God's nature, then let's take a look at the posture for friendship.

THE POSTURE OF FRIENDSHIP: THE IMAGE OF GOD

The sons of God are to look like their Father. We're to be "spittin' images," so to speak. And He is, at His essence, three in one. Reflect on that, Christian. The sons of God are to look and live like He does—a plurality practicing unity. A unit practicing oneness. I think this is somewhere close to the mystery of the image of God and near the mind boggling nature of the Trinity.

If you believe in the Trinity, you are beginning to understand that the whole point of Truth is relationships. To live in light of God's truth is to experience deep, interpersonal relationships with Him and one another.

In fact, when you think about it, that is the very nature of salvation itself. "Salvation" is one of the words and concepts closest to the heart of Scripture. "Saved." Saved from what? Well, sin. And the first-fruit of sin is separation. Isolation. Death. Physical death is the separation of the soul from the body. Spiritual death is the separation of the soul from God. Marital death is the separation of marriage partners. Sin and death are nothing more nor less than separation—isolation.

Recall that the first sin in Eden isolated the first couple from both God and each other. They "hid" (Genesis 3:7-8) from Him and began throwing stones at one another ("God, that woman You gave me..."). And all the rest of Scripture is one great story of God "saving" His people from separation, isolation, and death.

That's why another word for salvation is *reconciliation*. The reconciliation of man to God. And the reconciliation of man to man.

That's why another word for reconciliation of man-to-man is "together."

And why another word for together is "friendship."

And why another word for friendship is "church."

The local church is nothing more nor less than a biblical circle of friends.

I will admit to being more than a little weary of small-minded preachers who spend all their time beating people over the head with the "truth," and destroying relationships in the process. One without the other is neither. There is no real truth without the relationships. And there are no bona fide relationships without the truth. It's not truth *or* relationships, it's truth *in* relationships. If you can't live out truth in relationships, you probably aren't even close to the truth. So, Christians, we'd better get along and together.

I remember a good friend in seminary named Eric. He'd grown up in a church denomination that enjoyed a wonderful sense of getting along in warm relationships. I'd grown up in a denomination that prided itself on "upholding the truth." Now in seminary, we reversed roles. He was a youth pastor in my boyhood denomination. I became a youth pastor in his. We would meet regularly for lunch on the seminary campus and try to decide which was better—a church where people loved each other but knew very little about the Bible and theological truth, or a church where people really knew the Scriptures *but hated each other.*

What a disaster! Of course, neither kind represented Christ. The one had a low view of His Word. The other had a low view of His Body. And they both misrepresented Him terribly. You can't reflect the Triune God without both. His Word in the flesh. Like Jesus. "Full of grace and truth" (John 1:14).

I'm going to ask you to stick with me here. That last "bite" was a big one. We're going to have to chew on it for awhile, so we can digest it properly—so we can gain nourishment from it and grow up to be like our Father. He'd like that. So let's stay at the table a bit longer. One more chapter's worth.

And like you would any good steak, let's savor the flavor—a plurality practicing unity. This is at the heart of what we're working on here: the rediscovering of masculine friendship in a world of isolation. It's a masculine ecclesiology of sorts. And, like our Father might say, "It's good for you, son." It's the "meat and potatoes" of both friendship and churchmanship—two very similar character traits our Father wants developed in all His wide family.

Nothing pleases the Father like the oneness of His kids.

1. "You can do everything well, but if you forget where you're going, you will lose." The basketball game started well, but somehow, during the half, they became distracted. Still ready to play, but somehow turned around. How about you? Still know where you're going? Still on track? Could it be in some area of your life you still want to "play ball," but you've been distracted and turned around? Think about it. *"If you forget where you're going, you will lose."*

2. Do you know someone else who may have gotten his eyes on the wrong goal? Are you going to let him go? Are you going to let him make a play that could cost him a great deal? Can a real friend say "it's none of my business?"

LOCKING ARMS

1. God wants His kids to live lives that reflect four aspects of His character. How does each apply to you as a true friend to someone?

　　a. sacrificial

　　b. transparent

　　c. heart-to-heart

　　d. united

2. "So what do you do when you're deeply discouraged and need a fresh vision of God?" Do friends help you? How?

3. "Sin and death are nothing more nor less than separation—isolation." What makes people live out lives of lonely isolation? Why is it so important for us, as friends, to overcome isolation?

4. Friendship's purpose: the glory of God. How? Why?

5. It was said John was Jesus' best friend on earth. How do you suppose John was able to be a friend to Jesus, to meet relational needs in His life? Jesus called us friends and brothers as well. Do you ever think of Jesus wanting a relationship with you, individually? How do you respond?

6. "All the rest of Scripture is one great story of God 'saving' His people from separation, isolation, and death." Have you ever thought about the role you're having in the overall plan of God every time you befriend someone, lend a hand, rescue the needy?

CHAPTER SEVEN

History's Greatest High Five

The Theology of Friendship (Part Two)

"Standing firm in one spirit, with one mind striving together."
PHILIPPIANS 2:7

I love high school athletics. You've probably guessed that. Unlike their "bigger" college and professional counterparts, high school sports are more elemental and pure. It's the real stuff, and it's all there. The mountain peaks of emotional highs and the pits of emotional lows. Vast pleasures and bottomless sorrows. Grand moments and goofy youthful blunders and extra helpings of grit and courage and grace. To me, it's American sports at its finest.

Nothing in my experience, however, comes close to matching the intensity of championship high school basketball. I think of all those spontaneous on-court celebrations. The wild joy. The tears of frustration. The times when the guys just can't hold their passions in, and they explode in jubilation. Pressure and pleasure—all in the same few moments. Intensity and hilarity back to back. These games mean something to these kids.

Life's great moments are usually moments of intensity. Or hilarity. Or both.

That's why our family calls the state basketball tournament the "Annual Passover B-ball Championship"—to be "celebrated to all generations." It's fun just to watch the spectators between games. You see "game faces"…super-serious "go for it" faces…just-in-from-the-back-side-of-Oregon bewildered faces. And lots of arms-extended-over-heads-with-big-smiles faces. There are hugs, backslaps, and high-fives in abundance.

If there were high fives in the first century, I can think of a couple of scenes where Jesus likely would have practiced them. In fact, in one of those scenes His arms actually were extended, though not over His head. But His shout was a victory shout. It was a shout of great pressure and great pleasure (see Isaiah 53:11). There on the cross, when He had paid the price for our sins, with arms fully extended, the Lord of the universe shouted, *"It is finished!"* It was the greatest arms-extended, high-five moment in history!

In that singular moment, while the cosmos held its breath, Jesus experienced intensity, unspeakable suffering, and the consuming joy of accomplishment all at the same time. He had successfully paved the way for salvation, reconciliation, oneness. He had provided for the answer to His own prayers. He had provided for the realization of the Father's dream. The Firstborn had made a way for the brothers. He had sacrificed Himself for the church.

A FIRST-CENTURY ROUND TABLE

Another scene in Jesus' life that called for high-fives took place on a retreat. He was well into His public ministry. In fact, He was about to turn His eyes toward Jerusalem. He was about to begin His own death march, eyes focused, will steeled, and heart set. Not to be distracted, Jesus was in the process of getting on His "game face." This was it. The big one. The moment on which time and eternity hinged.

In preparation, He called a retreat for His team (see Matthew 16). The King assembled His somewhat rusty knights there in the foothills of the north country, not far from the slopes of Mt. Hermon. On that retreat at Caesarea Philippi, "around the table" so to speak, He reviewed the game plan.

It all began when He asked His men a few questions.

"Who do people say that the Son of Man is?" More importantly, "Who do *you* say that I am?"

Peter, the big guy, answered clearly and succinctly, "You are the Christ, the Son of the living God." In essence, *You're our King. We'll follow You anywhere.*

It was the right answer, and more than the right answer. It was the radiant key to a divine plan that had been in effect for centuries. It was the dream of the Father that His Firstborn would clear the way, set the pace. It was the Father and the Son, the King of kings and Lord of lords, preparing a table, an eternal feast. And He was preparing the way so that tens, hundreds, thousands, and millions would follow to join them at the marriage supper of the Lamb. This was the big one. The Lamb was about to carry the family colors onto the field of battle.

And Jesus could not contain His pleasure!

He shouted, "*Blessed are you Simon Barjonas,* because flesh and blood did not reveal this to you, but My Father who is in heaven!"

You've got it! Dare we think of the Second Person of the Trinity throwing back His head and laughing out loud? Yes, it was the right answer. The key. I like to think it was at that point that Jesus and His disciples would have exchanged high fives. Can't you picture Jesus on His feet, moving around to each of His men in that little circle, their hands over their heads, big smiles on their faces, and hands slapping?

(To be sure, there was a Judas around that table. A guy who never got with the program. Never played team ball. One guy who always did his own thing. One guy whose favorite song was, "I did it my way"...and the end thereof is death.)

And, yes, even Peter tripped, so soon after that glorious high-five moment. Like a high school athlete who plays magnificently over his head one moment then turns right around and makes a sophomoric blunder the next. When the King said He intended to die in this battle—that the way to victory was through the ultimate heroism of sacrifice—the Big Fisherman decided to take Him on. Bad decision, Peter. For a moment there, the King had to tell that rusty old knight to dismount and stand behind.

Peter was talking like the devil. In this King's army no one, I mean *no one* does his own thing. No man leads his own parade. We go together, the King's way, or we don't go at all. They were harsh words to old Peter, and probably cut like a whip. But the words had to be said.

How about you? Do you find yourself more like Peter than Jesus? Can you ask His forgiveness for bulldozing through life on your own course? Can you humble yourself? Can you get back in line? When the King calls, can you "fall in" without insisting on your own way? If you intend to ride with the King of kings, you'd better.

And I like to think it was at that point that Jesus—with jaw set and full game face—spoke His vision and heart. Loud and clear, in five little words. Five monosyllabic words that would change the course of human history.

"I...WILL...BUILD...MY...CHURCH!"

Message delivered! These are high-five moments. This is His team. This is His plan. This is His outfit. No one else calls the signals. Get in line, boys. Jesus has one and every intention of building this Body, and He will do it His way. It will look like Him, it will reflect Him, it will be a plurality practicing unity. It will be many in one. Many members, one body. One Spirit. One Lord. One faith. One hope. One baptism. And "one God and Father of all who is over all and through all and in all" (Ephesians 4:6).

And if you insist on chasing your own plans and goals, if you insist on leading your own one-man parade, you will look more like Judas than Jesus. More like Ananias and Saphira than Jesus and those who are serious about His church. So get in line and take orders. Stop acting like you're giving them.

"I WILL BUILD MY CHURCH"

Yes, it is Jesus' church, and when you take Jesus seriously you will take His church seriously. Mark this: *Building His church is the only thing on earth He is choosing to do.* And if you ride with Him, it has to be somewhere near the heartbeat of your life. If you're a knight called to

His table, but you're a bit rusty, let's figure how to knock off the corrosion and ride with the kind of spit n' polish that reflects the Commander we serve.

When you ride with Christ, you ride in a company. Never alone. And may I add a word here? This church is not just some spooky, ethereal, spiritual, universal body. No, not by a long shot.

It is visible. It is physical. It is real. It is local. And it meets in your town. Roughly the modern equivalent of the pillar of fire and cloud, the church is the glory of God!

Of the hundred plus uses of the word "church" in the New Testament, the great bulk refer to the local church. The one on the corner near your home. Come on, guys. Come on back to the church. Without you His body looks more like a ladies' aid society than the Body of the King. Let's get with the program.

And may I say one more thing about that program? It starts with men. I want you to consider a statement from Pastor Jack Hayford that speaks for me. It is a statement that is, at one and the same time, altogether politically incorrect and biblically and historically accurate. Here are Pastor Hayford's insightful words:

> In most of His workings (throughout history and Scripture), God *starts* with men. Get that. *Men* are God's "starting place."... *The shaping of a man is foundational to anything God sets out to do.*[1]

Taking great pains to insure no misunderstanding, Pastor Jack properly insists that men and women are indeed equal in value before God, that "God has not perpetuated this order or sequence because men are wiser, or more intelligent, or more gifted...than women." He rightly and skillfully debunks male chauvinism. At the same time, he accurately and correctly notes that "God is unapologetic about this plan He has of 'starting things' with men.'" Pastor Hayford traces the pattern throughout God's Word, noting specific examples to which I've added a few:

- The human race began with a *man*—Adam.
- The covenant of the testaments was given to a *man*—Abraham.
- The twelve tribes of the nation of Israel began with a *man*—Jacob.
- The redemption of Israel was delivered through a *man*—Moses.
- The occupation of the Promised Land was led by a *man*—Joshua.
- The royal prototype of Messiah was a *man*—David.
- The Savior of the world came as a *man*—Jesus.
- Jesus began His ministry and founded His Church with a gathering of *men*—the Twelve.

And I must include here one more insightful statement from the good pastor that is reflective of the entire purpose of *Locking Arms:* "A man who would become the maximum person God can cause him to become is a man who discovers the power and blessing of partnership with other men."[2] He's right. "Rise up, O men of God, the church for you doth wait!"

Back to the main point—Christ is calling for commitment, and it is not commitment in the abstract. The universal, invisible church has never met. It is the *local* church that reflects His glory. It is impossible for the universal church to do that inasmuch as it has never yet been together! His glory is visible. And "together" is the heart of His glory. So get it together, boys. Fly the company colors. Show up. Take part. Enlist. Serve. Be all that you can be. In the local church. If you're not, you're doing your own thing again. And that one-man-against-the-Enemy stuff is deadly. It can kill you, and those you love.

All my life I've wanted to see a church work. For the last eighteen years I've been privileged to be part of an assembly of people who are determined to see it work, too. We know we're far from perfect. We know "we'll never do it perfectly around here, but we'll always do it together." Because that's what our Father and our firstborn Brother have asked of us.

Our driving theme, our motto, has become "Learning Together to Live Like Christ." Everyone is "learning." No one has arrived, *especially* the pastor. We are "together." No one pursues his own agenda. We want "to live" the truth, not just "know" it. We want to flesh out truth *in* relationships. And we want it all to look "like Christ." To be a reflection of the Living Triune God.

We want to be part of the answer to Jesus' most earnest prayer, "that they may all be one, just as We are one; I in them, and Thou in Me...that they may be perfected [matured] in unity, that the world may know that Thou didst send Me" (John 17:21, 23).

Now I grew up in the church. And I have to make a confession to you—I hated it early on. As a youngster I didn't enjoy it at all. I remember when my dad made the decision that Jesus was either everything He said He was or nothing at all. Dad made the right choice. He decided to get with the program. I was about eight years old at the time. Mom didn't yet know the Lord, and she wasn't about to go to church. At that point it was bothersome to her that Dad had, in the words of the street, "gone and got religion."

But I had no choice. Dad said the two of us were going.

I remember my first introduction to church in that little town. Some stranger herded me toward a room where a bunch of kids were singing "This is My Father's World." Well, it wasn't *my* father's world. And I was uptight. Some other kid kicked me under the table, and before I knew it we were rolling around on the floor in a fight. My first experience of church was a fight.

And, you know, over a lot of years it was pretty much that way. Churches are known for fighting. Too bad isn't it? The one thing Jesus prayed for—our oneness—is the one thing we're worst at.

Perhaps you've heard the story told by comedian Emo Phillips. He states:

In conversation with a person I had recently met, I asked, "Are you Protestant or Catholic?" My new acquaintance replied, "Protestant." I said, "Me too!" "What franchise?" He answered, "Baptist." I said, "Me too!" "Northern Baptist or Southern Baptist?" "Northern Baptist," he replied. "Me too!" I shouted. We continued to go back and forth. Finally I asked, "Northern Conservative Fundamentalist Baptist, Great Lakes Region, Council of 1879 or Northern Conservative Fundamentalist Baptist, Great Lakes Region, Council of 1912?" He replied, "Northern Conservative Fundamentalist Baptist, Great Lakes Region, Council of 1912." I said, "Die heretic!"[3]

Hilarious. Funny. And maybe just a little bit too close to reality for comfort. Our Lord's dream turned into a nightmare, and that's our big point in this chapter on the theology of friendship: NOTHING PLEASES THE FATHER LIKE THE ONENESS OF HIS CHILDREN.

That is true in my family, your family, His family, and any family that understands the meaning of the word "family." Any kind of rivalry, enmity, comparing, or posturing is destructive to a family circle.

Pleasing the Father through oneness is the primary purpose of friendship. It is the primary purpose of the church to reflect His glory…to live like He does…to project His image on the screen of this life so others can catch a glimpse of bright eternal realities. It was so crucial to Him, He called it the bottom line:

> A new commandment I give to you, that you love one another,
> even as I have loved you, that you also love one another. By this
> all men will know that you are My disciples, if you have love
> for one another (John 13:34-35).

Jesus wrapped the concept in strong words. Listen…the only way the world is going to know that the Father sent the Son is by your treatment of your friends in the Body of Christ. The way you and I treat each other *is* the bottom line. It is the mark of the Christian. It is the flag of those who follow in this King's train.

It is also at the heart of the Father's promise. Millennia ago, the Father began to fulfill His dream. The creation had been stained by sin (Genesis 3). Death was the prevailing theme of the planet (Genesis 5). He had sought to wash it up once (Genesis 9). But the generations to follow Noah had continued in the ways of their fathers—chasing their own lusts, drinking the cup of sin and rebellion against God down to its dregs. It became unbearable.

By the time we arrive at Genesis 11, it is so bad that even God's greatest gift for plurality practicing unity—the gift of language, common understanding, communion, communication—humans had turned against Him. They began to use this heaven-sent blessing of one language to go their own way, to build their own kingdom.

God had to do something. The Father whose dream was for His children to live together in oneness had to scatter them. Separate. Disperse. Send apart. The thing He hated most, He had to do. And I believe it broke His great heart.

But that's why Genesis 12 follows Genesis 11. The Father would not let His dream die. Out of the ashes of the scattering came the beauty of the covenant. God at His heart is a promise maker and keeper. He made a promise to a man that through His family "all the families of the earth shall be blessed." One day all of these scattered peoples would be gathered again—through the Seed of Abraham. That covenant with Abraham governs all the rest of Scripture. Everything that follows Genesis 12 is geared to fulfill that promise and see the people of the earth come together again around the Father's table.

The elements of that covenant called for sacrifice. Abraham's son Isaac became a living prophecy of the Greater Son of Abraham who, like His type Isaac, would crawl up onto the altar of His own will at the Father's direction.

There was a major difference, however. When Isaac and his father climbed Moriah, there was a substitute ram in the bushes. When the

Heavenly Father and His Son walked up the hill called Calvary, there was no substitute ram in the bushes. There would be no staying of the Father's arm this time. The knife would fall. Jesus was, indeed, the Lamb. The Father had to see His own Son die. For His Son was the Passover Lamb whose blood washed and bore away the sins of the people and provided a way out of the bondage of sin and death to a new land of promise.

There was a new day coming when all the people would gather together again. It was that day which Jesus had in mind when He sat with His eleven rusty knights just prior to His ascension and they reviewed the game plan one more time:

> And gathering them together, He commanded them not to leave Jerusalem, but to wait for what the Father had promised, "which" He said, "you heard of from me; for John baptized with water, but you shall be baptized with the Holy Spirit not many days from now" (Acts 1:4-5).

Just ten days later, it happened. The Father blew the doors off with the coming of the Spirit. Watch what happened.

> They were all together in one place…they were all filled with the Holy Spirit and began to speak with other tongues, as the Spirit was giving them utterance. Now there were Jews living in Jerusalem, devout men, from every nation under heaven…each hearing them speak in his own language. (Read Acts 2 in its entirety.)

Did you notice? It was the *reversal* of the Tower of Babel and the scattering of the people. The Tower of Babel where one language became many, and the people were confused, was turned around. The Church became a new "tower" of sorts where the many people with many languages came together and understood one another. They were beginning to learn together to live like Christ—the three-in-one God.

It was the birth of the Body of Christ. It was the fulfillment of the blessing of Abraham. It was Father's dream come true. The kids were together again.

Let's take just a moment to bring this scene into even sharper focus. The emphasis of Acts 2 is not the early verses, but the latter verses. Acts 2:1-11 records the historical facts, while Acts 2:41-47 is the Spirit's *summary* of what has happened. In the first-century language and genre, we call it the "period statement." Read it carefully:

They were continually devoting themselves to...teaching and to *fellowship,* to the breaking of bread and to prayer...and all those who had believed were *together* and had all things in common...and day by day continuing with *one mind*...they were taking their meals *together* with gladness and sincerity of heart.

They were continually in the process of, to quote our little motto again, "learning together to live like Christ." They were becoming a plurality practicing unity. They were starting to look like the Body of Christ, they were beginning to reflect His glory.

You see it again in the next summary statement of the book of Acts just a couple of chapters later in chapter 4. Same song, second verse.

And the congregation of those who believed were of one heart and [one] soul; and not [even] one of them claimed [was acting like] anything belonging to him was his own; but all things were common property to them. And with great power the apostles were giving witness to the resurrection of the Lord Jesus, and abundant grace was upon them all. For there was not a needy person among them, for all who were owners of lands or houses would sell them and bring the proceeds of the sales, and lay them at the apostles feet; and they would be distributed to each, as any had need (Acts 4:32-35).

Man, these guys were getting the picture! This was one Body. One faith. One hope. This was the Father's dream and the Father's glory. And did you notice something else? Sandwiched in between all the talk of their oneness is the statement about witnessing to the resurrection of the Lord Jesus—almost as though the greatest evidence of the resurrection in the first century was the oneness of the Body. Makes sense, doesn't it? The unbelievers—the many who had not witnessed the resurrected Christ—could *see* with their eyes the glory of God when Christ's Body got together. Jesus was alive among His people, and folks were beating the doors down to find this Messiah for themselves.

No wonder the great apostle of the New Testament, Paul himself, told the believers at Philippi to act the same:

> Conduct yourselves in a manner worthy of the gospel of Christ...standing firm in *one spirit,* with *one mind* striving *together* for the faith of the gospel (Philippians 1:27).

A little later Paul goes on to tell them to look even more like our living Triune God:

> ...Being of the *same mind,* maintaining the *same love, united* in spirit, intent on *one purpose...*not...looking out for your own personal interests, but also for the *interests of others* (Philippians 2:2-4).

Paul goes on in that same chapter to describe several individuals whose lives are marked by that kind of character—Jesus, Timothy, Epaphroditus. We're instructed to hold them in "high regard" as models of the kind of behavior we're to practice—others oriented, body oriented, "kindred spirit" kind of behavior. And believers all over, who are careful with their Bibles, are waking up to it.

Norman Kraus captures the spirit of the early church:

> The whole [healthy, mature] person is person-in-community. The autonomous [self-governing] individual is not a whole

person. The autonomous person is not a saved person. The religious ideal of Christianity is not the ascetic mystic who has cut himself off from others…Neither is it the self-sufficient individual secure in his victory through Christ…*to be saved means to be in authentic relationship with fellow humans under the Lordship of Christ.*"[4]

Amen to that! Robert Webber has caught the same element:

Christianity is not "my experience" with Christ, as important as that may be, rightly understood. Rather, Christianity is the objective event of God incarnate in Jesus Christ who died and was raised again to establish a new humanity, the Church. It is *in* and *through* the *Church* as Christ's body that the experience of Christianity is *realized.*[5]

Ed Dayton says it still another way:

God calls us out of the world one by one. But what so many evangelicals have missed is that He also calls us into community, and community where the first thing we are to put aside is our individualism. "Now you are the body of Christ, and each one of you is part of it" (1 Corinthians 12:27).[6]

It was the promise of Genesis 12 and the dream of Jesus that was fulfilled in Acts chapter 2 when the Church, the Body of Christ and the Family of God was born. The new Body was baptized in the Spirit as the mark of the Father's pleasure and presence. The Bible says Christ died on the tree of Calvary, "in order that in Christ Jesus the blessing of Abraham might come to the Gentiles, so that we might receive the promise of the Spirit through faith" (Galatians 3:14).

NOT PERFECT, BUT TOGETHER

Let me try to describe the Weber home of recent years:

Three boys. One home.

Three personalities. Same last name.

Three perspectives. One family.

And, of course, three doses of "attitudinal testosterone" or, what is sometimes referred to as "the male ego." Left to itself, this family formula was one powerful recipe for disaster—sibling rivalry off the charts. But the key words here are "left to itself." Left to ourselves we humans self-destruct. The simple solution—never leave anything to the self! In the words of the last chapter, see that the plurality practices a unity. We don't do anything "my way," but work ceaselessly to do everything His way.

Over the years in our home, a little theme song developed that became the antidote for the toxin of sibling rivalry. "We'll *never* do anything around here *perfectly*. But we'll *always* do everything around here *together*." Never perfectly. Always together. You see, it's important that the main thing always remain the main thing. And the main thing was the family, the unit. Not the individual, the self. If God was to be reflected in our home, we were going to have to learn to live together...like Him.

It's the same with God's family. Even though there are all kinds of opportunity for sibling rivalry, the Father insists that we get along. That the kids love each other. That the brothers act like brothers. That we bond like the "kin" we really are.

So let's take a look at how God runs His family. Let's chew on a plurality practicing unity as the route to genuine friendship. We've already noted that such plurality in unity is the heart of the Trinity.

And Jesus pretty much said that was the point of the whole Bible when He answered that testy question from that arrogant lawyer: "Which is the greatest commandment of the Law?" Jesus didn't hesitate. He responded with full authority, "All the Law hangs on two principles." Jesus articulated them this way: "You shall love the Lord your

God with all your heart, and with all your soul, and with all your mind." Jesus said the second principle was just like the first one and could not be separated from it: "You shall love your neighbor as yourself" (see Matthew 22:34-40).

Jesus Himself suggested that the whole point of the Bible and therefore of the Christian faith was to love God and each other. To love the Father and His kids. And when you think carefully about it, you'll have to agree that theme is everywhere in Scripture.

Togetherness was the point of Creation itself. Our great Creator God determined to reflect Himself, His Spirit, in a very material world. It is a world that is extravagant, just like He is. It is a world that operates with an incredible concern for detail, just like He does. It is a world both simple and complex, like its Creator. And the capstone of that creation is the human being, made in His image—male and female made for one another in marriage, the first and most basic earthly plurality practicing unity.

Togetherness is the point of the first social institution God ever created. "It is not good for man to be alone," He'd said.

Togetherness was the point of the first nation of people He commissioned. "Hear O Israel! The Lord your God is ONE." The implication? *Reflect* that oneness.

Togetherness was the point of His creating the Church. History changed forever on the basis of just five simple words, "I will build My Church!" And Jesus meant it. This Church would be like no other assembly. This Church would look like the Living God. This Assembly would look and act like a family: the children of one father.

That's why Jesus prayed so earnestly at the end of His earthly life for just one thing: "that they might be one, Father, like we are one."

It's no great revelation to those of us pushing forty, fifty, or more that life is amazingly brief. The little time we've been given to walk the surface of this planet, taste the fruits of the land, and feel the warmth of God's sunlight flashes by like a toy boat in a fast-running river. And then comes the great sea of eternity, in all its mystery and wonder. We may not know much about what lies ahead for us, but one thing's for sure: If we're going to serve and please the One who purchased life for us with His own blood, we have to get after it. There's no time to waste or fritter away in our own narrow, selfish preoccupations.

So let me ask you this: If you could give Jesus only one thing in your lifetime, why not let it be the one thing He wants more than any other?

ONENESS among His brothers.

It's yours to give, and yours to receive.

1. "Building His church is the only thing on earth He is choosing to do." Of all the ways God could be working in the world, He's decided to do it through the Church. What kind of influence/impact are you and your friends having in the local church? Do you just go to receive, or are you making a difference? Are you content to simply "enjoy an inheritance," or are you building a legacy?

2. God has given you responsibility as a man. You are expected to influence your wife and your children, other men around you, and to be involved in the building up of the local church. Are you actively influencing each? Feel like you just don't know what to do in some areas? Aren't those reasons enough to develop friendships with men that will help you to grow?

3. "If you could give Jesus only one thing in your lifetime, why not let it be the one thing He wants more than any other. ONENESS among His brothers." Are there some damaged or neglected relationships among your Christian brothers you need to pray about and tend to?

LOCKING ARMS

1. Nothing pleases the Father like the oneness of His children. Why?

2. Why did Jesus say our close Christian friendships—our unity—was going to be a message to the world? Did the early church fulfill His desire? What was the effect?

3. God did not make anyone self-sufficient. We all have strengths, but we also have shortcomings—things we don't do well. God's purpose was to show us our need for one another and to draw us together. Why, then, do so many of us refuse to acknowledge our shortcomings or our need of others, and remain so fiercely independent?

4. What aspects do you like about the motto, "Learning together to live like Christ"?

How the Journey Begins

Four Mileposts of
Masculine Friendship (Part One)

"Make the most of the best, and the least of the worst."
ROBERT LOUIS STEVENSON

T he wide open spaces.

Living as I do in the western United States, that expression always triggers a collage of impressions for me.

It's a phrase that smells like a hundred square miles of sage brush on a cool morning…feels like sunlight spilling over a purple line of distant mountains…looks like a ribbon of gray asphalt winding toward a far horizon…sounds like the whisper of wind on a golden ocean of wheat.

Yes, I'm a western boy, and the "wide open spaces" lodge in my soul.

But that little expression never came home to me quite so keenly as in my freshman year in college. Until that watershed year of life, I had never ventured farther than that distant "eastern" outpost known as Idaho. But that was the year I boarded a train for the Midwest, and later visited a number of newly made friends on the East Coast.

Honestly, I had trouble believing my eyes. There were towns and cities *everywhere*. One after another. Strip cities. The end of one was the beginning of the next. The distance between two "cities" was the width of the sign post. One side read "Welcome to Monroe." The other side said "Welcome to Smithville."

Not so out West. Where I grew up you could drive for hours between cities under that big sky, with nothing in between but those "wide open spaces." Along state and federal highways, you measured your progress by mileposts. Mileposts were the significant indicators of location in sparsely populated country with few stand-out landmarks.

That is still true today. You can tune a CB radio to channels 17 or 19 and you'll likely hear a trucker saying, "Where you at, good buddy? What's your '20'?" And then, crackling through the speakers, you'll hear something like, "Headed east at Milepost 237, good buddy!"

So let me ask you, as we roll toward the midpoint of this book, where are *you* at, good buddy?

Or...do you even have a good buddy?

If you do have a buddy, how close are you? Which milepost are you passing? I like to think our friendships, like any highway headed for a worthy destination, have some mileposts along the way. Simple indicators of "where we're at." For our purposes here, let me suggest four mileposts that are critical indicators of where every friendship is headed.

MILEPOSTS ON THE FRIENDSHIP HIGHWAY[1]

Milepost #1—Acceptance:

We choose to accept each other as we are, no conditions. *"You will be my friend. I will keep your confidence. You can trust me."*

Milepost #2—Affirmation:

We commit to building each other up through genuine expression of interest and regular encouragement. *"I will focus on meeting your needs, not mine."*

Milepost #3—Accountability:

We will regularly check in with one another in key areas of our personal and spiritual growth. Our goal is to become godly men. *"Because I care about you, I will warn you when I see danger ahead of you."*

Milepost #4—Authority:

We recognize and if necessary remind one another of God's ultimate authority in our lives. To fully grasp that authority, we must delve ever deeper into His Word. *"I will submit to the leadership of Christ in everything."*

Every friendship should enjoy traveling toward those four "A's." Every friendship should see itself as an "A-team." Specifically, a "Four-A" team. Big-league friendships are all in the AAAA category.

So let's get back to the highway and get started. Fire up your engines, and let's roll. And when you get your speed up and merge onto the highway of friendship, I want you to check out that first milepost, Milepost #1. In any friendship, that very first marker stands for *accepting* other people where they are. Taking your friend as he is.

That's exactly what Prince Jonathan did so many years ago, on an unforgettable stretch of the friendship highway.

MILEPOST #1: ACCEPTANCE

Their friendship was the stuff of legends. David and Jonathan enjoyed to the hilt what may have been history's most celebrated masculine friendship. God Himself describes it in superlatives—their hearts "knit" (1 Samuel 18:1). It doesn't get much better than that. These guys were connected.

Just how did it get so good? How do you account for such a bond? Was there some singular quality that characterized their relationship and allowed it to go so deep? I think so. And I think that very same quality is present in *every* truly meaningful friendship. They started where you and I must start. At Milepost #1. With acceptance.

Take a look back at their lives together. Walk through their adventures and track their conversations. Measure their hearts for one another and see what you come up with. I think you'll find all four mileposts along that glorious length of highway. But none so sturdy as Milepost #1.

Could you identify just one word that seemed to characterize the relationship of these two young men, from beginning to end? What was it that cemented these warriors? Unselfishness? Commitment? Loyalty? Shared Values? Transparency? Common interests? (See Appendix A.) Yes, they were all there. As they are, to one degree or another, in most healthy relationships. But I like to think there is another, even more fundamental ingredient written right over the top of these magnificent relational qualities.

I think the one word that distilled David and Jonathan's legendary friendship, that spoke its heart, that accounted for everything else they enjoyed, was—*whatever.*

Whatever?

Yes. Take a look.

Jonathan spoke it first. As the Crown Prince of Israel, he held the high ground. David, after all, was just a rancher's boy from north Judah. Early in their relationship, at the point of David's great need, after he had ducked Saul's spear more than once and wore a bounty on his head, David felt his life was as good as gone. "There is hardly a step between me and death," he had said. It was at that point Scripture states, "Then Jonathan said to David, '*Whatever* you say, I will do for you'" (1 Samuel 20:4).

I wish we had that conversation on tape so we could hear Jonathan's voice, his tone. Maybe he looked David in the eye, maybe his voice quavered with emotion, maybe he embraced his brother. The account doesn't say for sure, but I do know their spirits met and the message came through crystal clear!

"David, I accept you as you are. You're okay with me. Our friendship is a safe place."

Acceptance, the first milepost of friendship, says, "Whatever."

"Whatever you need, that's what I will do. I welcome you as you are and give myself away to you. Whatever you lack. Whatever you've been through. Whatever you're going through. Whatever you say. Whatever you do. Whatever you don't do. Whatever. I'm here for you. You can count on me. You can be real with me. You can be *you* with me. I accept you as you are."

The apostle Paul drove that first milepost infinitely deeper into the roadside gravel when he commanded believers to "accept one another as Christ has accepted you" (Romans 15:7).

This is the bedrock of friendship, the living core of any relationship. A-c-c-e-p-t-a-n-c-e. Come as you are. I like you. I love you. I will do anything for you. And nothing you could ever do could turn me away from you.

To me, these words of man-to-man acceptance flash like bright, brief reflections of an Ultimate Friendship so powerful, so blindingly radiant that it can't be contained in human language.

THE ULTIMATE FRIENDSHIP

"While we were yet sinners, Christ died for us" (Romans 5:6-10).

"When you were dead...He made you live" (Colossians 2:13-14).

Take a few million years and savor those two sentences! Let's see...I am imperfect; God is perfect. I am unholy; He is holy. I am finite; He is infinite. I am a sinner; He is sinless. I like to get; He thinks it's better to give. Come to think of it, God and I don't have much in common. There isn't much to draw us together. Most of my most natural qualities are...well...repugnant to Him.

But He doesn't start there. He is the Ultimate Friend. In spite of all there is about me that should turn Him away in disgust, Jesus always starts with acceptance. He smiles His welcoming smile and says, "I like you. I want to be there when you open your eyes on the new morning. I want to walk with you in the cool of the day. I want to know you. I want you to know Me. I will do anything for you. *Whatever* you need, I will provide. In fact, I *accept* you as you are. I will even die for you. You have My Word on it. It has been My intention from the beginning."

And He went out and did it! Died for you to demonstrate—prove—His love and acceptance. It's the subject of entire books. Vast libraries. The hymn writer Frederick M. Lehman tried his hand at portraying the concept in verse—and did a yeoman's job of it, I think.

Could we with ink the ocean fill
And were the skies of parchment made,
Were every stalk on earth a quill

And every man a scribe by trade,
To write the love of God above
Would drain the ocean dry,
Nor could the scroll contain the whole
Though stretched from sky to sky.[2]

Yes! *Well said,* Mr. Lehman.

The bright stream of Acceptance, that fills our dry, thirsty world with refreshment and friendship, flows from deep springs in the high country of heaven. We give and receive love in friendship, because we have been loved by our Ultimate Friend.

But Scripture carries this idea a quantum leap further. Romans 15:7, remember, tells us to "Accept one another *just as* Christ also accepted us."

The virtually unbelievable truths surrounding Christ's acceptance of us are the basis and impetus for our exercising acceptance in our relationships. Christ did not require "performance" before extending to us acceptance. And that acceptance of Christ is the cornerstone of both our admittance to heaven and our friendships on earth.

Now let's check it out. Is this real? Let's listen in on a brief conversation, right in the heat and sweat of daily living.

HIGH NOON IN SAMARIA

Remember that woman at the well in Samaria, described in John 4? She was a mess. The talk of the town. She certainly didn't appear to have any meaningful relationships. She was alone, and friendless. The poor gal even had to go to the well in the broad daylight of the Middle Eastern noon-time sun when no one else was moving about. Normal people drew their water in the cool of the morning, and normal people drew *away* from her. With the exception of the transient "husbands" that stopped by from time to time, she was left to herself. Rejection was all she knew.

SNAPSHOTS: MY FRIENDS TELL THEIR STORIES

He's a rugged "man's man." He can operate a backhoe, ride a galloping horse, build a house, and hunt a deer. He's also the owner of his own company, an army veteran, and deeply involved in service to others through his local church.

We were working on a project a few days ago. He was teaching me how to run a jackhammer, to break up some concrete in preparation for a remodeling project we were doing. The subject of a man's friends came up.

"You know, I guess your wife ought to be your best friend," he said. "But there's just something else that a man needs. It's hard to understand. My wife's father once told me that the true test of friendship is whether someone would be willing to die for you. And you know," he continued, "I don't know that I have one friend like that."

Deep calls to deep. There's something in my heart that seems to be designed, from birth, to connect with a handful of other men, at a deep "soul" level of friendship. Guys I'd be willing to die for…perhaps because I enjoyed living with them so much.

Then she ran into that most unusual Galilean. Almost immediately, He began expressing His acceptance in non-verbal ways. To begin with, *He was there.* Just there. (Ever notice how "just being there" is such an invaluable quality in a friendship?) A Jewish rabbi facing a Samaritan woman spoke volumes to her. In fact, it was so startling and revolutionary, she felt highly uncomfortable. She tried to put Him off. Accustomed to rejection, she was actually more comfortable with it. At least she knew how to handle that!

This friendship stuff was foreign territory to her. So her initial response was a quick stiff-arm. "What are you doing here? Get a clue. I'm a Samaritan—and a woman. You're a Jew—and a man. We have nothing to do with each other. That's the way things are, and let's just keep it that way!"

A WORD ABOUT "RISK" IN FRIENDSHIP

You can understand the poor woman's reticence, can't you? Stepping into a new friendship is a risky business. Intimidating. And most of us feel and act a bit awkward, at least at first. But Jesus, the Ultimate Friend, is altogether unintimidated by it. He invented friendship. And He, of all people, knows it involves risk—a willingness to be vulnerable. Masculine to the core, He was willing to take all the risks involved.

Did you ever wonder why Jesus was so willing to take risks? Why He was so utterly fearless? Could it be because He *accepted Himself?* Yes. The Bible says as much in John 13. As Jesus and His friends approached the upper room for the Passover meal together, there were some uneasy moments. To begin with, there were no servants on hand to wash feet. This was simply inconceivable to the men with Him. Believe me, when you *reclined* at table as they did in the Ancient Near East, and your head was next to the other guy's feet, foot hygiene was more than a luxury. It's kind of tough to work up an appetite with some man's dusty, reeking, size twelves virtually under your nose.

But there was a problem. Even more unacceptable than unwashed feet was the job of washing them. And no one would do it. Normally it was the servant's job to wash the guests' feet before dinner, and the least of the servants, at that. But there was no servant in the upper room that evening. The Son of Man didn't have a household staff. Didn't even have a place to lay His head.

You can't believe how socially embarrassing and uncomfortable this situation was for Christ's men. It would be like walking around all day with your fly unzipped and no one being willing to mention it to you. *Everyone* could see what was happening, but *no one* would say or do anything about it.

Jesus did. It didn't daunt Him one bit.

Despite His kingly stature, He readily assumed the role of the lowliest of household servants. Despite the high-octane tension of that evening (He was about to go out and die for this bunch), Jesus had His wits about him. Of all people present, He certainly had license never to stoop so low. But no one else was about to do so! And we know why, don't we? No one else was *confident* enough to do it. No one else knew themselves well enough to do it. No one else accepted themselves well enough to do it. No one else was man enough. Jesus was.

Remember—the Bible says it clearly, "Jesus *knowing* that the Father had given all things into His hands, and [*knowing*] that He had come forth from God, and [*knowing* that He] was going back to God, rose from supper, and laid aside His garments, and taking a towel, girded Himself about [put on the uniform of the slave]" (John 13:3).

Jesus knew who He was. Jesus accepted Himself. So the "risk" was reduced. The "threat" eliminated. And that's the way it can be for you in your friendships!

"Yes," you object, "but Jesus is *God.* Of course He wasn't intimidated! Good grief, I wouldn't be either if I had going for me what He did."

But you *do* have what He had, if you'll just stop and think about it for a minute! The Bible says you are "clothed in the righteousness of

Christ." When God looks at you, He sees the sinless, shining purity of His Son. And if God accepts you as His Son, what do you have to sweat?

Here's another way to look at it that may be helpful to you. When you find yourself tip-toeing on the station platform of friendship, climb aboard this train of logic: All of the good and desirable things about you are gifts from God, right? By the same token, all the negative things about you are derived from this world's sinful system and, as such, are "common to man." That means we all have essentially the same problems. Our struggles may differ in degree, but not in kind.

You know what I mean. Can we just say it? The most common problem men share is lust. For most of us the lust monster first reared its ugly head somewhere around junior high age. When it happened, each of us figured we were the only one.

As the hormones flowed, we periodically lost our struggle with this relentless beast. We convinced ourselves (after a year or two) that there was no one else as vile as we. Couldn't talk to anyone about it. Surely God hated us. For many guys, an extra dose of anger compounded already overwhelming guilt.

Those were rough years. If only we'd only known that our struggles were common to everyone. And if only we'd known that God didn't hate us. He accepted us just as we were. And He still does.

So then, if all my assets are gifts, and all my liabilities are pretty much common to everyone—why am I "threatened" and feel I must hide? I shouldn't. I can take the "risk." I can be a man and reach out, extending myself to another in friendship. It's just a matter of thinking biblically. I like the way Paul put it to the Romans:

> As your spiritual teacher I give this piece of advice to each one of you. Don't cherish exaggerated ideas of yourself or your importance, but try to have a sane estimate of your capabilities by the light of the faith that God has given to you all (Romans 12:3, Phillips).

How then, do I consider myself? Just the way I am. I don't view myself in a phony, puffed-up way. Nor do I view myself in a groveling, totally worthless and incompetent way. I don't think too highly of myself, but neither do I think too lowly. I'm not an angel and I'm not a worm. I'm a man, who has both a sinful, fleshly nature and the very Spirit of the living God living within me.

And if for some reason my reaching out is not accepted, if my potential friend "rejects" my overtures, it's really not something that should blow my circuit-breakers. Actually, it is *his* loss, and may even indicate he is suffering from insecurity of his own and is unable to accept me *or* himself.

So don't let the "risk" factors scare you away. Go for it. The best returns are derived from the greatest risks. And a friendship is worth it!

BACK TO HIGH NOON AT THE WELL

Jesus and the woman continued their conversation at the village well. The woman persisted in shoving Him away. He stayed at it. He'd even given her the high ground—humbled Himself and asked her if she would be willing to help Him out. "Could you give Me a drink, ma'am?"

As they continued the dialogue, He offered to serve her—at the point of her deepest need. He communicated clearly and genuinely to her, in such a manner that she was able to catch a glimpse of His great heart. This was a Friend who cared. He was genuine. He really meant what He said. He wasn't put off. He hung in there. "Ma'am, if you could see My heart, you would let Me serve you, too. And I guarantee, you would not be disappointed with the eternal quality friendship I can give you—Life itself—all you've ever really wanted and needed."

Yes, she was suspicious of His motives. In her insecurities she still tended to put Him off with some banter about history—Jacob and wells and mountains and such. But that's typical of us, isn't it? When conversation hits close to home, it's difficult for us. We tend to change the subject. But in our heart of hearts we really do want to continue. Because real friendships dwell "close to home." It's just so fearsome early on, until we can actually believe we're accepted as we are.

Acceptance is the bedrock foundation of all relationships. Jesus, the Master Friend, accepts us completely, insecurities and all. Without that foundation, a relationship can crumble at the first major tremor.

Acceptance, Affirmation, Accountability, and Authority—in that order—are the four mileposts which any solid friendship or relationship must reach. Acceptance is where you enter the highway. *Affirmation* occurs as the relationship picks up speed.

MILEPOST #2: AFFIRMATION

The task of affirming another person involves tuning in to his emotional needs. It involves a decision to compassionately extend yourself far enough into his heart (walking far enough in his emotional moccasins) to feel his hurts and see life through his eyes.

A good friend of mine who grew up in Alaska recently told me this story:

> Tuffy was a boy my age. Tuffy wasn't his real name, but that's what we all called him. He lived in a small tar paper shack just down the hill from us, right at the edge of the community playground. On that little playground we made angel shapes in the snow, and shot marbles on the first patches of springtime mud. A bunch of us would strap on snowshoes and play a hilarious and clumsy game of softball in fresh, deep snow. Right behind home plate there was a swing set made of weathered spruce logs. In the wintertime the swings took a recess, but through the all-too-brief summer days, they carried us to thin-aired altitudes and imaginary distant places.
>
> Tuffy lived with an alcoholic live-in father and a passive mother. I remember when his older sister committed suicide. Home was hell.
>
> When I think of my friend Tuffy, I feel an ugly set of words forever etched on my memory. Cutting and hateful words screamed out the door of the ramshackle house toward an

embarrassed and angry ten-year-old boy who stumbled up the hill toward the playground. As he ran, he wiped hot, bitter tears on dirty jacket sleeves.

And there was Tuffy's father, gray stubble-bearded Bobby Burns standing in the doorway, one fist shaking, the other clutching a stubby brown bottle. He bellowed, "Who the ____ do you think you are? Shut your _____ mouth and get the ___ outta here or I'll beat the _____ outta ya..."

I hated old man Bobby for my friend Tuffy.

Before we can affirm one another, we have to get a handle on *where we come from.* Many little boys, grown to manhood today, carry wounds from tyrants like Bobby Burns. They don't know what it means to be loved and affirmed by another man.

Earlier this year the men in our church's weekly "High Ground" meetings listed words that came to mind to describe "father." Some offered positive adjectives. For others, a single word brought tears.

"Father"

Committed	Absent
Consistent	Abusive
Example	Alcoholic
Faithful	Angry
Godly	Bitter
Joker	Dead
Loving	Disciplinarian
Prayer	Defeated
Protector	Domineering
Provider	Frustrated
Sacrificial	Helpless
Stable	Isolated
Strong	Passive
Successful	Quiet
Submissive	Weak

For a lot of guys, the word "father" isn't a Sunday school picture of a smiling dad bouncing Junior on his knee. Yet deep in his chest every man longs for the approval of Dad.

It's been that way from the beginning of time. Sons have needed fathers. Little men have needed big men. Grown men have needed each other. A man cannot affirm himself.

When healthy male relationships—especially father relationships—are absent, little boys grow up with a gnawing sense of vacancy and lostness. As a result, society doesn't work right, families weaken, marriages disintegrate, and deep friendships don't develop.

If a man didn't get the affirmation of his father, where does he go for it? At another High Ground meeting, our guys suggested places where many of us attempt to find affirmation.

Car
Job
Sex
Wealth
House
Sports

But all these things are like veggie burgers. They may look great on the grill, but they surely don't replace the real thing.

By the way, a man's great need for affirmation is not the result of sin. It's not a manufacturer's defect. God designed us that way—on purpose. He made us to need each other.

So if a man grew up without affirmation, is he sentenced to a forever-hunger for something that's on permanent back order? Not at all. Just as with the Acceptance milepost, the Affirmation marker belongs to God. He made it and He planted it in clear view of the Friendship Road. He didn't want us to miss it.

When I was a boy of about ten or eleven, my dad was moonlighting at Sears Roebuck after his shift at the fire department. He was clerking in the sporting goods department, and one night I got to stop in and say hello. As we stood together in front of the counter, another man who knew my dad came in. He and Dad greeted each other. And then something happened that I will never forget. Dad put his hand on my shoulder, and said, "This is my son, Stu." I nearly exploded with pride! It was all I could do to "act normal." My dad had just identified and affirmed me in the company of men!

I imagine that Jesus Himself must have experienced something of this joy when His Father affirmed Him (at age thirty we still love it, don't we?) saying, "This is My beloved Son, in whom I am well pleased."

A big argument for sitting down every day to a healthy meal in the Scriptures is to simply hear affirming words from our Father. Maybe you didn't hear those kind of words from your earthly dad. You hoped for them, longed for them, worked for them, wept for them…but they never came. Yet the Bible tells us the truth over and over, again and again, in a thousand different ways. It's a fervent cry in the mouth of the prophets. It's a triumphant song in the psalms. It's the warm, brotherly call of a God-man and Savior in the gospels, and the soul-building assurances of the epistles.

He tells us He has inscribed our names on the very palms of His hands. He tells us that He thinks about us constantly, that He will deliver us, make our footsteps firm, and bring us to live in His house forever. He says He loved us enough to give His own Son for us, that He is with us always, no matter what, and that He is preparing a spot in heaven just for us. He calls us His children, His friends, and even the Nobles of His kingdom (1 Peter 2:9). Is that affirming or what? If God says such regal things about you and me, how should we be talking to each other?

As you might expect, the apostle Paul is ready with an answer:

Let no unwholesome word proceed from your mouth, but only such a word as is good for edification according to the need of the moment, that it may benefit those who hear (Ephesians 4:29).

"Edification" is an architectural term. Architects don't tear down, they build up. They dream positive dreams, they sketch a beautiful future, they imagine "what can be." That's what friends do for each other, too. They choose to focus on positive qualities, not weaknesses, to see aptitudes, not obstacles, to dream of what a man can become—regardless of where he's come from. Brothers of the same Father choose to view each other through their Father's eyes.

Jesus, the One who opened the door of Acceptance for us, is also the Master Affirmer. Dr. Luke gives us the funny, moving, highly-unlikely account of one unhappy little man who found himself looking into the eyes of pure affirmation.

A LITTLE MAN IN A BIG TREE

Every culture has its quislings. Every culture has its money-grubbing, small-minded, I'm-out-for-me kind of guys. The city of Jericho was no exception. You know the story of Zaccheus:

> And He entered and was passing through Jericho. And behold, there was a man called by the name of Zaccheus; and he was a chief tax-gatherer, and he was rich. And he was trying to see who Jesus was, and he was unable because of the crowd, for he was small in stature. And he ran on ahead and climbed up into a sycamore tree in order to see Him, for He was about to pass through that way.
>
> And when Jesus came to the place, He looked up and said to him, "Zaccheus, hurry and come down, for today I must stay at your house." And he hurried and came down, and received Him gladly. And when they saw it, they all began to grumble, saying, "He has gone to be the guest of a man who is a sinner." And Zaccheus stopped and said to the Lord,

"Behold, Lord, half of my possessions I will give to the poor, and if I have defrauded anyone of anything, I will give back four times as much." And Jesus said to him, "Today salvation has come to this house, because he, too, is a son of Abraham. For the Son of Man has come to seek and to save that which was lost" (Luke 19:1-10).

Contrary to the cute children's Sunday school chorus, this was no sweet, demure, little fellow. Zaccheus was a selfish, ambitious, white-collar thief! Jericho's answer to the Keating Five. As big as the infamous junk bond thief Michael Milliken. Zaccheus, to be perfectly blunt, seems to me to have been a sniveling little twit. A weasel. A Quisling. Probably suffered from a case of "small man's syndrome." He was a Jew who represented Rome. He was a "tax collector," a description virtually everywhere referred to in a negative, evil context. And he wasn't just any tax collector. He was a *chief* tax collector. He worked in the high tax district. He taxed the poor to benefit the rich. Namely, himself. He taxed heavily enough to meet both Rome's demands and his own. This guy made Prince John, the "phony king of England" in the days of Robin Hood, look like a saint. He was a lying, deceiving, cheating, selfish little money-grubbing jerk who thought he was really something. Innocent people everywhere in the community suffered constantly because of his greed and thievery.

It is likely *everyone hated Zaccheus except Zaccheus* (and deep down inside he probably hated himself, too) *and Jesus.* But whether you agree with my assessment of the man or not, you would likely have to agree Zaccheus was not the kind of man most of us would choose to befriend.

But Jesus did. Again, Christ took the initiative.

What did Jesus see up in that tree?

He saw everything Zaccheus was! Jesus saw that dark, greedy heart...and more. Nothing got by the burning, penetrating eyes of God's Son. He saw *everything* Zaccheus had done—and the hundreds of innocent people suffering because of his sin. And Jesus loved Zaccheus anyway. He valued him. He felt compassion for him. He approached him open-armed. And He was about to make a very affirmative declaration. Affirmation is a powerful force.

So Jesus said, "Let's go have a talk, friend." He even suggested it be in privacy and on Zac's own turf. "Let's go to your place." Now, as you might expect, that pretty much ticked everybody else off. "He has gone to be the guest of a man who is a sinner." And how!

Now we don't know all that transpired inside the walls of Zac's home that day. (Don't you wish we could get a tape of that conversation!) But I'm pretty sure, judging from Jesus' relational style with others, there wasn't a lot of finger pointing. I don't think Jesus beat him over the head with the Bible. And from what I read in the gospels, even "the Holy One" Himself never put on "holier than thou" airs. What you *don't* see here is a ranting, raving, guilt-manipulating attack that treats the man like evil personified. But you do see a caring, compassionate, personal approach to the core of a soul. And that's a friend!

No, we don't know all that was said. But because we know Jesus, we know it dealt warmly with Zaccheus' heart. And it dealt honestly with Zaccheus' sin. In this case, Scripture drew a curtain of privacy. What went on behind those walls was between one little man and one great friend, God Himself. But we do know when it was said and done Zaccheus was a changed man. His encounter with the affirming Savior changed everything! A true friendship can be like that.

I like to picture the two of them coming out of the front door onto the front step in the shade of a big palm, where the crowd waited with furrowed brow. I see the two of them standing there before the crowd. Perhaps their arms rest across each other's shoulders. I see two men wearing smiles. It's hard to tell which one is smiling largest. And then the taller one, the Messiah, says joyfully and authoritatively, "Today salvation has come to this house!" How is that for affirmation!

A man will do anything for affirmation. Even die for it. But he shouldn't have to. That's what a friend is for. The mileposts of friendship—first Acceptance and Affirmation, then Accountability and Authority—are so named because there may be distance and time between each. These are *mileposts*, markers on what may be a journey of many miles and many years through life's tight passages and wide open spaces. There may be a great distance, for example, between the milepost of Affirmation and the milepost of Accountability.

The trouble comes when we get impatient, assume too much, and try to short cut the process. Sometimes we even try to approach the friendship journey backward; we want to start with tough-minded Authority and work our way back to Acceptance. ("If you will change your behavior and do thus and so, I will accept you.") That's not what Jesus did.

Yes, we love to reverse the divine order of things. We like to come from the position of power. We want to start with the advantage. We don't like being out of control. So we swagger into a relationship thinking, If I'm really cool, or if I project the right "I've-got-it-all-together-image," maybe they'll like me and we can be friends. I'll just be Mr. Big and wow 'em."

It will never happen. Or if it does, the relationship will never be deeper than rainwater on a sidewalk. So stay at it...*whatever*...as Jonathan would put it.

Because true friendships, by definition, can never be superficial.

Stay on the highway, traveler. We're coming up on a glorious stretch. The road climbs sharply, yes, but you won't believe the view.

1. Since all our strengths and assets are gifts from God, and all our liabilities are common to man, it seems we should be pretty accepting of one another. But chances are, you may not even be able to accept *yourself.* How does that fact hold you back from accepting others?

2. More men than you might imagine are hungry for affirmation. Not flattery, but real affirmation. Look around you for someone who needs affirming this week. You might be surprised how many opportunities you find to build up a brother.

LOCKING ARMS

1. We're told that the first milepost on the friendship highway is Acceptance. Can Acceptance be conditional? Why is it called the "bedrock" or "foundation" of all relationships?

2. What's the one word used in this chapter to capture the spirit of Milepost #1? Why is that word important to remember in building and maintaining a friendship?

3. Romans 15:7 says, "Accept one another as Christ accepted you." In a word, how has He accepted you? Now give some examples of how that fact applies to you when it comes to accepting others.

4. Why is "just being there" an important part of Acceptance?

5. Milepost #2 is Affirmation. What does that word really mean? Give some examples.

6. "A man cannot affirm himself." Why not?

7. "Before we can affirm one another, we have to get a handle on where we come from." Why is that important?

8. If you have a good buddy, how close are you? Which milepost are you passing?

9. Do you have some relationships that seem to bounce back and forth between what seems like an encouraging friendship one moment and "just an acquaintance" the next? What might be wrong with the relationship? What steps might you take to change it?

10. Explain why the four mileposts need to be in this order: Acceptance, Affirmation, Accountability, and Authority. What's wrong with putting them in another order—or reverse order?

Every High Road Needs Guard Rails

Four Mileposts of
Masculine Friendship (Part Two)

*A friend is one who knows you as you are, understands where you've been,
accepts who you've become, and still invites you to grow.*

e didn't have much money. And we didn't have much time.
But the experience was unforgettable.

I was a Second Lieutenant in the 2d Brigade, 3rd Armored
Division. Linda was pregnant with our first son. We were in
Europe on an eighteen-month assignment, and though we never spoke
of it, we knew orders to Vietnam waited just over the horizon. The
Brigade was understaffed and the equipment was overtaxed—Southeast
Asia siphoned off the best of everything.

Back in the States, newspapers headlined the Soviet invasion of
Czechoslovakia. As Red Army tanks patrolled the streets of Prague, our
unit sat astride the Fulda Gap, the traditional invasion route into the
heart of the continent. No one knew what was going to happen next,
but we had to be ready. The Soviet bear was on the prowl, looking for
red meat; the threat was real.

As a result, the work was never-ending. The idea of taking leave
and "seeing Europe" just wasn't on the agenda. Long days, intense
weeks, and interminable months stretched one after the other.

That's why I'll never forget my surprise at the Old Man's words that
morning.

The colonel knew his officers—doing double-duty and stretched to their limits—needed a break. I can still hear that gravelly voice and see those level gray eyes as he looked up from a stack of reports on his desk.

"Lieutenant, if you hope to get any leave at all over the next year or so, it had best be next week. It's the only possibility—given our circumstances."

I wondered what he knew that he wasn't saying, but I wasn't about to push him.

The trouble was, Linda and I were in no way prepared for this. We were nearly broke. (This was before the big pay raises of the early 70s, and Second Lieutenants made next to zilch.) We'd made no travel plans. And this was November—a terrible time of the year to tramp about in Europe.

But hey, you don't question the boss. The colonel had said, "Six days. Starting *now*. That's it." This was a take-it-or-leave-it deal, and we weren't about to pass it up.

So we loaded our little '65 Mustang that gray November morning, and hit the road to Rome with a total of ninety bucks in our pockets. That was all the cash we had for the whole week, and somehow, we had to make it cover gas, food, and lodging.

It turned out that we couldn't afford motel rooms. So we "slept" in the car. I have to hand it to my wife—she was a trooper! Can you imagine being pregnant and sleeping upright in the non-reclining front seat of a cold Mustang?

So much for lodging. But we had to "economize" on meals as well. Before we left I grabbed a few outdated LRRP (Long Range Recon Patrol) dehydrated rations and threw 'em into the trunk. Then I tossed in an old fondue pot (remember those things?) and a few cans of Sterno to do some "serious cooking." That act alone would come back to haunt me for years. You see, Lindy had dreamed since girlhood about a "real spaghetti dinner" in Rome. I didn't think we could afford it. (Those were the days before I learned to speak "Woman," and was more warrior than tender.) So when we hit Rome, I pulled out a dehydrated spaghetti ration, dumped in some water, heated it over a can of Sterno in the fondue pot and *"Voila!"* Spaghetti in Rome!

Lindy didn't think it was particularly funny. But now, a couple of decades later, it will bring at least the trace of a smile to the corner of her mouth.

But the most unforgettable moments of our adventure were still ahead. It happened in a place called the Simplon Pass. We had headed north through Italy's Alps on the return trip. At the edge of the Swiss Alps, we got caught in a savage blizzard. It was bad enough that a work crew along the road actually stopped us. There was serious concern that the road was not only hazardous, but actually impassable.

One wizened old toughie on the road crew, however, scoffed at his fellows' fears. I can still hear him saying, "Bah! Road is *goot!* Yah, goot!"

That was all this soldier needed to hear. I got out, chained up our little Mustang, and we headed up the pass. We were going to conquer those mountains. After all, we were young, and had grown up driving on snow in eastern Washington. We thought ourselves invincible. At least I did. Lindy wasn't so sure. Oh well, as they used to say at Ft. Benning, "Drive on, Ranger!" So I did.

But the blizzard got worse. The banks piled higher. The road narrowed. The snow was beyond belief. I found myself thinking, *Well, Stu, this sure isn't Yakima!* By the time we had climbed high into the Alps, we found ourselves in a virtual white-out. Every once in awhile, the swirling winds would create a tiny break in the blizzard and we could see where we were—and that's when it got really scary!

The road was a tiny, icy ribbon climbing the steep flanks of enormous mountains. Just a few inches off the pavement, it was straight down. A sheer drop-off of thousands of feet. If you left the road, it meant certain death. And in Europe, evidencing that typical European disregard for public safety, guardrails were almost nonexistent.

Even so, there seemed little sense in stopping. We were, quite literally, in the middle of nowhere—and it was freezing cold. *Drive on, Ranger!* But by that time, all the smiles and bravado were gone. I had my wife and unborn baby in this dangerous mess. This was life and death.

As we rounded yet another white-knuckle turn, Lindy said, "Stu, you're going a little too fast!"

"We're only going seven miles an hour," I replied. And just as I said those words we began to slide. I tapped the brakes. As I feared, that only made it worse. We were sliding faster, out of control, and there was nothing I could do. This was crazy. It wasn't supposed to end this way! But there we were, shooting toward the edge of eternity.

I gripped the wheel. Our bodies tensed. We closed our eyes, waiting for the inevitable. But just when we thought we'd launch over the cliff into a white abyss, we heard a loud crack and found ourselves jerked around by a violent impact. Our necks snapped forward, then sideways, as the Mustang spun to the right and careened toward the other side of the road before plowing into a soft snowbank.

We blinked, glanced at each other, and simultaneously shouted in our wonder and relief, *"What was that?"*

Still trembling, I crawled out of our only slightly damaged car, walked through the blowing snow to the point of impact, and bent down. There, mostly buried beneath the snow, was the now exposed metal of a guardrail! (I thought about kissing that thing, but didn't want to leave my lips in Switzerland!)

It was only a short piece of guardrail—one of a few over the entire pass. But it was at just the right spot for Stu and Linda Weber! To our minds, a divine Providence had installed that one stout little length of metal on that treacherous road just for us. Just when we needed it.

It was time for worship! And gratitude! We thanked God for a life-giving, life-saving, future-preserving guardrail. Something so simple had literally saved our lives. Were it not for that guardrail, neither of us would be here today. And that little one in Linda's womb (now in graduate studies at Oxford) would not be here, either. Nor our other sons. An entire family...a beautiful heritage...whole generations would have been destroyed...were it not for that guardrail.

Today when we drive through the Cascades, Oregon's spinal mountain range, we see a lot of guardrails. And we see them differently than most people. Most are "oohing" and "aahing" over the wildlife or mountain scenery. But you may catch us saying something like, "Look at that wonderful guardrail. Have you ever seen anything so beautiful in your life?" Guardrails have come to mean the world to us. The fact is…

Life

    without

        guardrails

            can kill you!

Life is a risky prospect. Physical dangers abound. Spiritual dangers threaten the life of your soul—the life that matters forever. You can't even imagine how high those stakes are. Your personal future, your family's heritage, and the generations to come will feel the impact of how you stand up to those dangers. It's a far more dangerous passage than weathering a blizzard in the Alps.

The great and living God, who invented life, knows just how treacherous this earthly trip can be. That's why, from the very outset, He placed guardrails at strategic points alongside the road. His strong counsel? It is not good for man to be alone. No one should travel by himself. Every man needs a friend. Friends are divinely placed guardrails.

Despite what others may tell you ("Road is goot, yah!"), you are driving today on hazardous asphalt; the icy curves and steep slopes of moral decline in this country are growing worse by the day. Powerful storms are descending. You'd best travel with a friend. A strong friend. One who won't collapse when you need a life-saving guardrail. The best of us need them.

I've often wondered how David's life would have been different had Jonathan lived. Had Jonathan been beside him, I doubt there would have been a Bathsheba episode. Crown or no crown, throne or no throne, Jonathan knew his buddy well enough to have cut through the royal bull. Jonathan wouldn't have kept silent when David elected to brood at home instead of riding out with his armies. Jonathan would have been aware of David's mid-life struggles with lust. Their hearts were close enough to allow total authenticity. They read each other's souls. Like true friends, they were guardrails in one another's lives. The thought of looking into his friend's calm, penetrating eyes might have made David pause before dialing Bathsheba's number. Most likely, he would have quickly left the palace roof, taken a cold shower, and that would have been the end of it.

But Jonathan wasn't there. And David slid over the edge.

This road called "life" can be a rough one. It's full of jarring potholes and hairpin curves. And just at the road's edges are sheer cliffs that spell death for the unwary. You have to keep the wheels between the lines. And you need some guardrails to protect you from the precipice when you find yourself moving too fast and beginning to lose control. Friends, rock-solid friends who Accept and Affirm us, can provide the much needed Accountability and Authority when we're in a spin.

FRIENDSHIP'S CUTTING EDGE

Accountability and Authority are the muscle fibers of friendship. They comprise the kind of strength spotlighted in Proverbs 27:17: "As iron sharpens iron, so one man sharpens another." Accountability and Authority in a friendship are iron meeting iron. They are the sharpening elements as one man sharpens another. But you have to get it just right. They must be used very carefully. Go at it the wrong way and keen blades can be damaged and blunted. Get sloppy and those sharp edges can cut deeply.

Here in Oregon's great outdoors, a knife is an invaluable commodity. Hunting and fishing, hiking and camping all demand a good blade. A sharp blade. Nothing is more frustrating than finding yourself with a dull edge. When you need a knife, you need a *sharp* knife. And putting a sharp edge on a good knife is something of an art form. I'm not nearly so good at it as my brother-in-law. I understand the science of it. But Rich has mastered its art.

Rich will tell you it's all in the coming together of a number of elements—a good blade to begin with, a quality stone, a smooth lubricant, and a precise angle where the steel and stone come together. When you know the elements, he tells me, you develop a "feel" for how they must come together.

So it is with friends.

You have to blend the elements rightly. The friction of Accountability must be soothed and smoothed by the oil of Acceptance. The strength and force of Authority must be softened with the confirming touch of Affirmation. The only way iron can sharpen iron is when the two pieces are held together by a force greater than either piece. With the blade, it's the strength and skill of a man's hand. With the friendship, it is the strength and value of mutual commitment between two friends. That's what "makes or breaks" the friendship—commitment. Staying power. Strength and touch.

The mileposts of Accountability and Authority have their proper and legitimate role in meaningful interpersonal relationships only *after* we are secure in knowing that we are devoted to one another.

Be devoted to one another in brotherly love (Romans 12:10).

That is precisely why both Jesus, the Lord of the Church, and Paul, the great apostle of the Church, continually exhorted their friends and followers to "be one," to be a "body." Anything less tends to self-destruct. It sharpens nothing. At best, anything less is superficial. It has been stated axiomatically that "authority wielded without relationship breeds rebellion."

Jesus flat out condemned such an attitude in His body. He insisted, "I will build *My* church." That is, He insisted that it be an assembly that bears His mark, possesses His characteristics. It must look like Him or it is not His body. And He always operates in the context of a relationship. He and the Father are "one."

Don't misunderstand. There is a proper and high place for Accountability and Authority in every relationship. But the meaningful ones don't skip the first two mileposts and *start* there. Normal "Gentile" relationships do. Jesus told His circle of friends, "You can see how it works among the pagans. They 'lord it over' one another, always throwing their weight around" (Matthew 20:25).

People tend to maneuver for strategic terrain. That's legitimate in a war but not in a relationship. And that's why the military model of "relationships" and the familial model start at opposite ends. In the military (whose purpose is to prepare for and, if necessary, engage in, war) everything hinges on Authority. But in the family (whose purpose is to nurture and develop whole human beings capable of deep relational "oneness") everything hinges on Acceptance:

Man's military model:

Authority —> Accountability —> Affirmation (earned) —> Acceptance (conditional)

God's familial model:

Acceptance (unconditional) —> Affirmation (freely given) —>Accountability —>Authority

Accountability and Authority are necessary aspects—mechanisms, dynamics—for control and structure which are, in turn, ultimately necessary elements of every meaningful relationship. Even the Trinity experiences them. But our natural tendency when we encounter even the slightest difficulty in a relationship ("interpersonal tensions" we call them), is to invoke Authority. That's why so many relationships become "dysfunctional"; they have degenerated to a series of "power plays." One-ups-manship. My dog's better than your dog. My dad's bigger than your dad. My case is tighter than yours. And that's the history of human relationships in one mocking, playground chant—*nah-nah-nah-nah-naaah.*

No, in our flesh we insist nobody's going to get the best of *us.* We're in charge here. And to secure our insecurities, we tend to hammer another. To elevate ourselves, we put another down. And the relationship dies. "Holier-than-thou" types make lousy friends. Our Lord said, "It shall not be so among you!"

HOW THE MILESTONES WORK TOGETHER

Remember, the route to quality friendship is marked by at least four milestones: ACCEPTANCE...AFFIRMATION...ACCOUNTABILITY... AUTHORITY. The tender side—Acceptance and Affirmation—creates the fertile seedbed for authentic friendships to grow. In those growing authentic friendships we recognize and enjoy the security that results from making ourselves Accountable to another person for our thoughts, words, and actions. It becomes a healing, even pleasurable experience, to reveal one's innermost realities within the context of unconditional Acceptance. We willingly submit to the care and Authority of those we trust and with whom we feel safe. That's the way our friendship with God operates. Through His Son we are unconditionally accepted and approved *prior to our Accountability* to God (for future reward) because of Christ's fully satisfactory sacrifice on our behalf. In other words, His Acceptance of us is *never* performance-based. In the same way Christ pleads for us to *reflect Him* in our relationship to others. This means we must learn the gracious, grace-full, often risky, always self-denying skill of accepting and affirming others because they, like us, have value as the very image-bearers of God.

Marriage, families, friendships, and Christian brotherhood should not be battlefields and the rules of the "military model" should not be invoked. Our "Christian soldiering" is to be focused upon being in a battle "against rulers, principalities and spiritual forces of wickedness in the heavenly places"—not in the kitchen toward our wives or in the body against our brothers! We are to be the best of friends. Jesus sees His Body, the Church, as a circle of very fulfilled best friends.

The biblical images for family and friendship—relationships—are to drive us toward unity and connection, not separation and isolation.

WHEN CONFLICTS RISE—THEN WHAT?

But everyone knows that even the best friendship highways have rough stretches—and maybe a speed bump or two. Not everything runs smoothly in friendships. Sometimes traffic on the highway jams up with personal conflicts. When it does, we need an alternate route. In fact, we may need to backtrack a bit just to stay on course!

Every friendship has its conflicts. And because most conflicts rise out of SELFishness or SELF-assertion, most conflicts take place at the Accountability and Authority levels of the relationship. Try this…at whatever level the conflict occurs, *take one step backward.* Put 'er in reverse and go back to the previous milepost. It'll feel like you're going backward, but if I don't miss my bet, you'll find it's really two steps forward! And you'll end up way ahead.

Here's what I mean: If you're struggling with the matter of Authority in your friendship, back up and reaffirm your mutual Accountability to one another. If you're finding Accountability a tough go, don't drop back and punt. Drop back and Affirm! If you're having a hard time finding anything to Affirm, drop back and Accept. And watch what happens! The upset relationship will settle back firmly on the bedrock of Christlike Acceptance.

Do you see how it works? The "step-back" is more an appearance than reality. Because the closer you get to the bottom-line of Acceptance, the more solid the relationship. One step "back" is really forward progress, because the bottom-line of a growing friendship is an accepting relationship. It's not who "wins" an argument. It's not who "makes the best case" or "proves his point." The point of truth is the relationship itself. Don't "win" the argument and lose the relationship!

Two men who have learned to "drop back and accept" each other through tough times are Dr. Joe Aldrich, president of Multnomah Bible College, and Paul Griffin, the college's vice president of finance and operations. Paul describes one "tight passage" in their friendship where lesser men and lesser friends might have parted company. But in this case, Joe Aldrich affirmed that the *relationship* was more important than a point of pride or winning an argument:

> Dr. Joe and I had been working on some heavy-duty issues at the college. These things had been weighing on both of us, almost on a daily basis, for a long time. We were on the edge, and—for me, anyway—the stress was off the scale. Well, I did something stupid. In Joe's office I started going on with a raised voice about the injustice of things, and in the emotion of the moment I delivered an ultimatum.
>
> Joe said, "Are you threatening me with that?"
>
> "Yes, I am," I yelled. "You can count on it!"
>
> In one of the few times I've seen him really angry, Joe said, "I *will not* be threatened. Don't give me any ultimatums!"
>
> "All right then," I responded, "so it's worth the relationship to you?"
>
> A strange look came over Joe's face.
>
> He looked at me and said, "No. No, Paul, it isn't worth the relationship."
>
> We both changed—right there, in the heat of the moment. His answer enabled me to see what I was doing to one of my closest friends, and helped me back off. I apologized, said I could trust Joe to do the right thing, and would support whatever his decision was. We went out to lunch, and the friendship took on a whole deeper level of commitment for me. In the fire of anger and disagreement sometimes deeper trust and friendship get forged. That is what happened here. We could be angry with each other, and I could even yell at the president of a Bible college, and we could still be friends. That's the real stuff.

Here's the point—when you're trying to find and win friends, major in the tender qualities of Acceptance and Affirmation as opposed to the stronger side of Accountability and Authority. Let's take a closer look at those latter two mileposts.

MILEPOST #3: ACCOUNTABILITY

SAY IT GENTLY AND FIRMLY

There's something about that word "Accountability" that sticks in the craw just a little. At first, it doesn't sound all that inviting. It's like seeing a road sign that says "Steep Grade Ahead: Slower Vehicles Use Right-Hand Lane." Milepost #3 gets you into the high country. It's the mark of friendships that refuse to stall out—friendships that keep climbing and climbing. From this panoramic vantage point, you'll discover a whole new vista on the crests and canyons of life. It's worth going for.

The thrust of Accountability is not meant to be punitive, but preventive. It's not to yell after your brother as he plummets over the cliff, "See what you get, you jerk?" It's to say, "I'm committed to your good. When you need me, I'll act as a human guardrail for you. I'm not made of steel, but I cannot watch you go over the cliff without warning you. And I want to warn you right at the road's edge where you still have an opportunity to regain control."

I always look forward to driving into the church parking lot at 6:15 Tuesday mornings for our weekly High Ground men's meeting. If it's a clear day (we do have an occasional one in Western Oregon) an 11,235 foot silhouette of Mount Hood rises regally against a luminous sunrise. Crisp early mornings *are* for men, aren't they? As I pull into the church parking lot, it always amazes me how many men in our church drive full-size pickups. Dodge, Chevrolet, GMC, Ford. Once I noticed a three-quarter ton Ford parked in the first row displaying this message on its oversized chrome bumper. "Friends don't let friends drive Chevys."

That little bumper barb has probably led to more than one friendly fight. But it also nails the message of Accountability. Driving a Chevy is just fine, but there *are* certain things friends don't let other friends do. Friends don't let friends drive drunk. Friends don't let friends pick fights with NFL linebackers. That's the truth. And true Christian friends don't let their buddies slide off the road if they can do anything about it.

Friends *warn* soul-mates when they're moving dangerously close to the precipice of adultery or other life-wrecking sins. They challenge them to measure their position by the center stripe of God's Word. Fellow-soldiers help us see how we can be better husbands, brothers, fathers, grandfathers, and uncles.

A fellow-soldier-friend can say things that a wife can't. He listens attentively to things that wives can't relate to. A true friend is unconditionally committed to helping his friend become all he can be in the kingdom of God.

Sometimes that means saying, not just the pleasant words of "Acceptance" and "Affirmation," but the harder-edged truths of "Accountability."

Such as...*Jim, the last three times we've talked you've mentioned that gal at the club. You're gonna think I'm crazy, but I gotta tell you, you're heading for the edge.*

And by the way, "Accountability" is not a club you grasp and flail wildly. There are some well-intentioned but deluded people strutting around many churches who will tell you they have the spiritual gift of "confrontation." I have bad news for them. There isn't one. Accountability without relationship borders on fraud.

Accountability works best when it begins with prior permission to ask the hard questions, and a *commission* to do it whether either of you feel like it at the time. Scores of guys in our church have written up their own list of "hard questions" to be asked by a loyal friend. For others, it's not a written list. But there is total freedom to ask, to say, to be, *whatever* a friend needs to stay on the road.

- *Are you praying consistently for your wife?*
- *What have you been learning from Scripture lately?*
- *What's the purpose of your life right now?*
- *Describe your prayer life recently.*
- *Are you tithing regularly?*
- *How much time are you spending with your kids?*

- *Have you intentionally held onto any lustful thoughts in the last week? Have you viewed anything sexually explicit?*

Could I take a little "time out" right here? I want to say something about pornography. Some of you reading these words are struggling with pornography addiction. Might be magazines or videos. You could be dropping in on bars featuring "dancers"—where you know you won't be recognized. You may be a longtime church member, a Bible study leader, a deacon, an elder, or a pastor. Your reputation belies the awful secret that only you know. You think you're getting away with it. Know what? You're not. It's getting away with you.

Could I encourage you, no, could I beg you to get help? Know where to start? With a friend who has accepted you and who is willing to affirm you while he holds you accountable.

If you find yourself unable to resist pornography, you need help getting control. The ruts in your mind are so deep that the chances are you will never extricate yourself. Your struggle will only sink you deeper into the filthy muck. Eventually it will suck the life out of everything you cherish. Everything.

So get a strong friend who'll put his shoulder to it and push you past it. Start by telling him the truth. The whole truth. If you need additional professional help, get it. Ask your pastor to refer you to a Christian counselor. But please don't go on pretending. You're missing out on Life! You're playing with dangerous explosives you can't control. Mark my words. Someday they'll blow.

Accountability is not a restricting thing, it's freeing. When you're accountable, you have a brother to stand beside you, someone to call when temptation is really rough, an affirming friend who will praise your progress as you become more like Christ. Keep your arms locked with a brother. Don't let go of your Ranger buddy—except in the most unusual of situations. And I need to explain that one.

Sometimes, in extreme cases, it is necessary to pull away from someone who consistently and blatantly violates God's principles. To them your backing off may feel like rejection and disapproval. But if a friend shows utter disrespect and contempt for God and His Word you really don't have much left in common. Your partner has deliberately broken through every guardrail you could offer, and it's quite likely that the relationship will grow apart. And both of you will know the reason for the distance. It's okay. You've done your best.

MILEPOST #4: AUTHORITY

What does the Authority milepost add to this life journey called friendship?

In actuality, it's the underlying, load-leveling, roadbed that supports everything else on the highway. Authority is the underpinning, the foundation. Authority provides bedrock stability for relationships. The buck has to stop somewhere. And God, our final Authority in friendships and all of life, intends that it stop with Him.

There was a day when my younger brother Eric tested this "Authority thing" in our growing-up home. I think Eric was about four when it happened. Our sister Alison, who would have been ten, was temporarily left "in charge" while Mom and Pop stepped out for a moment. Now, Alison is about the most un-dominating and un-demanding person I know. But when sisters are left in charge they do sometimes test their "motherly oats" a little. Eric, on the other hand, understood the home economy to be such that Pop was the head of the house and that was about it.

So when Alison requested something of her bunny-sleeper-clad brother, the little man inside Eric thrust out his tiny chest and puffed, "You ain't the boss of me!"

It was the same thing Adam must have said to himself in the garden. We've been rejecting God's authority—using different phraseology of course because we're creative—ever since the beginning. Rejection of authority shatters relationship.

"I know my rights."

"Who do you think you are telling me what to do?"

"Who cares what the manual says. I'm doing it my way."

"I have eighteen years in this company. And I say…"

"You obviously don't understand. I should be an exception."

"Authority," the fourth milepost, stands for this: *God makes the rules.*

Come to think of it, He made everything, didn't He? He holds all the original patents, all the copyrights. He doesn't need to negotiate anything. Sounds a bit absurd, doesn't it, to think of the Creator negotiating with His creatures?

God is the boss of us. He has the right to say so and the power to reinforce it. But God isn't into cruel games. Our Father didn't want His children guessing about what was right and what was wrong. *"Oh. Sorry. The pea was under the other shell. Ha! You lose!"*

So the Creator carefully and clearly laid out His loving and wise plan for us in a Book. We pause at Milepost #4 to nod and say, "Yes. I am under authority. God's authority. And the only authority I stand on in my friendships (and the authority I *must stand on*) is the Bible."

Remember now, a milepost is not a nightstick or a battering ram. It's a secure foundation. A Source you can draw on when you have to say to your friend, "I am your brother, not your adversary. But I have to say something you may not want to hear."

That's what Proverbs says: "Oil and perfume make the heart glad. So a man's counsel is sweet to his friend" (Proverbs 27:9-10).

Make every effort to sweeten your counsel. Don't wrap it in bitterness or cloak it in anger. Let it come as if God Himself spoke it. And make sure your face looks like His when you say it.

Dr. David Eckman helps us with an illustration. Imagine for a moment that you're sitting alone at your dinner table. It hasn't been a particularly good day. It's been marked by failure. Then in walks God the Father Himself and pulls up a chair directly across the table from you. Now think about this. What does His face show? How does He look at you? What is His expression?

Did you know He is smiling at you? When God looks at His children, He sees them through the eyes of Acceptance. Because of what Christ has done, when He sees you, He sees His Son. You are in Christ. Pre-approved. Pre-accepted. Publicly affirmed. Accountable to Him, but totally safe, because you are living under His Authority.

God sees you this way every—hear it again—*every* time you look at Him. His face *always* says, "I accept you unconditionally."

ABUSING THE FOUR MILEPOSTS

One last thing about this AAAA highway. Let's take a look at what happens when we confuse or abuse the four mileposts of Acceptance, Affirmation, Accountability, and Authority.

We'll start with the one most easily abused.

The abuse of Authority usually involves some kind of power-play, some control technique, or a form of simple manipulation. When Authority is abused, everyone loses. Some sample abuses:

The Power-play:	"I'm right, you're wrong."
	"You must have a weak conscience."
	"Your attitude is crummy."
Control:	"I could reject you at any moment."
	"Do what you want. I can get along without you."
Manipulation:	"You haven't heard the last word on this."
	"I can figure out a way to make you look bad."

The only Authority you have in a friendship is that which lies in the pages of God's Word. But it is powerful. And it is enough.

The abuse of Accountability might sound something like this:

Power-play:	"I saved you."
	"You owe me."
	"I'm calling in my chips."
Control:	"You have to play by my rules on this one."
Manipulation:	"I'll decide when you've jumped through enough hoops."

Accountability is for the well-being of your friend, not to satisfy your own ego.

The abuse of Affirmation and Acceptance usually involves rendering them *conditional* as opposed to unconditional—sort of dropping "carrots" out there in front of your friend, stating in effect, "I will affirm you only a little and only as I see you are deserving of it." Or I will accept you when you comply with my expectations." Performance-based friendships are really no friendships at all. To quote an Assyrian king out of context, that sort of a friendship is "a splintered reed of a staff, which pierces a man's hand and wounds him if he leans on it" (Isaiah 36:6, NIV).

THREE SONS AND A FULL WARRANTY

If you need one dominant image to linger in your mind out of these two chapters on the mileposts of friendship, linger on the image of a Father with open arms. Linger on God's acceptance of you and me, that makes acceptance in every other relationship a glorious possibility.

I believe one of the reasons, perhaps one of the more critical reasons, God gives us children is so we will understand how much *He*, our Father, loves *us*, His children. I love and accept my three sons. That love is strong. It is subjective. It is emotional. It is a *gushing* kind of love.

I love my sons just because I love them! They are mine. And I am theirs. I love them not for what they do...not for right or wrong...not for what they will become. But for what they *are!* My sons! So when I read that my heavenly Father loves me as a son, my heart leaps! When I read that my heavenly Father loves me so much that He gave His first-born Son for me, my heart melts. When I read I am worth a son to Him, my heart rests. Because I know how much I love my sons. And I know I am not a better father than He.

Linda and I are empty-nesters now. The youngest one has now marched 2,300 miles away off to college. The house rattles a bit these days. It seems larger. Incomplete. This last Christmas as I anticipated the home-coming of all three sons, I experienced one of those emotionally-out-of-this-world musings.

It was at the end of a long day. My mind and body were weary. I was lying on my back in bed just before turning the lights out...and letting my mind wander. That's when the thought shot through me like a mild electrical current.

The boys are coming home.

It occurred to me that even as I was laying there—at that precise moment on the other side of the globe—Kent was wrapping up his final papers in grad school in England. He was tossing a bag over his shoulder and heading to the train station...then Heathrow...then the big bird home. As Kent boarded in England, Blake was packing his pick-up truck in Central Oregon. Soon he and his young bride would make the drive across the Cascade Range "over the river and through the woods" to his boyhood home. As Kent flew and Blake and Jami Lyn drove toward home, Ryan was completing his final exams at college in Wheaton, Illinois, and heading for Chicago's O'Hare to fly home to Portland as well.

They were coming home! Now I had not been with them in months. I couldn't have told you where my sons had been, what they had been doing, or what they had been thinking. But I knew one thing beyond questions: They were mine. And they were coming home! Would I receive them? You'd better believe it! They are mine. And I am theirs. And, to put it in Jesus' words, "no one can snatch them out of my hand." When it comes to these kinds of things, fathers can have pretty good grips! And I'll take 'em exactly as they are.

One day recently, as I wandered through a used car lot, a thought struck me. I'm glad my heavenly Father doesn't deal with his kids like this car dealer does with these cars. Remember those stickers on the windows of the cars in the used-car lot—"As Is/No Warranty"? That gives me the creeps. Makes me feel every one of those cars is a lemon. It says, in effect, "When this thing blows up, don't come see me." Our Father is quite different. Unlike the used car dealer, God gives us a life and in great love says, "If you ever have trouble with this thing, if it ever blows up in your face, please come see Me. I'll make it right." Across the forehead of each of His children, His eyes read, "As Is/Full Warranty!"

That's precisely what one friend needs to read in the eyes of another.

1. Have you ever developed a friendship to the point of Acceptance and Affirmation? Have you advanced to Accountability and Authority? If not, why not now? If so, are you working at it? Is your friendship *really* functioning at that level—or did you just catch a glimpse of that high ground for a moment or two?

2. Remember, a guardrail is an immovable object between a safe path and a dangerous precipice. Life without guardrails can kill you, but friends are divinely placed guardrails. Are you willing to stand anchored into solid ground between a friend and the disaster toward which he may be heading? What may happen if you're not there?

LOCKING ARMS

1. "Accountability needs prior permission." What does that mean? What does it require?

2. "The thrust of Accountability is not meant to be punitive, but preventive." So how does Accountability work between two friends? How can you practice it without causing a rift between you?

3. How can Accountability be a positive thing? How might it be a negative experience? What accounts for the difference?

4. Being accountable to another man, answering the tough questions men don't want to be asked, is said to be *freeing* rather than confining. Why?

5. What are we told to do if we find ourselves in tension or conflict in the midst of these relationships? How will that make a difference?

6. When we talk about Authority, Milepost #4, what are we talking about? Whose Authority? How does that Authority figure into a man-to-man friendship?

7. List five things that might cause men to back away from a friendship based on the "four A's." Now list five things that might actually *draw* men to such a relationship.

CHAPTER TEN

The Heart of a Genuine Friend

Why Some Men Make Best Friends

"For I have no one [like him] of kindred spirit who will be genuinely concerned for your welfare."
PAUL, OF HIS FRIEND, TIMOTHY

very now and then you meet a person who is immediately winsome. So authentic, so real, so open-hearted and positive that you walk away from the encounter thinking, *Man, I wish I could get to know him better. That guy would make a great friend. I'd just love to figure out how we could become buddies.*

Somehow you identified. You clicked. Some combination of personality chemistries melded into a quick shot of excitement, a barrelfull of laughter, or an explosion of mutual ideas and insights. Within a short amount of time, you found yourself wanting to know one another better.

How do you account for that? Was it appearance? Common interests? Similar personalities, education, or background?

Let me follow a hunch. I don't think it's necessarily any of those elements or any other commonly named "quality" of a friend. I think it's more illusive than any spontaneously-named (let alone acquired) trait. I think it may be something more basic, more intangible, and not easily identified as a "trait" at all.

Some people just seem to be born with it. Those who have it seem almost magnetic in their ability to attract others into relationship. Others seem oblivious to it. And some, those desiring to develop into mature and genuine friends, pursue it with great determination, discipline, and desire.

How might we identify it?

For want of any better term, let's call it "heart."

Or, more specifically, "a heart of integrity." You might call it "open-heartedness" or even "winsome transparency" or an "accepting authenticity." But whatever you call it, it involves an ability to accept one's self, to accept other people, and to humbly and authentically open one's heart to another.

Somehow when you meet such people, you're left with the undeniable impression that "What you saw was what you got." This person was Real. Honest. Sincere. And what came through on the outside was exactly what was there on the inside. No deceptive labeling. No camouflage. No "nice to know ya" with eyes focused across the room. This was the genuine item…and it was extended to you.

I think it was this kind of transparency or genuine innocence that endeared "Forrest Gump" to a surprisingly large chunk of America's movie-going public. This was one guy on the big screen who seemed real. He kind of ricocheted through life, but always with a simple consistency that had unfailing appeal. His genuineness enlisted strangers on benches, befriended other fearful soldiers, won over a hardened lieutenant, intrigued a bright-eyed hippie, appealed to presidents, and impacted an entire community. Forrest was real.

But, alas, the only way the public could accept such reality was by portraying it as a trait of the simple-minded. The unfortunate tragedy of the film was that such nobility and consistency had to be "justified" as a lack of intelligence. Certainly no "normal" person could be so transparent. No "normal" person could be so simple-hearted, so accepting, so lacking in prejudice, pretense, and hypocrisy. Or could they?

When you get right down to it—isn't that what you desire most in a friend? Real honest-to-goodness open-hearted authenticity? Of course it is. Without it, friendship goes nowhere. It's somewhere right at the center, the core, of what makes a great friend.

THE FOUNDATION OF GENUINE FRIENDSHIP

Let's take a look together at a man who radiated that kind of open-hearted authenticity. Consequently, he was a man who made an exemplary friend. For one sample case study, we could take a peak into 2 Samuel 16.

You'll remember that David and a contingent of his "mighty men" were pulling into a small town in the back country. As they were moving along a route leading into the village, a scruffy character by the name of Shimei ran alongside David's entourage shouting and screaming and cursing the king. At one point, the little runt went so far as to scrape up handfuls of dirt and throw it at David. He even chucked rocks at him—the ultimate insult. Not your basic approach to a relationship. (This guy was probably a graduate of the Sadaam Hussein School of Congeniality.)

The response of David's friend Abishai tends to bring a smile to the corner of your mouth when you read it: "Why should this dead dog curse my lord the king?" Abishai then asks David for permission to simply "go over...and cut off his head." Rather effective conflict resolution model, wouldn't you say? *Let's go to the source of this indignity, O King. There's a talking head—let's remove it and be on our way.* For that day, it was a pretty typical response. *Let me just wipe the little creep out for you, David, and we'll move along. That punk is nothing more than a momentary distraction, nothing more than the corpse of a Cocker Spaniel.*

But how did David see the situation? Judging by his reply, I picture David to be thoughtful, pensive, contemplative. No—more than that. He is honest, open-hearted, and unthreatened. Listen to the king's response to his loyal friend's request to—as the Green Berets used to say— "terminate with extreme prejudice."

David says, in effect, "No, hold your hand. Put your blade away. Let's hear the fellow out. He may have something solid to say. Who knows, he may even be speaking for God." David's actual words were, "If he curses, and if the LORD has told him, 'Curse David,' then who shall say, 'Why have you done so?'"

It was not insecurity on David's part. Quite the opposite. He was so secure the harsh criticism didn't intimidate him at all; he was even willing to accept it for real consideration. The man had enough humility to hear another perspective, evaluate it, test it, try it out, and if appropriate, adopt it.

While David was very human like the rest of us and had more than his share of faults, he was an open-hearted, authentic man. He was, generally speaking, a humble man, sensitive to people and circumstances, and usually willing to listen and learn. David *faced* life. He didn't try to run from it or bury it or wall it off. You can almost hear him saying, "Guys, life is real. Circumstances are real. Let's face up to them. Let's take life as it is, turn our hearts toward God, tell Him the truth about our feelings, and respond as we think He would want us to."

David's character snaps into even sharper focus when you lay the portrait of his life alongside that of his predecessor on Israel's throne.

TWO MEN IN CONTRAST

Some people record their past in a journal, diary, or autobiography. Not me. My life story seems to be written in my spinal column. You name it, it's there. Bike wrecks, football injuries, parachuting accidents, car crashes. I go in for myleograms like some people get family portraits at K-Mart. For the uninitiated, a myleogram is a specialized X-ray of the spinal column. In order to get the clearest picture possible, radiologists may inject a "contrasting agent" into the spinal column in order to make the structural elements stand out more visibly by contrast. That's how the good doctor is able to speed-read my spine.

Contrast, you see, helps things show up better. It works for stressed joints, abused back bones, and sometimes…a man's heart. Sometimes you can see a man more clearly by contrasting him with another man in a similar setting. Consider David and Saul. David was a small-town boy who became a king. He was a great athlete and a tender friend. He was a sheep keeper and a giant killer. A sensitive poet and a magnificent fighting general. A humble worshiper and a powerful king. A gifted musician and a capable statesmen. He was a husband, a father, and a sinner.

Saul was also a great man. Like David, he was a handsome, strong, naturally-gifted leader. Both men lived through great trials. Both experienced deep pain and crushing disappointment. Both clearly and flagrantly sinned. They lied and deceived. They failed to grasp all of their God-given opportunities and live up to their God-given potential. They had much in common with each other—and with us.

But their lives *ended* so differently. Saul died at his own hand in a lonesome, bloody suicide. David died in bed, at a ripe old age, surrounded by friends.

And they are *remembered* so differently! Saul is remembered as a pathetic, tragic, hapless fool. David is remembered as a champion, a great king, a linchpin in Messiah's royal line, and a hero and model for children. Jesus Himself enjoyed being called "the Son of David."

And by the way, it isn't a sky-blue and white "Star of Saul" that flutters in the breeze over Israel's government buildings as you read these words. Neither do diplomats and tourists stay at the "King Saul Hotel" in present-day Jerusalem. Even modern Israelis gladly acknowledge their kinship to the youngest son of Jesse.

How do we account for that great difference in these two men given their obvious and numerous similarities? There may be many reasons, but I believe the central one is—in a phrase—"the repentance quotient." Saul had an extremely low "RQ"; David's "RQ" was very high.

David learned from his failures. He was trained by his mistakes. He profited from the discipline surrounding his sin. He gained from his losses. He gleaned wisdom from his pain. But while David learned from his failings, Saul was hardened by his. When Saul failed, he retreated further into the shadows. Saul evidently believed the way to live and grow was to grasp, to consume, to hold on, to pursue. David discovered there is growth to be gained in losing. David came to believe that we live by being consumed, by letting go...by running *to* God instead of running away from Him.

David learned not to explain, excuse, or blame. He learned to be honest, confess, get real. David discovered what my insightful friend, Dr. David Eckman, has taught me: God doesn't require His friends to be sinlessly perfect, but He does expect them to be scripturally honest. And that simple-hearted authenticity before God provided solid ground for deep friendship.

It's at the heart of every great friendship.

I think that's why we remember David so well. And why we still name our sons after him. David does not owe his immortality to the fact that he was a great king. Others have built far larger kingdoms. Nor to the fact he was a great warrior. Others have been greater. He doesn't owe his reputation to his parenting skills. His family was rocked by sibling rivalry, incest, rape, rebellion, betrayal, even murder. And it certainly wasn't a holy lifestyle that put David's name on the biblical map. He did it all—lies, adultery, deceit, and murder.

A FRIENDSHIP "AFTER GOD'S HEART"

To what, then, does David owe his reputation as one who was "after God's heart"? I think it boils down to one thing.

David knew how to run to God.

David knew where to go when he was in trouble. David ran toward his pain rather than away from it. He picked it up in his hands and ran swollen-faced and broken-hearted to God. David ran out of the shadows toward the light when his own darkness overpowered him.

Evils beyond number have surrounded me;
My iniquities have overtaken me, so that I am not able to see;
They are more numerous than the hairs of my head;
And my heart has failed me.

Be pleased, O LORD, to deliver me;
Make haste, O LORD, to help me
(Psalm 40:12-13).

Isn't that classic? *God, I'm in deep weeds, I'm utterly screwed up, and it's totally my fault. Help me out of this mess, Lord. And by the way—could You please hurry?*

David tasted, a thousand years before Christ, what John learned explicitly while walking with Jesus. What John heard, what he saw with his eyes and handled with his hands concerning the Word of life was, quite literally, life-changing. He learned that our fellowship is with the Father and that our joy may be complete in Him. He learned that our God loves us no matter what, that He is genuinely gracious, that there is nothing we could ever do that could be bad enough to turn His great heart away from us. David knew that in his very worst moments, God still cared for him. So he felt free to run to the throne of heaven. David did what John encouraged. He ran straight to the Father with his heart in his hands and confessed his sin, refusing to deceive himself about himself.

Somewhere, thumb-tacked on the wall over David's littered desk, you could probably spot his favorite placard:

> *When the going gets tough…*
> *the tough go to God.*

Here's some excellent advice from a man who did it all and who developed the heart of a genuine friend:

In my distress I called on the LORD;
Yes, I cried to my God (2 Samuel 22:7).

He has redeemed my life from all distress (1 Kings 1:29).

Wash me thoroughly from my iniquity,
And cleanse me from my sin.
For I know my transgressions,
and my sin is ever before me.
Against Thee, Thee only, have I sinned
(Psalm 51:2-5).

The LORD lives, and blessed be my rock;
Exalted be God, the rock of my salvation (2 Samuel 22:47).

When I kept silent about my sin, my body wasted away...
I acknowledged my sin to Thee,
And my iniquity I did not hide;
I said, "I will confess my transgressions to the LORD,"
And Thou didst forgive the guilt of my sin
(Psalm 32:3-5).

Because David came to Him with an unlocked, unshuttered, wide-open heart, God spoke some very special words about his sometimes stumbling servant. Samuel speaks as the voice of God, "The LORD has sought out for Himself *a man after His own heart*, and the LORD has appointed him as ruler over His people" (1 Samuel 13:14).

David was "a man." A normal human being with weaknesses and strengths. As the feminists would say, he had "testosterone poisoning" like the rest of us. He could be foolish, impetuous, and intemperate. As a man, he fell. As a man, he experienced failure. David was a man, and there are no perfect men.

But he was a man "after God's heart." I sense the force of a verb in that little word "after." David was *after* God. He followed him. He patterned himself after Him. He ran to Him. He sought Him. He hung out in His presence. His heart was sensitive to the things that God's heart was sensitive to. He had a heart after God's.

It was David's heart that figured prominently in God's choice of him. God's choice of David, and an evident reflection of that heart, is contained in Psalm 78. Verses 70 through 72 note God's earlier choice of David to be king, and bear a beautiful summary of the man's life and character:

> He also chose David His *servant*,
> And took him from the sheepfolds;
> From the care of the ewes with suckling lambs He brought him,
> To *shepherd* Jacob His people
> And Israel His inheritance.
> So he shepherded them according to the *integrity of his heart*,
> And guided them with his skillful hands.

Did anything catch you there? Could you see David's heart? I believe those brief verses describe the heart of a genuine friend. I believe they reflect God's earlier words to Samuel, while David's older brother Eliab stood before him, "Do not look at his appearance or at the height of his stature...for God sees not as man sees, but the LORD looks at the heart" (1 Samuel 16:7). Further, I think they are somewhere near the center of what allowed the Lord to say a thousand years after David's death, "David, after he had served the purpose of God in his own generation, fell asleep" (Acts 13:36).

Wow! Think about it. David was a sinner just like the rest of us. In fact, he managed to get himself into more heartache and trouble than most of us could have stirred up in a couple of lifetimes. Yet how God loved this man! In His incomprehensible grace, God introduces him initially in Scripture as "a man after His own heart" and then writes over the top of his life, this is a man who "served the purpose of God in his own generation."

No ugly footnotes on his gravestone. No asterisks after his batting average. He was just a man remembered for his heart. What was it that made that heart so memorable?

From my perspective, those three words I've italicized in the psalm above capture the essence of David's heart. The man had a heart that was *servant*-oriented, *shepherd*-trained, and full of *integrity*. Just to keep them parallel and easy to remember, let's change their order and start them all with the letter "s." Let's say David was:

> Simple-hearted
> Servant-hearted, and
> Shepherd-hearted.

And let's look at those three elements as describing the heart of a genuine friend. I like to think those are the elements of David's heart that made him such a good friend of God's. And I think those are the elements of David's heart that made him such a good friend of Jonathan's. How can I find such a friend? By being one. So I must work at becoming simple-hearted, servant-hearted, and shepherd-hearted. Let's consider those critical elements one at a time.

1. A Genuine Friend Is Simple-Hearted

The word "simple" according to Webster means, "having or consisting of only one part...without additions, unembellished...without guile or deceit...without ostentation or affectation, unpretending." Now that's a "heart of integrity." The word integrity makes you think of the mathematics term "integer." An integer is a whole number. Non-fractioned. One. Singular. And David's heart, bottom-line, was singular. When he sinned (and he did it royally!) it crushed the soup out of him. He was absolutely heartbroken about it.

With all of his humanity and its sinful warts, David was open-hearted toward God, and toward his friends. You could read the man. He didn't complicate life with a lot of "what if's" or political posturing. David was real. David was authentic. He was an observer of reality. He took life as it came. Watch him before Saul, his brothers, the army of Israel and the freakish champion of Philistia in 1 Samuel 17.

Israel's army had ground to a fearful halt in the Valley of Elah. Israel's King Saul, head and shoulders above his own people and the natural champion of the nation, cowered in his tent after one look at the giant. He would not face him. He would not act as Israel's champion. He would not go one-on-one with Goliath. He would not be "the man of the in-between" the nation so desperately needed. That position was reserved for those with hearts of integrity, such as one called David and the Greater Son of David yet to come, who would stand in the gap for the people and face off with the Champion of Evil. Everyone and everything ground to a frustrating, fearful standstill in the steamy little valley. Everyone waited in sheer anxiety for all Sheol to break loose.

What would happen? How would it end? Enter a boy and a brown bag. David hiked into the valley packing his big brothers' lunches. Just an unknown country kid with a bag full of cheese sandwiches. As he was obediently making his delivery, he couldn't help but scope out the situation with the Philistines. He could feel the fear in the air, and sense the paralysis around him, and it absolutely baffled him. Fresh from the hills and flocks, and new on the battle scene, he began asking the naive, simple-hearted question: "Hey, who is this uncircumcised Philistine, that he should taunt the armies of the living God?"

David said in essence…"Let's see now. We're God's people. He watches over us. These idol worshipers have threatened our existence. Right? Well then, the situation isn't actually all that complicated. It seems pretty clear. The options are limited. Why isn't someone doing the sensible thing and facing off this evil in the name of Yahweh?"

It reminds me of a situation many years ago when I was a youth pastor and had my four-year-old son, Kent, with me in the meeting. Thirty kids or so were seated in a circle, and we were about to wrap up our time together. I asked that we spend some time in prayer with several different ones leading us as they wished. We bowed our heads.

Silence.

Utter, profound silence.

We might as well have been in a cave in Antarctica. No one said a word. You've been there, haven't you? It's awkward and embarrassing. Not one of these kids was about to single himself out by being so bold as to pray out loud. No way. Too risky.

"Hey!"

The silence was suddenly shattered as the voice of a four-year-old piped up in simple-hearted disgust, "HEY! I thought we were *praying!* Why isn't anyone *saying* anything?"

Whoa! All of us there learned something from the littlest guy in the room.

In a sense, that scene in the basement prayer meeting wasn't much different from the one in the Valley of Elah. Everyone there learned something from the little guy in the valley. Those who should have been leading, weren't. Those who should have been taking the initiative were sitting solemnly on their hands. Those "mature adults" who understood all the "difficult dimensions" of these "politically sensitive" and "abnormally complicated" moments, were immobilized by their lack of heart.

In walks the boy from the sheep pens, and history turns. Not because of political prowess. Or physical strength. Or military strategy. Or tactical brilliance. Or special gifting. But just because one young teenager, one simple-hearted shepherd boy with a servant's orientation, let his heart be known.

"Do not look at his appearance or at the height of his stature...for God sees not as man sees, for man looks at the outward appearance, but the LORD looks at the heart."

No, the situation wasn't particularly complicated. It was abnormally dangerous, but there wasn't anything confusing about it. It was really pretty simple when you thought about it. When you have a need, you meet it. That's what simple-hearted servants do. And David had such a servant's heart. So he did it. Just like Jesus. No wonder the Father liked that heart. It was "after His own."

2. A Genuine Friend Is Servant-hearted

This is a heart oriented toward God's purposes.

David was unusually aware that he served Another. He was sensitive to Another's needs. He was alert to Another's expectations. He was oriented to application, to *doing it*. Long before the Nike company came up with its splendid marketing slogan "Just Do It," David was. His attitude was

DEAL WITH IT…whatever it is.
FACE UP TO IT…even if it's your own failure.
WALK INTO IT…even at your peril.
DO IT…even if you have to go it alone.

These things weren't "someone else's" job. He served the King. His job title was "servant." His job description was "serve." So he just did it.

And David said to Saul, "Let no man's heart fail on account of him; your servant will go and fight with this Philistine" (1 Samuel 17:32).

David was willing to *walk toward the pain*. You see it everywhere in the Scriptures touching his life. Whatever it was, even his own disgusting sin, he came to the place where he was willing to walk toward it and face it. If it required confession, he'd say it. If it required sacrifice, he'd get after it. If it required a sling and a couple of stones, he'd jump in and get it done. After all, he was a servant. He served "the purpose of God in his generation." He was a servant with a sense of responsibility, something every good shepherd develops.

Out there under the stars, beside the sheep fold, David had developed a simple-hearted, servant-oriented, shepherd's sense of responsibility.

3. A Genuine Friend Is Shepherd-hearted

This is a heart with a sense of responsibility.

To David's uncluttered mind, the situation in the Valley of Elah really didn't seem much different than some of the issues he'd already faced as a young shepherd watching his dad's flocks. It differed in degree perhaps, but not in kind.

The hills could be lonely places—and dangerous, too. The flock had been threatened more than once, and the servant-oriented shepherd's heart had taken over. His dad, Jesse, had told him to take care of those sheep. The family had a lot riding on that flock.

Responsibility for the flock belongs solely to the shepherd. And David had developed his shepherd's heart to the full. For him it was a relatively simple transition from the hills of Judea to the Valley of Elah. Listen to this young man's plain-spoken, unvarnished logic as he speaks to the skeptical king of Israel.

> But David said to Saul, "Your servant was tending his father's sheep. When a lion or a bear came and took a lamb from the flock, I went out after him and attacked him, and rescued it from his mouth...your servant has killed both the lion and the bear; and this uncircumcised Philistine will be like one of them, since he has taunted the armies of the living God" (1 Samuel 17:34-36).

For David it was just one more day, albeit a stiffer one, in the life of a simple servant-shepherd. "When the lion attacked, I had to stand up to him. The flock depended on it. Dad expected it. And when the bear wandered in and drug off a lamb, it seemed like I should go after it, and get the lamb back. Didn't seem right to just stand there."

David's actual words in Scripture are a real treat: "When [the lion] rose up against me, I seized him by the beard and struck him and killed him." Of course. What *else* does one do when confronting a charging lion? You grab that old chap by his chin whiskers and throttle him about. Then you crack him across the noggin with a big rock and that's that. All in a day's work, old fellow. (Doesn't it make you wish you could see the video of that episode?)

A shepherd is like a soldier. You do what comes in the line of duty. A soldier knows that. One day it may be peeling spuds or scrubbing the

SNAPSHOTS:
MY FRIENDS TELL THEIR STORIES

At one point, early in our friendship, he said something to me that I never thought I would ever hear from a man (besides my father) without hitting him in the mouth. My friend said he loved me, and I knew he was saying this as the deepest expression of friendship, man to man. I'd never heard this level of friendship verbalized before, and felt like a kid wobbling around on a bicycle without training wheels when I tried to respond. But I said I loved him, too. We embraced and shed a tear or two in the process. This kind of talk was foreign to me, and yet I knew it was right. Plus, it unleashed a feeling of freedom I had never had before.

Two of my friends came early in the morning to the hospital, right before I went into heart surgery. We all prayed together and embraced. It was a special time I'll never forget, and it felt good to be able to share words that matched what I saw in their eyes.

latrines. The next day it may be digging a ditch. The next day it may be running into hellfire with an empty rifle and naked bayonet. *You do the next thing.* And you count on God for everything, great or small, all the way through.

Out there in the hills of Judea, beneath the hot sun during long days and under the brilliant stars during chilly nights, there beside the sheepfold, David had developed a simple-hearted, servant-oriented, shepherd's sense of responsibility. It made him a good man after God's heart. And it prepared him to be a great friend: to enjoy an unparalleled friendship with God and to experience one of history's most renowned masculine friendships.

That's the kind of friend I'd like to have—and be.

It may seem like a stretch at first, but when you think about it…you and I have the very same resources for friendship as David. And the same potential to pursue the very heart of God.

It isn't complicated at all. It's simple. So simple we may walk right by the best friendships life has to offer.

One of David's attributes was the humility to hear criticism. You know it's hard to be friends with someone who can never take advice, hear criticism, or consider another perspective. How about you? Do you distance friends because they're never sure when they'll cross you? Or do you draw friends because they know it's always safe to be "real" with you?

LOCKING ARMS

1. "Every now and then, you meet a person who is immediately winsome." You've met guys like that. What drew you to them? How could you project more of that spirit to others?

2. It was said that David and Saul were so much alike and experienced so many of the same things in life. Yet "while David learned from his failings, Saul was hardened by his." Why? What did David do differently? Which instinctive reaction to sin and failure best characterizes you?

3. David was given almost every advantage in life—the things men have always dreamed of having. Yet at the same time, he made almost every major mistake—adultery, murder, failure as a husband and dad. Why would God use a man like David as a positive example? Why would Jesus refer to Himself as the "Son of David"?

4. Remember four-year-old Kent? The reality of the situation was pretty plain to him. "Hey! I thought we were *praying!* Why isn't anyone *saying* anything?" Are you aware of a situation in your church or in your company of friends where someone needs to step up and take the spiritual lead on a certain task or issue? Could you be the one to exercise some servant leadership and help get things started? What comes to your mind when you think about David's willingness to step forward and take on "the next thing"—whatever it might be?

5. David was said to be—

   —"simple" or "single-hearted." What does that mean?

   —"servant-hearted." How did he show that?

   —"shepherd-hearted." How did he express that? What are some ways you might display these qualities in some specific situations you might be facing today?

CHAPTER ELEVEN

Real Friends Say So

Getting Past the Small Talk

"David rose from the southside and fell on his face to the ground, and bowed three times. And they kissed each other and wept together, but David more. And Jonathan said to David, go in safety…we have sworn to each other in the name of the LORD…"

I SAMUEL 20:41-42

riendship needs to be expressed. Two friends need to talk. Honestly. Openly. In specific terms. Using real words. Friendship needs to be defined and expressed. And for most of us men, that prospect is about as inviting as a leisurely swim in the East Siberian Sea.

I suspect that many of you are just like me—wanting our friendships to somehow go deeper. And you know what? I think they *would* go much deeper…if we would just say so. If we could just muster the courage to stumble through a few faltering first steps and try to express our hearts to one another, our friendships would likely take off. But as in any venture worth anything at all, it requires squaring off with a few risks along the way.

There is something about us men that hesitates to admit our need for another human being—whether male or female. But it seems especially difficult for a man to express his feelings honestly to another man. And lest you think that reluctance trivial, it's probably the same reticence that keeps us from expressing our need for God.

I have a good friend who enjoys a number of solid friendships with other men. They are all friendships that go beyond a few common interests and activities. They extend into the chest. I love the guy. He inspires me, stretches me, and makes me stronger just for knowing him. Because he is my friend, I want to be a better man. It's healthy. He is a prominent man and heads a strategic national ministry impacting many thousands, likely millions, of people.

On one occasion he candidly shared with me his difficulty in expressing his need for friendship. I have a hunch you'll identify with his words as much as I did:

> I will never forget the day I told a man, whose friendship I had enjoyed for a number of years, that I needed his friendship. It was interesting as I talked with my wife about my need to define and declare formally where this man and our friendship stood. As I called him and asked him to have lunch with me, I remember talking to my wife about what a difficult assignment it was to really bare my soul to another man and admit not only my need of him, but also to tell him I really needed his friendship. I think there is something within all of us that seeks the safety of obscurity and, as a result, we never define where our relationships are. Thus, men go through life like islands— only touching each other's coastlines occasionally, but never really letting another man in on the interior of his life.
>
> As my friend and I sat down for some mediocre Mexican food, I remember looking him in the eye and being severely tempted to chicken out. The thoughts rushed through my mind, *Why risk it? Why be this vulnerable? Why, he may not want a friendship with you. He already has too many friends. There are too many demands on his life. Why would he want to know you? Why dump this additional weight of another person's needs on him?*
>
> Resolutely, I pushed away the fears and stuck to my commitment that I'd made to my wife the night before. It was a good thing I knew where I was headed, because the fears of the moment would have absolutely overwhelmed me had I not already counted the cost of admitting my need of this already treasured friend.

I sipped a Coke and said to him, "Jim, I want you to know something that I have been thinking about for some time. I want you to know that I really value your friendship, that I need you, and consider you to be my best friend." The words did not come out as strong as I had hoped. There was a halting choke in my voice as I attempted to express what I was feeling. And at that point, I grabbed my Coke and began sipping on it as I pushed my chair back from the table. I fixed my eyes on my friend, wondering what his response would be.

To this day I am astounded by his response. He looked back at me with nearly total shock that I would consider him to be one of my closest friends. He went on to express how he viewed me as pretty self-sufficient, as a man who had many friends on the inside of his life. He even listed several names.

While sitting in that restaurant, I remember thinking: *This is fascinating. I wonder how many men would describe their best friends in similar fashion and yet never take the initiative to move the friendship to another level by admitting the need for the friendship and esteeming the other person by declaring them a close friend.*

He describes the experience well, doesn't he? You can just feel the knot in his gut and those sweaty palms. Was it worth the effort and risk? Listen again as my friend recounts the impact of that meeting:

I wish I could say that our relationship was permanently cemented and needed no maintenance from this point. But these are things of fantasy land and not of real life. Real relationships between real men take hard work, maintenance, and working through problems as they occur. Real deep friendships with men owe their value, like gold and diamonds, to their scarcity. Commitment is costly.

I can say this about our friendship today: I believe that lunch was a key turning point in defining our relationship and moving it to another level. I am convinced both of us would have continued to enjoy one another and to frequently spend time together. However, we would never have understood the value we had in each other's lives if there had not been a tremendous risk taken to define our relationship and to admit the need of another man.

I couldn't agree more! Take the risk. Start to express yourself. Verbalize. Build trust. And know that a truly valuable friendship, like a diamond, takes a lot of time and pressure to build.

In my earlier book, *Tender Warrior*, I told about taking what to me was a huge step in one of my friendships: I actually called my friend from O'Hare Airport just to tell him he was in my thoughts. Not long ago, after another trip away, that same friend stopped by my office to pick me up for lunch. I piled into the front passenger seat, and he cranked the ignition. But then, instead of dropping it in reverse and scooting out of the parking lot, this big man paused and deliberately looked me straight in the eye.

Slowly, and with feeling, he said, "I have *really* missed you."

It felt good to both of us. And I returned the favor!

Any woman who might be reading these pages is probably thinking, *So what's the big deal? That's what friends, do, isn't it?* Yes...but what comes so easily and instinctively for the feminine gender can loom as a massive hurdle in a man's eyes. A man's emotions don't lie close to the surface as a woman's. The emotions are *in* there, all right, but deep down. Sometimes it takes a mining operation to get at 'em. For the next few pages, let's put on our miner's hats and dig in together. Strangely enough, the place where we might begin our excavations is in the depths of limestone cave.

WORDS IN A CAVE

As I've said, the road to manhood often goes through the doorway of friendship. Similarly, the path to the deepest of friendships usually goes through the doorway of adversity. We become best friends when we stand by one another in the crunch of pain and need. And it's in those very pains and needs that we ought to be expressing ourselves to our friends.

In the previous chapter, we did a little mining of David's friendship with the Lord. Yet we hardly dug more than a shovelful or two of ore. This vein runs deep into Scripture, and I think we'll both benefit by tunneling a little deeper.

David's friendship with God, like ours, was significantly shaped in the dark places. Under the stars, David developed his heart. In the darkness, God shaped David's soul. In the deep waters, God molded the man's spirit. And in a cave called Adullam, David entered into an experience with his Friend that would mark the rest of his life. Psalm 142 is the wrinkled, soiled, tear-stained journal entry coming out of that miserable hole in the ground.

The theme of the psalm appears in verse 3:

> When my spirit was overwhelmed within me...
> But Thou didst know my path.

Do you see how that verse reads? For a moment there, David almost forgot. His spirit was *overwhelmed*. Like a tiny chunk of driftwood swallowed under a great wave. Like a little piece of straw swept away in the rush of a prairie wind. For a heartbeat or two, David thought it was all over. Then he caught himself, and recalled his good Friend, the God of Israel. Crouched there in the bitter darkness, he reminded himself what his Friend was like.

He knows. He feels. He cares. He rescues.

When we're at the end of our wits, ropes, and resources, our Best Friend understands precisely where we are...and meets us there. There in our darkness, we pause to remember His loyal love, and the remembering is sweet. Remember, when you're headed for the high country, it's usually the roughest and rockiest roads that take you to the most beautiful places.

My younger sister, Alison, does not enjoy heights. Nor does she appreciate rough roads and wild country. Tight places and precarious corners do not delight her soul. But she does love her husband, Rich, very much indeed. So when he suggested visiting a "beautiful spot" I'd described to him in vivid detail, she swallowed hard and consented to go along. Now Rich is a consummate outdoorsman. He *loves* the highest places, deepest canyons, wildest rivers, and windiest ridges. He exults in tight places and precarious corners. I had told him of this heart-meltingly beautiful alpine meadow only about an hour's drive from our home near Oregon's snow-capped Mt. Hood. I also mentioned that the old logging road leading to the meadow was a tad rough (which is probably why the place is still so beautiful).

So Rich and Alison went. Neither of them will ever forget it. But for different reasons.

Rich claims the fingernail marks are still there in the side of his car. Alison told me it reminded her of our early childhood when I used to harass her by leading her into some of the craziest predicaments—only now I was still doing it "in absentia" through her husband. But she did understand the truth that it's usually the roughest and rockiest roads that take you to the most beautiful places.

David experienced that truth, repeatedly. Mention the cave at Adullam and memories would flood his mind. He'd learned a lot worth sharing in those dank, cramped quarters. In fact, he deliberately set out to share the learning experience—which is why we have Psalm 142. The superscription over the psalm indicates it is a *maskil* or teaching psalm—teaching others among God's men how to pray, how to run to God in open-hearted friendship. That same superscription also identifies it as the time "he was in the cave." There were a couple of caves in David's life, but most scholars agree that the definite article and the psalm's content point to Adullam. This was THE cave of David's life.

The old cavern was actually not too far from his earlier exploits in the Valley of Elah. What took place inside his heart inside that cave so moved David, he sat down and captured the experience with his pen.

> I cry aloud with my voice to the LORD,
> I make supplication with my voice to the LORD.
>
> I pour out my complaint before Him;
> I declare my trouble before Him.
>
> When my spirit was overwhelmed within me...
> [But] Thou didst know my path.
> In the way where I walk they have hidden a trap for me.
>
> [You, LORD—] look to the right and see;
> For there is no one who regards me;
> There is no escape for me;
> No one cares for my soul.
>
> I cried out to Thee, O LORD;
> I said, "Thou art my refuge, my portion in the land of the living.
>
> Give heed to my cry, for I am brought very low;
> Deliver me from my persecutors, for they are too strong for me.
>
> Bring my soul out of prison so that I may give thanks to Thy name;
> The righteous (ones) will surround me, for Thou wilt (have) dealt bountifully with me."

Let's leaf back through the Bible and grab a little context. How did David ever get stuck in a hellish place like that? The story of the cave at Adullam is recorded in 1 Samuel 22 and begins with the words "so David departed from there and escaped to the cave of Adullam." We have to step back a chapter or two to catch what's happening. David is in big trouble. The jealous Saul is hot on his trail with murder in his eyes. His friendship with Prince Jonathan has been his salvation thus far, but even that can't protect him much longer.

David has to say to his friend, "As the LORD lives and as your soul lives, there is hardly a step between me and death" (1 Samuel 20:3). Jonathan assures his friend that their commitment to each other is deep and strong. "And Jonathan made David vow again because of his love for him, because he loved him as his own life" (1 Samuel 20:17). Jonathan then investigates and is forced to admit that the plot against his friend is truly lethal. The two friends meet in a field to say their goodbyes. "And they kissed each other and wept together, but David more" (1 Samuel 20:41).

What a picture of masculine friendship at its best! These men had given themselves to each other. Jonathan had sacrificed everything for David. David, in turn, had found his characteristic open-hearted authenticity going even deeper than ever before. This friendship meant the world to both of them. They had walked together through a lot. And now there was deep pain. Soul-wrenching, gut-twisting, face-contorting PAIN! Tears welled. Eyes met. Their arms wrapped around one another, and squeezed in a bear hug so strong their ribs flexed. And they kissed. And wept.

Don't be afraid of that kiss.

It's rare, to be sure. Very few friendships will ever draw that deep (because most of us tend to run from pain and open-hearted authenticity). But a few do go that distance. And when they do, it's like drinking from a cold mountain spring after years in a desert.

Let me walk you through a little progression in my own life. Trust me on this, I'm not a guy who goes around passing out kisses. But the older and more mature I become, the greater becomes my appreciation for their significance.

My early childhood wasn't oriented to a lot of physical expression. I come from a German family, and we're not exactly what you would call a "kissy-face, huggy-poo" kind of clan. You might get a handshake, and if it's really "intimate" the second hand might grab your elbow and give you a "two-handed" shake. But that's about the extent of it. We're just not a real touchy-feely outfit, if you know what I mean, and I've always tended to shy away from any overt physical expression. As a boy I didn't think much about it. I suppose I subconsciously relegated that sort of stuff to the feminine half of the race.

My later youth didn't expand me much in these areas. I ran with the "jocks"—consumed with athletics and in-your-face competition. Oh, there was physical contact all right, but it was hardly relational. A clenched fist, a stiff forearm, a quick hand-check, and a crunching, crack-back block every now and then. But nothing you'd call friendly. Yes, there were a few "high-fives" and other great celebrational moments, but nothing that was deeply personal. Certainly not intimate.

Then I went into the Army. Now *there's* a relational Mecca. Not quite! The military's primary concern is not that people feel good about themselves or others. It's basically just shut up, salute, and get the mission accomplished. Communication was crisp, functional, and often punctuated with words that my publisher would never print. Most military relationships were what Jesus might have called "Gentile" in quality; that is, they were built on relative rank and who was calling the shots to whom. Jesus called it "lording it over" one another. Again, that wasn't an environment that provided a lot of opportunity for developing significant personal relationships. That was for psychologists not soldiers. I didn't know a lot about that kind of thing, and, frankly, I didn't care to.

Even my marriage at the time didn't experience a lot of it. Love? Yes. Passion, uh-huh. Flashes of interpersonal intimacy, sure. Lindy and I have always treated each other with respect. But we did not experience that rock-solid, give-yourself-away kind of authentic intimacy that I now know to be the most desired wellspring of life.

Then we had children. And life took on a new relational dimension. Personally, I have now learned that life is where you live it—that wives, children, home, friends, and neighbors are what life is about.

Our senses of destiny and history must increase the quality of deep, personal relationships rather than leave them behind or merely use them as launching pads for something else.

I believe David and Jonathan had learned that as well. I believe their friendship had come to mean the world to them. And now they were parting. They kissed. And they wept.

When I think about weeping with another man, I think of my friend and younger brother, Eric. Many years ago he and his wonderful wife, Jeri, separated for a time. Today, they're together, growing, and happy. But at the time, and for a period of nearly two years, there was no communication. Only separation and hurt. Eric lived at our home during those days. His heart was broken, his spirit torn, his soul aching. Man, I love Eric. I remember weeping with him. And I remember hugging him strong...and intimately.

Let me tell you about another friend, another man with whom I have wept. And a man I have kissed. His name is Ryan, and he's my son. He is nineteen years old, 6'2", 200 pounds, and the delight of my life. The other night as it was time for the lights to go out, we ended the day together—as is our custom when he is home—stretched out on the bed, talking through the day, and concluding with prayer.

It had been a difficult season for both of us for quite different reasons. We began to talk through our lives, and the issues we were facing. The conversation went deeper and deeper. We prayed. The prayers went deeper, too—more and more real. The communion was something beyond anything we'd ever experienced together. There was pain, to be sure. But it was glorious, soul-knitting pain. Healthy pain. Life-shaping pain. We didn't want it to end. The tears came for both of us. I told him how I loved him. He told me. The tears felt warm and healthy, and I did not want to wipe them away. We hugged each other. Strongly. And I kissed him on the neck.

Now, my brother, my son, and I are full-grown men. We are emphatically, enthusiastically heterosexual. We own no distorted sense of our masculinity. And yet we hugged one another as if we'd never let go. I can tell you that there was not the slightest sense of awkwardness, let alone shame. Only deep love...and respect...and friendship. Soul for soul.

What do old men remember? Years from now, as I thumb my way back through the dog-eared pages of my life, those moments with my brother and my son will be underlined. Highlighted. Rehearsed. And tasted again. No one but the three of us can know the value of those moments. Your reading these words may let you in on just a degree, but the knowledge of our souls knitting belongs to us alone.

So it is for any authentically accepting friendship with time enough to go deep. It is so often that pain—that universally despised and avoided commodity—which opens the door to a friendship so deep that its roots entwine with the roots of life itself.

So it was for David and Jonathan.

So it was that David walked out of that field...and away from the friend who loved him as himself.

David fled to Nob, gathered some rations and heavy weaponry from the priest, and moved on to Gath. While seeking refuge at Gath, it became evident that he would not be received, that he was in imminent danger again. Fear gripped him to the marrow. He had enough presence of mind to feign insanity, but it wasn't a pretty scene:

> He...acted insanely in their hands, and scribbled on the doors
> of the gate, and let his saliva run down into his beard
> (1 Samuel 21:13).

David's life had come a long way...a long way down...away from his dreams.

At the end of the line, the end of his options, he ended up at the cave called Adullam.

> And when his brothers and all his father's household heard of
> it, they went down there to him. All those who were in distress
> or in debt or discontented gathered around him, and he

became their leader. About four hundred men were with him
(22:2, NIV).

Sound like a fun group, doesn't it? Four hundred scroungy guys in
a gloomy cave with little food and no sanitation could get on a fella's
nerves after awhile. This was no place for Emily Post.

By this time, "David the shepherd boy" was ancient history. "David
the teen-aged giant-killer" was a dim memory. "David the king's musician and golden boy" was a long time ago. The weight of David's current situation was staggering.

In short order, he had lost...
>   his home—he had to flee,
>>   his career—he'd been drummed out of the military,
>>>   his contacts—Samuel was out of the picture,
>>>>   his wife—Michel had been given to another,
>>>>>   and his best friend—Jonathan was left behind!

David was man without a country. He was a fugitive, an outlaw, an
exile with a price on his head. The development of character doesn't
come easily, does it? There are times when the bottom drops out.
Darkness falls. The sun disappears. Everything seems painful. A heavy
sense of sinking sets in.

There's another way to look at it. A strange and powerful cycle of
events is taking place—to make or break "a man after God's heart."
How will he respond? Where will he turn?

How about you? What is the cave in your life? There is simply no
way to glamorize a cave. It is lonely...dark...damp...disillusioning. It feels
like the truth can hardly breathe there! Equilibrium is smashed.
Bubbles are burst. Perspective is shot.

I can recall some of the unbelievable caves that I or my friends have
had to live in at different times. You can too. What do you do when...

- your mate has quit talking and served you divorce papers?
- your son has moved out in a fit of anger and lives on the street?
- you've just discovered your daughter is a practicing homosexual?
- your boss just told you the company is bankrupt and you no longer have a job?
- you've just closed the door on a totally disastrous interview?
- the doctorate you've worked on for five years is not going to happen?
- the investment of your life savings just failed and you're utterly broke?

Where do you go? How do you respond? Where do you turn? You need a friend. You need a friendship that goes deep, that accepts you where you are, that helps you find your own soul.

David had that kind of need. There in the cave. Look at the emotional stress on his heart. Go back to Psalm 142 and just stare for awhile at some of those pregnant phrases: "Cry aloud with my voice...make supplication...pour out my complaint...declare my trouble."

David was at his wits end. The verbs alone capture the depth of his pain. To *cry aloud* is a cry of anguish; it is a red-faced, ragged-breathed, broken-hearted vomiting out of the very soul. It is a kind of involuntary, spontaneous, sobbing from deep within. It's the emotional dry-heaves. To *pour out* indicates the bitter water has filled the cup to capacity, reached the brim, and begun to spill over. Can you imagine David sitting...staring...eyes off into space...and desperately wanting out of the human race? To *declare* is a more deliberate and likely repetitious reviewing of his utter helplessness.

Which brings us back to the climax in verse 3. *When my spirit was overwhelmed within me* is a picture of overpowering, unstoppable flood waters. The mind is drowned, the spirit crushed. He is smothered in fog and conquered by the weight.

But wait!

In the second part of the verse, there is a flash of hope! Some

Hebrew scholars tell us the construction calls for a pause, as though David never finished his thought—"when my spirit was overwhelmed within me..." dot, dot, dot—thought incomplete. And they tell us the next part requires at least a mild adversative to rightly understand—"but." But...You...You...You KNOW my path!" You know! Oh, wow, You *know!*

Like a diver coming up from the deep end of a pool, David breaks into the light and sucks in fresh air. He recognizes, at least momentarily, the loyal love and sovereign hand of his Best Friend. And his own heart revives.

In verse 4, he nearly loses it again as he, in imperative tone, instructs the Lord to take a good look at his situation. He's saying, Lord, You "look to the right." You see. You take a good long look at this mess. I'm flat out trapped. There is no way out. There is no one that really cares for me."

But after David slips into a few words of panic, maybe even a little self pity, he comes back to reality. He notes there is no visible help anywhere available. And that's when he opens his own eyes again. And in verse 5 he shouts, "Lord, You are my refuge, my Portion in the land of the living!" Perspective returns and David realizes that there is no visible refuge. This cave really doesn't amount to any kind of a stronghold. But the heart of God...now there is refuge!

At that point, David's heart jumps back into its customary high gear and he begins to envision the future. He tells the Lord he can hardly wait until He brings his soul out of the prison. And he visualizes the day when the believing people of God will gather around. Then he will tell them of the ways of his faithful Friend. For this Friend "will have dealt bountifully" with him.

There's David's hope again, his confidence in this friendship, and his vision that it will flourish. The word "bountifully" there in verse 7 is probably not the best translation. Perhaps "fruitfully" would be a little closer to the intention. The word is associated with a harvest, but the emphasis is not so much physical blessing as fruitful production. God is dealing with His friend. He has David's best interests at heart. He wants to see David's life become all it can be. And His every move in the friendship is oriented to that end.

David is realizing that this Friend is "for" him. This friendship is a trusting one, as are all healthy friendships. David is understanding that his God is sovereign, and he therefore believes that when He is involved in grinding our lives to nothing, it is not to end our life, but to re-route it. God is going to produce fruit in the life of David. David knows it well and can hardly wait until the day he can tell other "righteous ones" about it.

It reminds me of the wine company ad: "We will sell no wine before its time." In God's vineyard it might be understood: "The living God produces no maturity without due process." Miles Stanford said it well,

> It seems that believers have difficulty in realizing and facing up to the inexorable fact that God does not hurry in his develop-ment of our Christian life. He is working from and for eternity! So many feel they are not making progress unless they are swiftly and constantly forging ahead. Now it is true that the new convert often begins and continues for some time at a fast rate. But this will not continue if there is to be healthy growth and ultimate maturity. God himself will modify the pace.[1]

I'd like to suggest that our earthly friendships are to have the same driving ends as David's friendship with God. That the role of my friend is to walk beside me, through thick and thin, accepting me as I am but never leaving me to myself and my natural loss of perspective. And then, after years of developing the necessary elements—affection, loyalty, and trust—my friend and I are in a position to become full-orbed in our friendship. We can be continually expressing our acceptance and affirmation while we hold one another on course through accountability, and love enough to actually become authorities in one another's lives.

We can get real. We can acknowledge our emotions and express them…honestly…to each other.

Now that takes time. Lots of it.

And hear this…that means it is highly likely I must re-prioritize my life if I expect to have such friendships. For one thing, my weekly schedule is going to have to allow for it. And for another, my "career path" will as well. In other words, if this kind of life-growing friendship takes years to develop, I can't be jumping from job to job and city to city pursuing promotions and fatter salaries and leaving my friendships in the dust.

Friendships take time to season into trust. Like water in a deep well, honest expressions of the heart bubble up to the surface rather slowly. A man could go all his life and never taste the cold, bracing refreshment from such a well. But once you've tasted it, the tepid, surface stuff will never satisfy.

1. "David kept coming back...running...into the arms of his Best Friend." Do you ever think of God as your best friend? What do friends do together? What is God wanting the two of you to do together as friends? So...what are you going to do about it?

2. If you want to have a friend, you're going to have to make time for one—make it a priority, take some initiative. How could you begin to do something about that this week?

LOCKING ARMS

1. "I suspect that many of you are just like me—wanting our friendships to somehow go deeper." Is that true for you? If you could make a list of five things you'd like to experience in deeper friendships, what would they be?

2. "I think there is something within all of us that seeks the safety of obscurity and, as a result, we never define where our relationships are. Thus, men go through life like islands—only touching each other's coastlines occasionally, but never really letting another man in on the interior of his life."

   a.   Do you opt for the "safety of obscurity"? Why?
   b.   Are most men "islands" by choice, or because of fear? Why? Fears of what?
   c.   How many of your friendships might be enriched and deepened by some honest expression of feeling?

3. Suppose, as in the example in this chapter, you realized you really wanted to tell another man that you consider him a close friend and that you deeply value his friendship. What fears would you have about telling someone that? What if you were on the *receiving* end, and someone expressed those things to you? How would you feel? Does that make the prospect seem any easier?

4. "Years from now, as I thumb my way back through the dog-eared pages of my life, those moments...will be underlined. Highlighted. Rehearsed. And tasted again." How can we begin to look at friendship more from the perspective of what it will mean to us down the road, and less from how "uncomfortable" we might feel expressing ourselves now?

5. "You need a friendship that goes deep, that accepts you where you are, that helps you find your own soul." How does a friend help you find your own soul?

CHAPTER TWELVE

The Greatest Man-killer in the West

Even the Lone Ranger Wasn't

*"If one falls down his friend can help him up. But pity the man who falls
and has no one to help him up."*
SOLOMON

Anyone who spent time in the military in my generation will likely recall the joys of "Brasso." That stuff saved more soldiers' hides than you can imagine. A liquid rubbing compound used to polish metal to a high sheen, Brasso has been liberally applied to countless GI belt buckles. When a soldier stands at inspection, he has to be at his best.

Many a GI's heart sank as he rushed toward a surprise inspection, threw open his footlocker and pulled out his belt...only to discover the buckle badly tarnished. He'd left it alone too long. He hadn't rubbed it to a careful shine. And now he could expect the usual greeting from the tight-lipped noncom.

"What kind of ☆#@% soldier are you?"

How does brass tarnish? How does armor rust? What do you have to do to turn that beautiful, highly polished belt buckle into a dull and discolored lump of metal?

Nothing.

Nothing at all.

Just leave it alone. Don't touch it. Don't hold it up to the light. Don't rub it. Just leave it to itself. And an attractive, useful piece of "armor" becomes worthless.

What do you do to render a man worthless? Unrecognizable? A thin shadow of his glorious potential?

Nothing.

Nothing at all.

Just leave him alone. Don't let him rub shoulders with another man. Isolate him. Don't let him come into regular contact with other growing, capable men. Let him stay isolated, and before long people may well be asking him, "What kind of a man are you?" Certainly not a healthy man.

It is not good that man be alone. Period. We weren't made for it. And left to it, we die. Perhaps that's why solitary confinement is considered "cruel and unusual" punishment by some. Isolation breaks a man down. Ask any POW and he'll tell you the roughest part is the aloneness.

So where, for crying out loud, did we ever get the idea that real men stand alone? That the real cowboy rides by himself? That the real hero has few friends? And that "strong, silent, and independent" are the hallmarks of true masculinity?

It may have begun with the Industrial Revolution ripping men out of their "natural habitat." It may have been fostered by the great war. But it was most certainly popularized by Hollywood.

Somewhere along the line there developed the myth of "The Man Alone." Somewhere over the years we learned to think that true men were to be "rugged individualists." John Wayne usually rode alone. So did Clint Eastwood. Ditto the Marlboro man. And mega-selling Western novelist Louis L'Amour constantly had his hard-bitten characters telling us that to the degree a man depends on anyone or anything else, he's that much weaker. I wonder if old Louis really believed that himself. This is the same author who created the wildly popular Sackett series of Westerns. And one thing you could always count on about that far-flung, hard-riding clan: When one of the Sackett boys was hurt, in trouble, or in a tight spot, every other Sackett across the wide West would come a'ridin' with his Colt on his hip and his Winchester in the saddle boot. An insult or injury to one of the Sacketts was an insult or injury to all of 'em, and cowboy, you'd better check your passport, because America just ain't big enough to hide in.

Nevertheless, generations of men have bought into the dominant mythology that "masculinity carries it alone." And it's *killing* us. When men began to stumble toward isolation, when men began to lose touch with each other and the home, that's when men, marriages, families, and an entire culture began to die.

Think about it for a minute. When this country was founded, it was always those with a strong sense of community and interdependence that did the yeoman's work. They knew they would survive and grow together. Or they would die...one at a time...alone. Plymouth was a community from the get-go. So were the other colonies. We called them *colonies* because that's what they were. Look up "colony" in a synonym finder and you'll see words such as "community" and "flock." Early Americans stuck together. Close at hand. Heart to heart. The men involved had a sense of "commonwealth." Community leaders were governed by a vision for the common good. That attitude almost seems like something unearthed from an archaelogical dig, doesn't it? Today the statement of Ray Kroc, builder of the McDonald's empire, seems more typical of the modern prevailing attitude:

> It is ridiculous to call this an industry. This is rat eat rat. Dog eat dog. I'll kill 'em, and I'm going to kill 'em before they kill me. You're talking about the American way of survival of the fittest.[1]

Seems as though what it takes to survive in America has turned like a burger on the grill—a 180 degree flip-flop.

How did we come to this? How could a nation barely two hundred years old have changed so dramatically? The key word there is *change*. The changes of the last century or two have been like none other in all of human history. And the closer you get to today's date, the more rapid the changes accelerate. My own dad grew up minus indoor plumbing—not to mention television, microwaves, laser surgery, and a host of other whiz-bang innovations. But the changes are far deeper than technology. Something more fundamental has been going on. We have been toying with such basics as the nature of the family, and marriage, and womanhood, and manhood. In her excellent book, *Choices*, Mary Farrar calls what we have experienced "the great flash flood of history." She describes it well:

> Suppose we were to take the equator that stretches clear around the globe and use it as a time line representing all of history. If we were to put the last 175 years on that line, they would amount to a mere ink dot. Yet the change that has occurred with this "dot" exceeds that of any tens of centuries before...until this time, cultural change occurred slowly, becoming absorbed into life over centuries. However, from the beginning of the Industrial Revolution until the present day, the unprecedented rate and power of change have literally turned modern culture upside down. What's more, this great flood is far from over...
>
> The cultural revolution of the last forty years should therefore come as no surprise. The rise of feminism in the fifties, the sexual revolution of the sixties, and the "immoral revolution" of the seventies and eighties—are all natural results of the flood...
>
> The storm that brought us this Great Flash Flood of history hit our land in the early 1800s. Many historians date the beginning as 1815, with the onset of the Industrial Revolution...[2]

Most middle school history students (prior to Outcome Based Education) used to be able to tell you that the Industrial Revolution took men into the factories. What we don't always recognize is that walking into the factory took men away from the home, away from families, into more direct competition with one another, and in some hard to define sense, away from each other. It was a costly move. Mary Farrar captures it:

> Often overlooked...is the price that men paid for the great progress of the world. An industry worker's life was a year-round job, usually with poor conditions and pay. Men...lost control over their working and were increasingly at the mercy of employers and big business...
>
> In short, with the mentoring role taken out of a man's work, the focus shifted to promotion and success. Work now served the primary purpose of self-actualization and affirmation. American men latched on to this idea with such gusto that European writers noted the unhealthy work frenzy and addiction among the early industrial men of our land...
>
> The nature of the world of business allowed only one part of a man to be expressed—his warrior side. Business drew heavily on his aggressive, protective instincts, all the while holding his tender side at bay.[3]

Now hear Mary's punch line. It is a potent summarization that rings painfully true:

> As a result, relationships of depth and meaning in a man's working world were rare to nonexistent. He certainly could not express his feelings of anxiety or fear at work. Nor could he freely express emotions of love and affection. Conversation at work centered around the job at hand—success, competition, winning the race—not around relationships or personal feelings and needs. A man learned to ignore his deeper emotional and relational needs in order to function in the dog-eat-dog world. And so, in due time, the relational and emotional side of man literally began to starve. *Tenderness gave way to a hard exterior. Affection gave way to aloofness. Enjoyment of family gave*

way to drive for success. And, finally, teamwork and companion-ship gave way to authoritarianism [emphasis added].[4]

And *Voila!* Enter John Wayne, Clint Eastwood, the Marlboro man, and (in the words of David Smith) The Friendless American Male. One by one, men wandered off into themselves believing they could trust only themselves. The rolls of the toxic cult of the individual began to swell with a vengeance. And SELF-reliance, SELF-improvement, and SELF-realization became cultural bywords. "Deciding for yourSELF" became the modus operandi.

THE CULT OF THE INDIVIDUAL

More than one generation of Americans have grown up now under the mistaken impression that we are our own best authorities, that we don't need one another. Our entire culture acts as though each individual is his own highest authority.

From the earliest age, the American child is encouraged to decide for himself—to make up his own mind; he is encouraged to believe he himself is the best judge of what he wants and what he should do. Even in those instances where the American cannot decide for himself, he still prizes the illusion that he is the locus of decision-making. Thus, when he needs to consult a banker, teacher, counselor or expert of any kind, he perceives it is (merely) seeking information that helps him to make up his own mind. The expert is treated as a resource person and not as a decision-maker. The American believes, ideally, that he should be the source of his own information and opinions and, also, solve his own problems. Esthetic judgments are frequently equated with personal preferences, since the American often resents accepting canons for judging the worth of a work of art. He prefers that value reside in the self; if the individual likes it, it is good. *The result is an intense self-*

centeredness of the individual—so striking that an American psychologist has suggested this as a universal value.[5]

So how have we fared lately living by such isolationist, do-your-own-thing principles? Not so hot. How do we like life left to ourselves? Not very much.

A recent Gallup poll dubbed the decade of the 1990s "The Healing Decade." It seems that millions of Americans are seeking help of all sorts—psychological, physical, emotional, and spiritual. Here are the reasons stated for this growing trend:

- *Loneliness:* One-third of Americans admit to frequent periods of loneliness, and a recent...survey discovered that loneliness is the key factor in the high suicide rate.
- *Detachment:* One survey reveals that seven out of ten people do not know their neighbors. "Americans move around more than most people, and hence find it more difficult to sustain intensive friendships and bonds among neighbors...In an average year, some 40 million Americans move. Put another way, every ten years, between 40 and 60 percent of an average American town's population leaves."[6]

Perhaps it's time for a change of values. Perhaps we should start measuring our wealth in terms of friends rather than dollars. The average American keeps his job 3.6 years. No wonder Vance Packard says "Rootlessness seems clearly to be associated with a decline in companionship, a decline in satisfying group activities, a decline in mutual trust, and a decline in psychological security."[7]

- *Divorce:* Six out of ten new marriages will end in divorce, a rate that may be the worst in the entire world.
- *Addictions:* We appear to live in an addicted society—addicted to chemicals, possessions, success, wealth, and a self-indulgent lifestyle.

- *Privatism:* Privatism contributes in a major way to the go-it-alone philosophy in religious matters.[8]

Men, I think we were fed a line. Somewhere along the line we picked up the wrong idea about strength and independence. It seems as though we figured they were signs of maturity. We were led to believe the lie that "when I grow up to become a real man, I won't need anybody else." Nothing could be further from the truth. The mature man enjoys friends. Jesus, the Ultimate Man, made certain He had at least eleven close friends.

REAL COWBOYS RIDE TOGETHER

We're strangling ourselves by riding alone. And by the way, *real* cowboys don't ride alone anyway! Consider this statement from one who actually spent some time on the range:

> When I'm in New York but feeling lonely for Wyoming I look for the Marlboro ads in the subway. What I'm aching to see is horseflesh, the glint of a spur, a line of distant mountains, brimming creeks, and a reminder of the ranchers and cowboys I've ridden with for the last eight years. But the men I see in those posters with their stern, humorless looks remind me of no one I know here. In our hell-bent [good choice of words!] earnestness to romanticize the cowboy we've ironically disesteemed his true character. If he's "strong and silent" there's probably no one to talk to [at the moment]. If he "rides away into the sunset" it's because he's been on horseback since four in the morning moving cattle and he's trying, fifteen hours later, to get home to his family. If he's a "rugged individualist" he's also part of a team: ranch work is teamwork and even the glorified open-range cowboys of the 1880s rode up and down the Chisholm Trail in the company of twenty or thirty other riders. Instead of the macho, trigger-happy man our culture has

perversely wanted him to be, the cowboy is more apt to be convivial, quirky, and softhearted. To be "tough" on a ranch has nothing to with conquests and displays of power. More often than not, circumstances—like the colt he's riding or an unexpected blizzard—are overpowering him. It's not toughness but "toughing it out" that counts. In other words, this macho, cultural artifact the cowboy has become is simply a man who possesses resilience, patience, and an instinct for survival. "Cowboys are like a pile of rocks—everything happens to them. They get climbed on, kicked, rained, and snowed on, scuffed up by the wind. Their job is 'just to take it,'" one old timer told me.[9]

Let me tell you about a real cowboy I know.

Dave Spear manages Spanish Canyon Ranch for owner Clint Nichols. Dave's tucked way in Eastern Oregon about ten miles west of Dayville (population 38), fifteen miles east of Mitchell (population 233), twenty miles south of Kinzu (population 11), and forty miles north of Paulina, Suplee, and Izee—a string of communities of populations of 76, 23, and 0 respectively. Now that you have it pinpointed, you can pretty much tell it is rugged back country. The kind of place for hardy people only. And there aren't that many of them. You get the picture.

If ever you were looking for isolation, this is the kind of place you might expect it to rule. But it doesn't. Quite the opposite. Oh, you can find plenty of wide open space to sit by yourself if you're seeking it. Here, of all places, where the population is less than one person per square mile, where the wide open spaces are just that, here you would expect to see the macho man, the Marlboro man, or some other such Hollywood fictitious character. Not so. Out here, men learn to rely on each other. You work together until the job is finished.

Spanish Canyon, settled by hardy pioneers about 1860, is today a working cattle ranch in the middle of some of the most beautiful country a man could hope to see—sixty thousand acres of sage, juniper, pine forest, and grassland. About six hundred head of cattle roam those acres, along with majestic elk, mule deer, bobcats, and the ever present "Wile E." coyote. Here and there, at several little places scattered across the ranch, are the gravesites of pioneers who once upon a time called this good land "home."

And here, Dave and Carla Spear raised their family. Four sons and a daughter. I've never met their daughter, but I've seen those boys—strong, bright-eyed, and hard-working. Just what you'd expect of such hardy stock. The kind of broad-shouldered, square-jawed, and steel-eyed men you find in the cigarette ads.

When the Spear boys were 17, 20, 22, and 24, Troy—the 20-year-old—died suddenly of a congenital heart condition very few knew he had. His strong work ethic on the ranch had certainly never betrayed it. As you can readily understand, the family was devastated.

Dave gave me a small taste of what it had been like for him.

"You know, Stu, from time to time you see a movie or a news clip where someone throws himself across a coffin, utterly distraught. I'd always wondered just what kind of pain could cause someone to do that. Now I know. I've never experienced such pain. It stirs deep down inside you, just lays there aching, and rises to a point where you think your soul will explode."

Dave went on to tell me about Troy's funeral and graveside service.

The cemetery sits on a wind-swept hill. The undulating grass knows nothing of the history or the heartache. Friends gathered around the family. As part of their expression of deep respect for each other and their brother and son, Troy's dad and three brothers carried the casket to its final resting place.

That's the way real men operate. Together. To the end.

Troy's pastor, Clay Williams, shared a few thoughtful words, then prayed. And then...in most towns and communities, people would quietly depart for their vehicles. The cemetery crew would lower and bury the casket. And the day would be over.

SNAPSHOTS:
MY FRIENDS TELL THEIR STORIES

In 1965, as sixth graders, we became best friends. We spent our "wonder years" together. Side by side we'd patrol our turf, a few rural Oregon miles of rolling hills, open fields, and sporadic houses. Today, thirty years later, I ride my mountain bike over the same ground. Every corner, every driveway, every house and field trigger memories of times in my life when I was inseparable from a boy named Jerry.

I remember Jerry and I picking (and throwing) berries at dawn on summer mornings, then spending our afternoons swimming and listening to the Beach Boys and Simon and Garfunkel, switching channels on our squawky eight-transistor radios and reading Superman and Batman comic books. We'd talk about cute girls and adventures and exploits, and what we'd do when we grew up. We'd haul out our sleeping bags and camp out under the stars in my back yard with Champ, my Golden Retriever. We'd look through my telescope at Jupiter's moons and Saturn's rings and wonder what life was all about. (In those days we didn't know.)

At age 38, Jerry was dying of cancer. Chemotherapy had already left him bald. After he was diagnosed as terminal, he and I talked about suffering, healing, and heaven. I picked out lots of books for him, and he read them all. We talked about God's grace in giving him time to prepare for what awaits every one of us. We prayed together for his wife and children. In our final coherent conversation, after I'd read to him a number of Bible passages, I said to Jerry, "We were made for another world, not this one." He smiled and said with a weak voice, full of conviction, "Amen."

Not here. Not in country where men walk together, ride side by side, mend each others' fences, depend on one another, and stay together until the job's done. Dave told me of the final tribute to Troy, their fallen comrade. He turned silently to his three remaining strapping sons. They'd agreed together "to stay 'til the finish." Each brother reached for his waiting shovel. They began to fill in the grave.

Other men stirred. Their eyes caught one another's. Spontaneously...slowly...quietly...with respect and purpose...each man walked to his waiting pick-up, reached for his own shovel, and returned to join Dave and the brothers in a rite of community like we all long to experience. A circle of man-friends was at work. They even took turns with shovels, so each man could share in the brotherhood of the moment.

AND REAL SOLDIERS FIGHT SIDE BY SIDE

It's always been that way. Real men find strength in sticking close together. Real soldiers know never to go into battle alone. In the year 491, the Persians were determined to beat the Greeks into submission. With a fleet of 600 ships and an army of well over 100,000 men, the Persians pitched their camp near a place called Marathon. They chose the site believing it best for their cavalry in which they overwhelmingly outnumbered the Greeks.

The Greek countryside was in turmoil. The Persian military had never yet been defeated. It looked hopeless. Still, Greek men gathered from Sparta, from Plataea, and from Athens. When the opposing armies met, it was disheartening. The Greeks had something just over 20,000 men; the Persians five times that many. The battle ensued. Let Will Durant tell the story:

> The Persians were brave, but they were accustomed to individual fighting, and were not trained for the mass defense and attack of the Greeks. The Greeks united discipline with courage, and though they committed the folly of dividing the

command among ten generals, each supreme for a day, they were saved by the example of Aristides, who yielded his leadership to Miltiades. Under this blunt soldier's vigorous strategy the small Greek force routed the Persian horde in what was not only one of the most decisive battles, but also one of the most incredible victories, of history. If we may accept Greek testimony on such a matter, 6,400 Persians, but only 192 Greeks, fell at Marathon.[10]

It's no different today. When the going gets tough, the tough need each other (and all the rest of the time, too). Do you remember the dark days of 1979 through 1981 when fifty-two Americans were held hostage for 444 days in Iran? All America was angered. But seemingly helpless. Finally, on January 20, 1981—the morning of President Reagan's inauguration—those beleaguered captives were finally released.

They had been through extraordinary trauma. Psychologists all over America feared for them. Most thought it would be many years before the hostages could become "normal" again. But to the surprise of many, the former hostages simply picked up their lives and careers and moved on. Some felt they were stronger and better people than previously, actually strengthened by the ordeal. How so?

One psychologist, long interested in the effects of captivity upon a human being, was not surprised at all by how well adjusted the hostages were. Dr. James Segal had studied the American prisoners of war who had returned from Vietnam nearly a decade earlier. These men had been tortured and abused in unimaginable ways. But most of them adapted rapidly and healthily back into normal life upon their return. Why?

Dr. Segal feels there are really just a few basic principles necessary to enable people to endure the stress and anguish of captivity. Listen to his first and second principles:

1. *Stay in contact with others.* First and foremost, even the strongest of us need the support of others.... Take the case of Navy Capt. James B. Stockdale, who was once dragged from

his North Vietnamese prison cell to a hot unshaded courtyard. There, for three days, he was forced to remain sitting with his hands cuffed behind his back, his legs locked in heavy irons. Guards would not let him sleep. He was beaten repeatedly. After one such beating, Stockdale heard a towel snapping out in prison code the letters GBUJS. It was a message that would remain a source of strength through his captivity: "God bless you, Jim Stockdale."

2. *Help others in trouble.* Self-pity never increased anyone's psychological endurance. Compassion for others—shedding the martyr role and turning one's attention outward—has a remarkable healing effect. While serving as U.S. Ambassador to Colombia, Diego Ascencio, along with other diplomats, spent sixty-one excruciating days as a hostage of gun-wielding terrorists. He recalls, "I think what helped most was that I started working for the benefit of others. I wasn't just sitting in the corner. I was trying to take care of other hostages, and I didn't have much of an opportunity to brood."[11]

Did you catch the single common word in the two primary principles? Others! Stay in contact with others. Help others.

You and I may not be prisoners of war, but many of us are hostages. We are held hostage by all kinds of stressors—marital discord, family conflict, crushing financial burdens, serious illness, a disintegrating culture, job woes, and so on. And what we need is contact with others. Friends. Not independence. Listen...*there is no such thing as self sufficiency.* Such a concept denies the image of God in man.

We have to stick together if we're going to survive.

We have to ride together if we're going to stay in the saddle.

It's about time that phony Marlboro Man image blew away like the puff of smoke it really is.

1. *The Friendless American Male.* Is that book title a good description of you? If so, is it because friends aren't available—or because you haven't made cultivating friendships a life priority?

2. With the industrial revolution, men left the teamwork and quiet mentoring of the farm for the intense competition and demands of the workplace. They became more self-aware, more "success" oriented. Try this: On the top of a sheet of paper, list some of your personal and career goals. On the bottom half of the paper, write down some goals you hold for your marriage and family. Is that second list as sharp and complete as the top one...or is it a little fuzzy? What might that indicate about your emphasis in life?

LOCKING ARMS

1. A friend or acquaintance really messes up, sins, blows it big time. What usually happens? Do people rally to him, or back off? What's the usual result? How can we avoid the appearance of condoning sin, without avoiding the brother in need?

2. "Perhaps we should start measuring our wealth in terms of friends rather than dollars." How would that change the way most men make decisions? Does that thought even seem reasonable? What might the result be—years from now?

3. Dave buried his boy that morning on the lonely hillside. His other sons grabbed shovels and soon those standing nearby did the same. Would that have happened where you live, or would men stand back, afraid of butting in or being embarrassed?

4. "You and I may not be prisoners of war, but many of us are hostages. We are held hostage by all kinds of stressors..." What two things do we need to remember when we become hostages to the pressures of life?

5. In the end, we pretty much choose the life we live. How about you? Have you chosen to have friends? Or have you chosen to live the role of the friendless American male? Are you satisfied with your choice?

friendly Is as friendly Does

Choosing Your Friends Carefully

"He who walks with the wise grows wise,
but a companion of fools suffers harm."

PROVERBS 13:20

When I was born in the 1940s, there was no such place as "Disneyland."

Some old guy in Anaheim with a straw hat and bib overalls was putt-putting his John Deere through a grove of navel oranges on the same acreage where one day Mickey and Goofy would preside over a "magic kingdom." But Walt was picking up steam. In those years he created a movie that rocked our little minds. Disney, as he used to do regularly, produced a potent proverb in animated form. Who can forget *Pinocchio*?

Think back with me to the last time you saw that amazing little cartoon parable. Remember how it starts? The Good Fairy waves her wand and the little wooden puppet on Geppetto's work bench comes alive.

"Am I a real boy?" he asks.

"No," she responds, "to make Geppetto's wish [for a son] come true will be entirely up to you. Prove yourself to be brave, truthful, and unselfish, and someday you will be a real boy."

"A real boy!" he exclaims.

"It won't be easy," she warns. "You must learn to choose between right and wrong."

After the Good Fairy leaves, the would-be boy and his newly awakened conscience (Jiminy Cricket) have a conversation. Jiminy tells him, in effect, "If you want to be a good boy, you need to know the world is full of temptations. There are wrong things that seem right at the time. (That's a pretty solid insight for Hollywood, don't you think?)

So, with that excellent coaching from Jiminy and the Good Fairy, two of the truly best friends a guy could have, it's off to school for Pinocchio. He's about to meet some people and make some friends. It's pretty heady stuff for a kid carved out of a hunk of pine.

But the poor little buddy never gets there. Alas…his road to the schoolhouse is intersected by two seedy characters coming off a sideroad. The two new "friends," a slippery fox and a slow-witted cat, convince him there is "an easy way" to success, bright lights, music, applause, and fame.

Jiminy's pleas go unheeded, and the Good Fairy fares no better. She tells him, "A boy who won't be good might just as well be made of wood."

But what's that to Pinocchio? He has friends to see and places to go. His new companions—the fox, the cat, and a fat guy—talk him into a trip to "Pleasure Island."

You can probably visualize right now those famous and painful animated scenes that follow. The little wooden-headed puppet piles into a coach full of other youngsters—a slug of new friends—all determined to have the time of their lives. They transfer to the boat which delivers them to Pleasure Island. As they draw near, it's odd how the place looks so dark and foreboding at first. But, hey, what the heck. Smiles come to their faces. This place is unbelievable. Their eyes nearly explode. It's even better than they'd been led to believe. That fox and cat really were jolly friends!

Pleasure Island has it all. A Rough House for roughhousing. A "Model Destruction Home" to tear apart. Stained glass windows to throw bricks through. Cigars for everyone. And a pool hall. The party is on, and boy, do they party! Finally, the night slips away and the revelry spends itself. Pleasure Island looks more like a graveyard now.

Pinocchio and Lampwick—his cigar-smoking, tobacco-spitting buddy—wander into the pool hall. Lampwick prods his little friend to "quit smokin' like me gramma!" With his pal's encouragement, Pinocchio takes a real drag on that thing. (Yes, he inhales.) And before long, the poor boy is completely disoriented. His eyes refuse to focus. He feels sick. He begins to lose function. Finally he collapses, utterly helpless, sprawled across the pool table in the now abandoned pool hall—just a trembling shadow of his former self.

It was an incredible progression. Make that deterioration. And Disney portrayed it well. From health, vibrancy, and an extremely bright future as a "real boy," to a confused, collapsed pile of wood and strings in a greasy pool hall.

All because of a couple of lousy choices.

All because of a couple of lousy friends.

In the space of five short minutes, Pinocchio's demise can be documented. The clues are visible and progressive. His voice loses its innocence. His wide, innocent eyes begin to close down. His hat, once on the back of his head displaying his bright face, is now cocked forward and to one side, shielding his eyes. He begins to talk like those around him—slow, slurred, and out of the side of his mouth. He begins to walk like his new friends, swaggering and cocky. Pinocchio has been transformed…no, deformed.

What Disney portrays in a brief clip usually takes longer in real life. But not much longer. The point is painfully clear. Friendship is a road, and it is a road that *leads* somewhere. Walk with the wrong friends long enough, and you will end up where you never wanted to be.

Three thousand years before Disney animators inked their first frames, a wise man put it like this: "He who walks with wise men will be wise, *but the companion of fools will suffer harm"* (Proverbs 13:20).

Someone else along the way took that same bit of wisdom and gave it this familiar twist: "One bad apple spoils the whole barrel."

The point of that potent little proverb, obviously, is not to solicit concern for the bad apple. *Ah, the poor little apple.* The point is to warn the good apples—the fellow barrel-dwellers. Watch out who you bump up against, or you could end up soft, mushy, and good for nothing. In a word, rotten.

That's the nature of association with things that are breaking down. When you closely associate with deterioration, you tend to deteriorate. Rot, you see, spreads.

Ever noticed the phenomenon in neighborhoods? Apples, friends, and neighborhoods tend to take on the characteristics of those nearby. Homes seem to run in groups. "Nice neighborhoods" are just that. "Run down" neighborhoods are just that. Seldom, if ever, do you find one really "nice" home (sterling, well-maintained, fastidiously kept) in a neighborhood of deteriorating, trashy, run-down, used-up homes. People who care about their homes try to move out of bad neighborhoods, if they possibly can.

> Apples deteriorate...
>> Weeds proliferate...
>>> Disease is contagious...
>>>> Rust corrupts...
>>>>> Cancer spreads...
>>>>>> And the wrong kind of friends can kill you.

Scripture says it right up front, in simple, straight-forward terms: "Bad company corrupts good morals" (1 Corinthians 15:33).

Back in the book of Genesis, the Bible paints a life-sized mural of two men who chose different neighborhoods...and what became of them.

TWO MEN, TWO ROADS

So Abram went up from Egypt to the Negev, with his wife and everything he had, and Lot went with him. Abram had become very wealthy in livestock and in silver and gold.

From the Negev he went from place to place until he came to Bethel, to the place between Bethel and Ai where his tent had been earlier and where he had first built an altar. There Abram called on the name of the LORD.

Now Lot, who was moving about with Abram, also had flocks and herds and tents. But the land could not support them while they stayed together, for their possessions were so great that they were not able to stay together. And quarreling arose between Abram's herdsmen and the herdsmen of Lot. The Canaanites and Perizzites were also living in the land at that time.

So Abram said to Lot, "Let's not have any quarreling between you and me, or between your herdsmen and mine, for we are brothers. Is not the whole land before you? Let's part company. If you go to the left, I'll go to the right; if you go to the right, I'll go to the left."

Lot looked up and saw that the whole plain of the Jordan was well watered, like the garden of the LORD, like the land of Egypt, toward Zoar. (This was before the LORD destroyed Sodom and Gomorrah.) So Lot chose for himself the whole plain of the Jordan and set out toward the east. The two men parted company: Abram lived in the land of Canaan, while Lot lived among the cites of the plain and pitched his tents toward Sodom. Now the men of Sodom were wicked and were sinning greatly against the LORD (Genesis 13:1-13, NIV).

Note the ominous change of tone at verse 13. Note the people with whom Lot was beginning to associate. He had chosen his friends poorly! He was on a road, now. And it was leading somewhere.

Abram, having chosen well, moved on to a greater quality of life, a deeper friendship with God, children, a healthy family, and the pleasure of the enormous covenant relationship with God and His people. Abram, by choosing wise associations and values, left his family a heritage you and I are still enjoying today.

Lot, on the other hand, was on the road to becoming a debased man. The next time we see him, he is living in the midst of the city that personifies the ultimate den of sin and evil, the city whose very name epitomizes rotten choices and lives…and it isn't Pleasure Island. It's Sodom. He has offered to give his daughters away to associates for the most denigrating and immoral activity—group sex (19:8). He has completely lost the respect of his wife and children. When he speaks, even in honest urgency, they think he is a joke (19:14). He ends up getting his wife killed. He falls into a drunken stupor and becomes involved in incestuous relationships with his own daughters.

And it all started with a choice.

A fork in the road.

Lot chose to associate with the wrong kind of people, and he paid for it. Dearly. So did his entire family. The only heritage he left was the fathering of two ungodly peoples who became intractable enemies of God's people for generations on end: the Moabites and the Ammonites. These two nations were nothing but a barbaric, idolatrous thorn in the side of Israel for centuries.

Quite a contrast between those two men, Abram and Lot. They started out together, but chose different values and friends that led them down separate roads to far different destinations.

I'll never forget the time—even though it was twenty-five years ago—when I watched that same dynamic unfold before my own eyes.

THE TWO MUSKETEERS

Vietnam wasn't a happy experience for anyone.

Mrs. Roberta Johnson was particularly unhappy. No, she never set foot in Southeast Asia herself, but her son did. Eric Johnson was her pride, her joy, and her hope for the future. "Such a good boy," in her words. And truthfully, he was. You could see it in his eyes and you could see it in his ready smile.

Eric had always done well in the schools of the little south Georgia town where he'd grown up. And his first two years of college had gone exceptionally well. A bright and thoughtful young man, Eric had declared a major in Literature. British Lit was his favorite. But for reasons many members of the class of 1967 couldn't understand, Eric felt he should set Shelley and Shakespeare aside to do his part for his country. Eric enlisted in the U.S. Army and was sent to the Republic of Vietnam.

Unlike many of the more self-centered members of Eric's baby boomer generation, he had actually *believed* John Kennedy, when America's young president had encouraged America's youth to "ask not what your country can do for you, ask what you can do for your country." Eric wanted to be part of carrying the dream of Camelot to a little country threatened by dark forces. He, like many young men in the Army of his day, was willing to "pay any price, bear any burden, support any friend, and oppose any foe to ensure the survival and success of liberty." (Why do those words now seem so far-away and other-worldly?)

Eric arrived in Nam just a few weeks after a young man named Darryl, and they became inseparable chums. Tall and well-built, with dark, chiseled features, Darryl Wilson looked like he'd stepped right off an Army recruiter's poster. He fit the classic, swaggering-young-buck Green Beret image to a T. An earlier generation might have called Darryl a "man of the world." He knew how to "get along" most anywhere. He knew how to use the system...and how to abuse it. For Darryl, life was just one big smorgasbord of unlimited taste-tests—some legal, some not. But all quite acceptable—by his standards, at least.

They were an unlikely pair. Darryl had been around the block. Eric hadn't...but he was about to. One miserable step at a time.

Far from home, overseas in a combat zone where all social inhibitions have a way of fading, Darryl intended to get his money's worth at this "all you can eat" buffet called life. He sampled everything—off duty, on duty, legal and illegal.

Here were two strong, young men. Two friends. Both Green Berets...America's best. And both bright enough to have been specially selected for assignments in the Intelligence Operations shop of the 5th Special Forces Group. At that point, their similarities ended. They were fast friends, to be sure, but they weren't good for each other.

One was there for a cause. One was there for himself.

One believed in patriotic words. One mouthed them with a wink and a smirk.

One was innocent. One "experienced."

One naive and gullible. One a high-stakes gambler.

One eager to please. One eager to experiment.

And, as was perfectly predictable, the gambler led the gullible. The "worldly wise" fox led the wide-eyed Pinocchio. The strapping kid with the flair led the sweet kid with the heart. The immoral corrupted the moral. Darryl led the friendship down a path neither believed at the time to be destructive. But they walked down it together, one leading the other, one pleasure-yielding, life-destroying step at a time.

It started with nothing more complicated than late hours of conversation. Yet they were hours that should have been used responsibly for rest because of the critical job demands upon them. The mission and their fellow soldiers' very lives were at stake.

Then they drank together. Couldn't blame a guy for that. Beer was often the only cold, wet thing you could get your hands on in the base camp.

Then they decided to "slip downtown" to NhaTrang just to "have a look around."

Then the "looks" became extended visits to experience the exotic, perfumed "pleasures of the Orient."

Then there was the venereal disease. No problem, what was penicillin for, anyway?

Then there was the more serious strain of VD, that didn't respond so quickly.

As the days went by, there was less and less sleep at night, and more and more wild nights in town. Inevitably, key responsibilities began slipping. You could almost see the physical, mental, and spiritual deterioration at a glance.

It's not as though they weren't warned. The two soldiers were regularly confronted by others, and eventually even threatened with a "bust," or reduction in rank. Too late, young Eric opened his eyes and saw his own reflection. The Georgia boy panicked when he began to realize what had become of him. He was little more than a trembling shadow of his former self, now *unable* to function responsibly. He was dismissed—in humiliating disgrace—from his assignment.

In his confusion and distress, the young man wrote home. Maybe he thought a cleansing confession could set his shattered life to rights. Maybe he simply didn't know where else to turn. Whatever his thoughts may have been, Eric spilled out his whole painful story to his mom back in south Georgia.

To Eric's deep chagrin and embarrassment, Mrs. Johnson fired back a bitter, angry, accusatory letter to her son's commanding officer in Vietnam. The bottom line? "Just look at what *your* Army has done to *my* precious boy!"

It fell to me to respond to her. I told her what she most likely already knew in her heart. The Army had done nothing to her son; it had only provided him the opportunity to make choices for himself. And he had made some poor ones. But all of those poor choices ultimately stemmed from the initial one: Eric Johnson had not chosen his friends wisely. One "friend" had taken him a long way down a winding, downhill road. It remained to be seen if he could ever find his way back to the point where that wild, plunging sideroad had branched off from the main highway.

The point is agonizingly simple. Friends, when chosen carefully, are a wonderful—even essential—part of life. That's what this book is all about. But friends who are poorly chosen can kill you.

Friendship—real, solid, life-enriching friendship—always takes the high road. True friendship travels the straight path. Friendship never lurks in alleyways; it never hangs out in darkness. Friendship doesn't point to the alleys, it leads to the free-ways.

Friendship never leaves you in a trap. It always pulls you out of ditches, bandages wounds, dusts you off, washes you up, and sets you back on a healthy course.

The writer of Hebrews may have had the fellowship of believers— the company of friends—in mind when he wrote:

> Therefore, strengthen the hands that are weak and the knees that are feeble, and make straight paths for your feet, so that the limb which is lame may not be put out of joint, but rather be healed (Hebrews 12:12-13).

That's what friends do. They encourage each other's strengths, help each other to heal, and keep each other on the straight path.

Friendship, true friendship, always lifts. It never drags. Oh, it can be heavy, but it is not destructive. Friendship leads you out of the woods and into the sunlit meadow. Friendship never hangs in the shadows, but always presses toward the light.

You see, friends don't let friends run amuck.

Friends don't let friends self-destruct.

Friends don't lead friends where they shouldn't go.

The great Creator God, who knows the heart of man better than anyone else, is well aware of the power of friendship to bring a man up out of the valley...or drag him into a bottomless swamp. That's why He put clear road signs—biblical principles—along the way: to alert us, to warn us, and to guide us away from disastrous detours and fatal dead-ends.

Principle #1: Not everyone is a friend who appears to be.

Reading the book of Proverbs is like walking through a grove of ancient sequoia redwoods. Like those mighty giants of the west, the proverbs are thousands of years old, they are straight and true, *and they are alive.* Listen to this piece of wisdom that has stood strong for over three thousand years.

"A man of many **friends** comes to ruin, but there is a **friend** who sticks closer than a brother" (Proverbs 18:24).

Be careful how you define "friends." All that seems or acts "friendly" is not truly friendship.

The first word translated "friends" in that old proverb is a word that refers to friends pretty loosely. It's really speaking of "acquaintances," "associates," or "companions." We're talking about shallow, surfacy friendships here. It's those we come across, share a few activities with, hang out around, and casually call "friends."

But the second word is to be taken more seriously. We're talking *friends,* here. Real friends. True friends. The kind worthy of the word. This is a different word, stronger and deeper. It could even be translated "lover"—one who really and truly loves. The difference between the two words is the *focus* of the relationship. On the one hand you have self...fun...activity. On the other hand you have soul...core...depth. The second word for friend is really the only word for friend—the kind of person who puts his friend's well-being above his own.

Principle #2: Friends are like highways; they lead somewhere.

Stand for a moment in the shade of another towering sequoia. Here's another truth that's three millennia old—but as current as this morning's sunrise: "The righteous is a guide to his neighbor, but the way of the wicked leads them astray" (Proverbs 12:26).

Contemplate that towering, ancient proverb for a moment. Think about it. How does God get His people to grow? Answer: God uses a number of change agents, fertilizers, growth inducers, if you will, to help us grow. He uses His Word, His Spirit, and His people. And who are His people? *The church.* Christian friends! The church, if viewed rightly, is really a circle of friends.

You see, we were created to live in company, in plurality. God, who is Three in One, created us in His image. Like Him who always lives in company, we were made for communion. It is by divine design that we tend to take on the characteristics of those to whom we are closest.

You've seen it in your friends, you've seen it in your kids, you've seen it in yourself. We begin to talk like each other. We tend to adjust to each other. We pick up each other's accents and expressions. We laugh at the same kind of dumb jokes and hum the same tunes. We begin to act like one another, and even dress like each other. It's all a part of *belonging,* of living together in a company, of being accepted. And the fashion industry capitalizes on it every day of the year. The tendency to stick together is so strong that "style," as we call it, becomes an entire industry. We tend to switch "styles" even when we don't like them just because it's "in" to dress in a particular way. And some people are getting rich off our tendencies, aren't they? I think a large part of it is because we were created as gregarious beings.

So, given our propensity to conform, who we hang out with becomes a large factor in our lives. *Who* we hang out with has an incredible influence upon *how* we live. *Who* we travel with has a way of determining *where* we end up.

Highways have destinations. Outside my office window runs a federal highway. U.S. Highway 26 climbs toward Mt. Hood that rises majestically out of the Cascade range about fifty miles from where I'm sitting. Now I've been down ol' 26 many times—I can't count how many. I know where that highway goes. I know where that road leads. And when I see—even through the limited perspective of my office window—a car traveling on it, I can tell you where it's headed. Even though I'm neither a prophet nor the son of a prophet, I can tell you where those folks will end up unless they turn off or turn around.

And that is life. When I see people speeding down a particular road

—such as a man or woman flirting with adultery

—such as a teen playing with premarital sex

—such as a couple that gets caught up in frantic materialism

—such as a family that becomes consumed by non-stop recreational pursuits

—such as men and women who gradually "lose interest" in spiritual things—I can tell you how and where they will end up unless they turn around and get off that road. I've seen where those roads lead. I've seen the ruins, the pain, the emptiness.

Roads lead somewhere. Highways will inevitably bring you to a destination, and ending point. And so will the wrong kind of friends. That's why, if we care at all about where we want to end up in life, we must choose those friends carefully.

Don't do as Rehoboam, the phony King of Israel and the Pinocchio of the Old Testament, whose life and reign were marked forever by self-induced tragedy. Why? Because "he forsook the counsel of the elders which they had given him, and consulted with the young men who grew up with him" (1 Kings 12:28).

Let me repeat another proverb from Rehoboam's time. His dad Solomon wrote it, and Rehoboam should have known it. "He who walks with the wise grows wise, but a companion of fools suffers harm" (Proverbs 13:20).

A companion of fools suffers harm. Those words are as cold and biting as wind rolling down a glacier. Yet they are true. If taken wisely, they ought to serve like a chill playing up and down your spine, or like a stinging slap in the face. This is reality. This is truth. This is God's own word. A clear warning from God Himself. That alone ought to raise the hairs on the back of your neck.

Principle #3: Certain kinds of people—like certain roads—should be avoided in our drive for friends.

Ready to walk a little further down the grove and look up at another giant sequoia or two?

> Do not associate with a man given to anger;
> Or go with a hot-tempered man,
> Lest you learn his ways,
> And find a snare for yourself (Proverbs 22:24-25).

> A perverse man spreads strife,
> And a slanderer separates intimate friends.
> A man of violence entices his neighbor,
> And leads him in a way that is not good (Proverbs 16:28-29).

Both of these ancient, immeasurably wise sayings are encouraging you and me to avoid certain kinds of people—angry people, hot-tempered people, slandering people. Scripture indicates all kinds of people are to be avoided when it comes to choosing your close friends: perverse people, gossiping people, greedy people, people on the prowl, people without direction, without values, or without faithful intentions. The Bible is saying in simple, proverbial form, "Don't find your friends among _____ people." You fill in the blank. Seriously. Make up your own list; it's not that difficult. Don't find your friends among...materialistic people, self-centered people, people with no regard for authority, undisciplined people, loose people—in the precise words of Scripture, "fornicators, adulterers, nor effeminate, nor homosexuals, nor thieves, nor the covetous, nor drunkards, nor revilers, nor swindlers." They have no place in the kingdom of God. They have no place among your closest friends. (See 1 Corinthians 5).

My wife, Linda Weber, provides a clear example of what I'm talking about in her book, *Mom, You're Incredible!*

> Preventing negative experiences requires positive planning.
>
> I remember clearly a time when [we] had to take preventative steps with our son Blake. When he was thirteen or so, a boy named Dan on his soccer team really took to Blake; he almost seemed to worship him. Blake, in turn, was drawn to Dan.
>
> The phone rang regularly as the two buddies stayed in constant touch. Whenever there was an event to attend, a game to see, or just an urge to go out and do something, those boys wanted to be together. It's great to have friends, isn't it?
>
> From my perspective, however, Dan had an attitude problem. He didn't respond well to authority, any authority—parents, teachers, coaches, even suggestions from friends. He often kept information from his parents. And his language was laced with profanity.
>
> In addition, Dan's family was seldom home. (Do you see any connection?) Both parents worked long hours, so he received little supervision and had virtually no boundaries placed around him. As a result, he was trouble waiting to happen, and when it did, I didn't want Blake anywhere near it.
>
> To put it bluntly, I was uncomfortable with Dan being Blake's best friend, because I knew that especially with teens, peer influence is strong. Already I was seeing a new defensiveness developing in Blake. He would make excuses for Dan, who seemingly could do no wrong in his eyes. And he wouldn't listen to any of our concerns about Dan's attitudes and actions.
>
> Because of this negative effect on Blake's personality and loyalties we decided we had no choice but to step in. We warned Blake of the tendencies we saw growing, and we said that rather than helping build his life and character, Dan was

actually serving to tear them down. Though we didn't forbid Blake to see Dan, we did ask him to phase out gradually his close friendship with Dan and start doing more with other buddies. (Had he failed to respond in distancing himself, we would have ultimately forbade him to see Dan. As it was, he did respond.)

Blake listened, but he wasn't very receptive to our point of view. Nonetheless, because of the solid relationship of mutual respect that we had built with him over the years, little by little he started seeking out other friends to fill his free time. He didn't like our request, but he chose to honor our desires.

In the years that followed, the two boys went down different roads. Dan, unfortunately, chose a path of drugs, alcohol, and disposable relationships. And today (years later), when Blake looks back on that friendship, he understands why we acted as we did. Not long ago, something brought Dan to his mind, and he told us, "Thanks, Mom and Dad, for steering me when I couldn't see the potholes in the road."[1]

Principle #4: Certain kinds of people, like certain roads, *should* be sought in our drive for friends.

When it comes to finding your friends, seek out *wise* people, committed people, growing people, honest people, mature people. For, in the words of Scripture, "Wisdom will deliver you...from the man who speaks perverse things; from those who leave paths of uprightness, to walk in the ways of darkness...whose paths are crooked...who are devious in their ways...who flatter with words" (Proverbs 2:12-16).

When I think about choosing, I can't help thinking about Naomi and Ruth. Check out the book by that last name: one of just two books in Scripture named for a woman. Naomi married a man. She went where he went. Eventually, some hard times drove the couple out of Israel into the neighboring kingdom of Moab. There her young sons grew up and married. Both of them married Moabite girls; one by the name of Ruth, the other named Orpah. Apparently through some sort of congenital family weakness, all three men ended up dying in Moab. Broken and bitter, Naomi decided to return to her own people, the nation of Israel. As she readied her return, she encouraged her daughters-in-law to choose whether they would stay or go with her. Actually, she encouraged them to stay in Moab among their own people. It made "logical" sense.

But Ruth knew something beyond logic. She knew that her young life was at a crossroads and that the road she chose would write her destiny. So she made a decision; a decision that changed her life, and in God's providence, has changed countless lives since. Ruth chose Naomi over her own people because she identified true friendship with the quality of life prescribed by Naomi's faith. Orpah opted to stay with the familiar...and with her idolatrous friends.

The result? Ruth ended up in the royal line that led to the birth of David, and ultimately, the great Messiah Himself. Orpah simply disappeared. Her life flitted by like the shadow of a bird across a pool of sunlight. Listen to the words of Scripture as the three women stood together at the major intersection of their lives:

> And they lifted up their voices and wept again; and Orpah kissed her mother-in-law [saying goodbye], but Ruth clung to her. Then she said, "Behold, your sister-in-law has gone back to her people and her gods; return with your sister-in-law." But Ruth said…"Where you go, I will go, and where you lodge, I will lodge. Your people shall be my people, and your God, my God. Where you die, I will die, and there I will be buried" (Ruth 1:14-17).

Ruth chose her friend well. In so doing, she chose her destination...and her destiny. It made a difference in her life—*the* difference—and her life is still impacting people today. We still name our daughters after her, some three thousand years later!

How about Orpah? Well, when was the last time you heard of a lady or a little girl by that name?

WE'RE ON OUR WAY...TOGETHER

It's a truism—our friends and families affect us in an incredibly powerful way. Spend time with people you know you should want to be like—because people who like to spend time together usually grow to resemble each other.

Friends are like highways. They lead somewhere. They take you to a destination. They shape your destiny. And a true friend always takes the high road. True friendship, like its potent first cousin, true love, never seeks its own. Friendship never acts unbecomingly. Friendship never rejoices in unrighteousness. It always rejoices with the truth. A true friend bears all things, believes all things, hopes all things, endures all things. But friendship never destroys anything. It always builds. It never drags. It contributes to character. It does not dilute it.

We're all on the way...somewhere. And in my heart of hearts, I know where I want to be. And I know the few good men who will take me there. Do you? If you don't, there's no better time than right now to make the connection.

Let's lock arms, friend, and aim for the high country.

1. List six of your closest friends. Now, beside the name of each, record a number to indicate the "milepost" you've reached and consistently enjoy in that relationship. #1: Acceptance; #2: Affirmation; #3: Accountability; #4: Authority. Are those relationships at the level where you want them to be? Realistically, what level could each of them achieve?

2. "Friendship is a road, and it's a road that leads somewhere." Is there someone you're leading like the "righteous guide" of Proverbs 12:26? Is anyone growing and maturing because of your influence in his life? Can you think of someone who could use your influence in his life? Your friendship?

LOCKING ARMS

1. Neglect always has its consequences. Do you think about the need to maintain relationships? Do you purposely do things to maintain and build your relationships…or do you find yourself assuming they'll just "hang in there"?

2. Principle One: Not everyone is a friend who appears to be. Complete this sentence with several examples: A friend is *not* a friend if he…

3. Principle Two: Friends are like highways; they lead somewhere. It's said that in choosing your friends, you choose your destiny. Do you buy that? Why or why not?

4. Principle Three: There are friendships we should avoid. Who we hang out with influences how we live and how we think. But in the workplace, you can't always control who you'll be with. How can you be friendly without being friends? How can you influence without being influenced?

5. "We come to reflect one another." Sometimes, that's the "kindred spirit" that attracts us to one another from the start. Sometimes,

that's the result of spending time together. Share a couple of relationships where you "reflect one another."

6. Principle Four: Certain kinds of people should be sought out as friends. Do you seek out friends or do you tend to wait for them to come to you? How can you actively seek out a new friend?

Big Tracks

Leaving a Trail Friends Can Follow

"Since we have such a huge crowd of men of faith watching us from the grandstand, let us strip off anything that slows us down or holds us back...and let us run with patience the particular race God has set before us."

HEBREWS 12:1, THE LIVING BIBLE

I t was early evening, crisp and cold. A silhouette of towering firs stood dark against the pink, snowy sky. Great silent flakes swirled in the headlight beams as the old Pontiac rounded the bend and came to a lurching, sliding halt on the snow-covered gravel. The driver piled out, leaving the engine running and the door flung wide open. There had been movement between those trees—just at the top of the ridge. Was it a martin? The rump of a retreating mule deer? A coyote slinking after a winter feast? Or just a rabbit? The driver had to see for himself.

With a quick shout, he leaped the roadside ditch and plowed up a clearing, soon disappearing over the ridgeline. Behind him, emerging from the old car, was a small boy, shoes untied, coat open and flapping as he ran, trying hard to follow after the man.

"Dad! *Wait up!*"

But Dad was far ahead, and soon even the sounds of his heavy breathing and the crunch of the snow under his feet grew faint and faded away.

"Dad!" the boy cried again. "WAIT! Please! I can't see where you're going! *I can't keep up!*"

But the father's attention wasn't on the son following after. It was on the chase ahead…the fleeting glimpse of what might be. Excited by a vision in the corner of his eye, the man left an erratic track in the dancing snow as he lunged through drifts and dodged among dark, drooping fir boughs.

The boy was left behind, the faint evening light giving few hints of which way to go. There were only the hurried, chaotic tracks left by his father, spaced too far apart for the boy to step from one to another.

Would his dad come back for him? How far could he go without losing his way? There were tracks, but not for a boy to follow. The only thing worse would have been…

NO TRACKS AT ALL

Not long ago, on a day like a thousand before it, I walked absent-mindedly from our mailbox, thumbing through a stack of envelopes on the way back up the drive. One of the pieces stood out from the handful of junk mail and bills. It was personal, carefully typed. As it turned out, it was a letter that moved me as deeply as I'd been moved in a long time.

The letter was from a naval officer. He'd been at sea for a number of months, and he'd just finished reading my earlier book, *Tender Warrior*.

> Why did *Tender Warrior* strike such a chord with me? Because I understand life without a father.
>
> When I was nine years old my father abandoned my mother and his four children. I loved him more than anything in the world. I wanted to be with him…he was so strong…so caring…and then he was gone.
>
> He drove a road grader for the county. Every day at five o'clock I would meet him at the turnoff to our house about three quarters of a mile away and ride the grader back to the house with him. I admired him so much because he could handle a machine that was so huge.

One day I went to my usual place and waited...and waited...but no dad. I was there the next day...no dad. I went there for four days...and no dad. Over the next twelve years of my life I saw my dad a total of only five minutes.

You know, people say divorce and abandonment don't bother kids. They say kids are "resilient, strong, tough." Baloney!

Three months after my dad left us I had a nightmare. My mom was on that road grader and she was leaving me behind. No matter how much I cried, or ran, or yelled, she went farther and farther away.

It *does* hurt when a parent—especially a father—leaves with no explanation or excuse. Even today, this thirty-six-year-old son is still crying because he's still waiting by the roadside...and there's no dad.

Where did his father go? WHY did his father go? What was happening in that man's soul? The story breaks my heart. And it's all too familiar in a society where men don't know what a real man is, where men lack staying power and conviction.

We'll never know what was happening in that father's heart when he walked away from his home and family. But I can guess what was *not* happening. My guess is the man didn't have any close friends—no one to whom he could bare his soul, unload his burdens. No fellow soldier to help him carry the weight that pressed down on his chest. No Ranger Buddy. No guard rails like accountability to keep his ol' grader on the high road.

I'd lay odds no one in that county shop even had a clue the man was about to snap. There was no one to throw him a rope when he needed one. My guess is that in all his days that man never knew what it was to lock arms with a caring, adult male friend.

As a result, the dad on the road grader left a son who adored him...standing by the road...with no tracks to follow. And even now, after all these years, the grown up naval officer—on a ship in the middle of an ocean—feels the desolation of a little lost boy. A boy who got left behind.

Real men leave clear tracks—big, steady tracks—that others can follow.

WHAT KIND OF TRACKS ARE YOU LEAVING?

Will those who come after you, both children and friends, follow the same path you've taken? Will they be able to see it? Is it even a path you would want them to follow?

The tracks you leave are your legacy, your children's heritage, and your friend's treasury. You're a man. You have influence. Whether you're married or single, a father or not, you're leaving tracks every day. Tracks of one kind or another. And it will make a difference. Will you "walk in the way of good men, and keep to the paths of righteousness" (Proverbs 2:20)? Or will you join those men like the one on the road grader who "leave the paths of uprightness, to walk in the ways of darkness...whose paths are crooked" (Proverbs 2:13-15)?

A friend of mine said he never felt very close to his father. His dad had been a military career man, an MP, and, unfortunately, an alcoholic. He always wondered why his dad seemed unable to connect to him and to his brothers as they grew up. Years later, as an adult, my friend asked about his grandfather, someone he'd never heard much about.

His dad said the last thing he remembered about his own father was one summer day when he was a small boy. A trail of dust along the dirt road to their country home alerted his mother. He remembers her yelling out to where his dad was working, "Run, run, the revenuer's comin'!"

He saw his father drop what he was doing, run across the field and hurl himself into a creek bed, where he could escape unseen. That was the last he ever saw or heard from his father. *No wonder* he didn't know how a dad was supposed to relate to his sons.

SNAPSHOTS:
MY FRIENDS TELL THEIR STORIES

When I first met Dave, I admired his humble and yet friendly, confident manner. As I got to know him, I grew to appreciate him as a professional, a newspaper editor. Dave says he felt the same things about me. It didn't take long before we were having lunch once a month, working on projects together, asking each other our opinions on various things, discussing our families, and starting a weekly men's group. Our relationship is now to the point that we are regularly pushing each other to examine particular parts of our lives, and holding each other accountable in various ways.

Dave and I are not afraid to say, "I am concerned about _____ in your life." We ask each other about our marriages, our families, our jobs, our priorities, and our time. But we also do things for each other. Last week Dave and I had arranged to have lunch in a local pizza place. That morning I went and purchased a copy of a book I had just finished and I thought would be valuable to Dave at this time in his life. I wrote an inscription on the inside flap that expressed what I appreciated about Dave and how much his friendship meant to me.

I arrived at the restaurant about twenty minutes early, and paid for Dave's lunch in advance. When Dave arrived he wondered what was going on. I just asked him to trust me and have a seat. I simply said, "You are a special friend, and I never want to take that for granted. Thanks for being my friend." Dave was obviously touched. He didn't have too many words. But our friendship just took another step in the right direction…deeper.

Different men leave different tracks. Some of us tend to walk so lightly—like Tolkein's light-footed elves—we leave little or no impression at all. Others walk so erratically there's no clear path for anyone to follow. Others walk so heavily they crush all around them. Like driver-less bulldozers locked in gear, they leave a path of random destruction in their wake.

What kind of tracks are you leaving? What kind of heritage? What kind of treasury?

DOES HERITAGE STILL MATTER?

In Psalm 16 David wrote, "Indeed, my heritage is beautiful to me." Is yours to you? Mine certainly is to me.

Whenever I can, I visit an old cemetery in a small town in the mountains of Central Washington (not far from the film site for television's popular sitcom "Northern Exposure"). The little coal-mining community has seen its glory days. When the railroads replaced steam engines with diesels they left the coal fields behind. Both my dad and his dad worked in those mines, and my heritage from those hills is still beautiful to me. In fact, on my home office wall hangs a framed, counted cross-stitch reminder that reads: "Though my path may wander up and down, my heart will stay in my hometown—Cle Elum, Washington."

I guess you could say my path *has* wandered up and down a bit. From college in the Midwest to Army service in Germany to the heat and chaos of Southeast Asia and back to the Pacific Northwest. But that little town among those beautiful mountains holds memories that can't be replaced. I recall with pleasure a hard-working, perspiring-in-the-kitchen grandmother and an equally hard-working, coal-mining, candy-carrying grandfather (who loved his Pepsi Cola). I remember parents who thought the best form of family entertainment was a drive with the kids through the woods on an early winter evening.

Heritage matters. People need clear, steady tracks to follow. It's by divine design. We're linked to people who've walked the long path before us. We're linked to those who tread the trail behind. Not so very long ago, God Himself left clear human footprints in the dust of our little world…tracks infinitely more indelible than those left by Apollo astronauts on the airless moon.

Memory is the great encourager of spirit and life, of connectedness. And rehearsing the past is a sacred practice. It sets the present on course. It gives perspective.

Locking arms, you see, is more than walking with contemporary friends. In a larger, more ultimate sense, it's locking arms with *generations*. It's gripping the legacy before me and making sure I pass it off to those following behind.

Do you remember when people passed down special family possessions with pride? I do. My Grandpa Weber's well-worn Bible rests in a place of honor in my office. I still officiate weddings holding my grandmother's "special New Testament." Grandma's old dining room bureau sits in stately glory in our family room. Even her old chrome-legged kitchen table—standard for the early 50s—is the breakfast table we eat at daily. Some would regard it as an out-dated monstrosity. Obviously, I don't. Oh, sure, Lindy sometimes sighs when she looks at it, but she understands and appreciates the meaning of it, too. She indulges me.

Today, many of the old possessions are sold just to gain a few bucks. As one writer laments:

> Most heirs want only the money, not family heirlooms, treasures, or Bibles. The past means nothing to them, nor the future. However much education they have, they are barbarians. The modern barbarian may be a university graduate, a scientist, an artist, a person of prominence and wealth, but he is someone with no respect for the past, nor roots in it, nor any concern for the future. If he receives an inheritance, he wants to liquidate it, to turn it into cash. Rootless people live rootless lives.[1]

Inheritance is priceless. Heritage is a treasure. Clear tracks left behind are the pathway for tomorrow. That's why our Lord gave His people so many sacred signs, symbols, and memorials, saying, "You shall remember the way which the LORD your God has led you...beware lest you forget..." (Deuteronomy 8). Looking back to remember the past helps us to look ahead and live well for the future. That's why He left us with the rainbow and the Communion table, among other things. They are unmistakable footprints.

You, too, will be remembered. The question is...

HOW WILL YOU BE REMEMBERED?

Let's go back to that front porch of chapter 1. Who's sitting there after you're gone? Family and friends. What are they talking about? How are they remembering you? What heritage have you left behind? What kind of tracks lead over the horizon?

A few weeks ago, some friends and I were sitting outside at the end of a ripe, summer day. The sun had just slipped behind the hills. A chorus of crickets sang in the fields, and the flowing waters of a small creek nearby added its background music. It was a good time. The best. One of those wonderfully mild, quiet, reflective times that come all too infrequently in the rush of life...the kind that just demand some reminiscing.

And together, in that peaceful interlude, our thoughts went to our friend Owen.

We talked about his life, his character, his skills. We spoke of his maturity and servant's heart. We remarked how much his life had touched each of ours.

For years, the three of us—John, Owen, and I—along with our families had camped and hunted together back in the Eagle Cap Wilderness of Northeastern Oregon. For me it was a fantasy land come alive—high country chock-full of alpine lakes, crystal clear rivulets streaming right out of the granite, short-needled evergreens, quaking aspens, abundant wildlife. It was (and is) magnificent.

No one would think of missing the July family campout. Even the little ones in the earlier years wanted to go on the hikes. We watched the elk and deer graze along hillsides. The kids played tag on horseback in the meadow. Garbage bags became sleds on the deep snow drifts that remained in the high-altitude shadows and sheltered spots. It was a summer week of heaven, filled with fun, firesides, and friends.

And no sooner was it over than the three men would begin planning the fall deer hunt. We called it our "annual Passover deer hunt—to be celebrated to all generations." And no way were we going to leave that next generation behind! We hauled our sons along even before they were old enough to carry rifles. After all, the point of the thing was really the companionship, not the game.

THAT UNFORGETTABLE MORNING

It was 4:30 in the morning when we crawled out of our sleeping bags—the first morning of that hunting trip. And it was cold! Stars burned white in the black vault overhead. A heavy frost bent the meadow grass. We warmed our hands around cups of coffee or cocoa and thawed our bodies around the campfire. Then, with one last swig of hot stuff, it was time to get rolling.

We drove a mile or two from camp, gathered at the foot of a ridge, checked our rifles and headed up an old, overgrown logging road. At the top, like football players in a huddle, we chose our routes and positions for the morning, wished each other luck in frosty whispers, and moved out.

John and his boy Nate headed south. Owen and young Todd moved north. My boys, my brother, and I moved quietly a couple hundred yards east. We settled above a dark sage-and-juniper-filled draw and watched the eastern sky pale with first light.

Suddenly, the crack of four or five rapid-fire shots pierced the dawn. Good grief, were there other folks in the area? Had some inexperienced hunter become overly excited at sights and sounds in the shadowy light? Had some "newfer" seen a buck and fired in panic?

Then—very faintly—I could hear someone shouting. Strange. For a second I sat transfixed.

Suddenly I understood. The shots were a signal—a desperate call for help.

I set my gun down and took off toward the sound, telling my brother to stick with the boys. As I ran up the long, sloping hill to the west I could see John silhouetted at the top, running full speed in the same direction.

Fear gripped my heart, twisted my gut. The shots and shouting had come from Todd. There was trouble. *Get to him, Stu. Move! Run!* It seemed to take forever to cover the frozen ground between us. It felt like a bad dream—running and running in that eerie half-light and not getting anywhere.

John got there a half-minute before I did. When I topped the ridge I could see Owen down and John hovering over him, desperately administering CPR.

Too late.

Owen was already gone. He had died instantly of a heart attack. The rattle in his chest and the dilated eyes were testimony enough.

Owen was already beyond the rising sun that now crested the nearby hills. He was with His Lord. He was home. But his friends and his son weren't home at all. We were in a wilderness of our own...one of pain and emotion.

None of us noticed the sunrise that morning. We were stung. Dazed. Shocked. Sick. As if in another world, we gathered our friend in our arms, carried his unoccupied body back to our rig, and drove to the ranger station miles away to report the situation.

The days that followed were filled with reflection. *What matters? What really matters?* We wept with the family. We planned and conducted the funeral. The church was filled. Hundreds of people attended, including many who'd never seen the inside of a church and thought they never would. But Owen's life drew them. It seemed all of us, family and friends, had needed a man like Owen in our lives. He'd made deep impressions on many of us.

He'd left tracks.

Owen was my friend, a millwright by profession, a life-impacter by calling. Our families had shared life together. Although trim and fit, he knew his life span would be limited by a genetically high—and medically uncontrollable—cholesterol level. He understood that his heritage and legacy would not wait; his tracks had to be purposeful, and direct.

CLEAR TRACKS

Known simply as "O" to most of his friends, he was so much the kind of man we all wish to be—gracious, compassionate, skilled, wise. His commitment to Jesus Christ was the centerpiece of his life. His loyalty to his wife, Linda, was a model for others. His dedication to his children, Todd, Sheila, and John, was matchless. His care for his elderly parents was extraordinary. And his sensitivity to his neighbors and friends left us shaking our heads with appreciation. Owen gave you an honest day's work and more. And his skills were sought after and admired.

Owen Raynor was a Christian. And we all knew it without him having to say it, though "O" always enjoyed telling others about Christ. He wasn't just a "Sunday" Christian, he lived faithfully each day.

He had his faults, but no one ever focused on them because they were so buried in all the good. The man was a delight to be around, a champion, a friend.

I think the quality I appreciated most in Owen was his ability to reach out to others and include them as friends without qualification. He certainly met a special need in my life. He allowed me to be his friend without being a "pastor" every second. He knew me well, understood my shortcomings, and accepted me anyway.

PATH STRAIGHT AND TRUE

Owen was a man of biblical conviction. Tempted just like the rest of us, Owen did not compromise. He believed God's Word and believed it fully. God was simply the Ruler of his life. What God said, Owen did. As a result, his behavior was consistently righteous. He had the ability to say "no" when his faith demanded it. And by his example, the rest of us were stimulated to live well, too. He was a friend to lock arms with.

Owen was also a churchman, in the finest sense of that lofty word. He was an elder in his small, local fellowship. He was always available. Always faithful. He never sought nor liked the limelight. He stood at the back of lines, and on the edge of crowds—never at the center. He never regarded himself as a leader or a spokesman, or any kind of "up-front" person. It was a scary thought to him. But he always did what needed to be done. And if that meant saying something in front of a group, he'd swallow hard and do it. He figured that's what His Lord would want.

Too many guys tend to sit back polishing their hobbies. Owen didn't want to be numbered among that breed, although he grew up with a passion for fast cars, motorcycles, and airplanes. As a kid he built a dune buggy with nothing more than a frame, dual wheels, a seat, and a huge engine—nothing else. When one police officer pulled him over and inquired as to why he had no windshield, Owen deadpanned that he didn't need one. He wore glasses.

Once in high school he wired a Model T coil and battery to a bank of lockers to enjoy the shock and shrieks of his classmates when they reached for their combination locks. Exceeding even Owen's expectations, school authorities soon evacuated the whole building, fearing major electrical problems. As the students filed out, Owen sneaked back in to disconnect the battery and then join his friends for some unscheduled time out of classes. That same coil went to summer camp and greeted more than one counselor reaching for his cabin doorknob.

Owen had a lot of fun in life. He just knew it could be clean fun, the kind that wouldn't detract from his convictions. He walked a straight path, but it was one filled with laughter along the way.

I think his greatest efforts were probably spent seeing that his three children—two sons and a daughter—came to know and love Jesus Christ. It was "O's" fervent hope that, no matter how long he was given to live, his kids would be grounded in spirit and character before he was called to his eternal home. And he succeeded. He was the anchor between generations—caring for his elderly parents on one hand and marking the path ahead for his children at the same time.

A PATH OTHERS ARE DRAWN TO FOLLOW

To his newly-widowed wife fell the task of selecting the words that would appear on Owen's gravestone. During those days following his funeral, she and I would talk about the words to summarize his life, words that would appear in granite to describe a life equally rock solid.

How could such a thing be summarized? How could such a life be reduced to a few words on a stone? Just yesterday, on a blustery October morning at sunrise, I stood again before that stone. And yet again I found myself nodding in appreciation at how three words could so capture one man's two-score and five years…

Owen Rex Raynor
Gentle, Faithful, Strong

And with those words I'm reminded of Psalm 112, speaking of every man who—like my friend Owen or like the great King David before him—would seek to "serve the purpose of God in his own generation" (Acts 13:36) before he "fell asleep and was laid among his fathers."

Linger with me for a moment in this grand and glad song, as we come to the end of this little journey together…

Blessed is the man who fears the LORD,
who finds great delight in his commands.
His children will be mighty in the land;
the generation of the upright will be blessed…

Even in darkness light dawns for the upright,
    for the gracious and compassionate and righteous man.
Good will come to him who is generous and lends freely,
    who conducts his affairs with justice.
Surely he will never be shaken;
    a righteous man will be remembered forever.
He will have no fear of bad news;
    his heart is steadfast, trusting in the LORD.
His heart is secure, he will have no fear;
    in the end he will...TRIUMPH
    (Psalm 112:1-2, 4-8, NIV).

Owen triumphed. On that unforgettable Saturday morning, on a hilltop at first light, in the presence of his son and his friends, Owen had been ushered instantly into the presence of Christ. His lifetime ended. His impact did not. Owen left family and friends a treasured legacy—footprints that are visible, consistent, and pleasant to follow. "He being dead, still speaks" (Hebrews 11:4).

HOW ABOUT YOU?

What kind of heritage are you leaving? Where do your footprints lead? How will you be remembered?

If your family, like my friend Owen's, had to come up with just three words to summarize your life, what might they be?

What matters, really matters, to you? It's a question that grabbed me by the throat on a muddy hillside in the Republic of Vietnam. In the end, for each of us, it will be a question that determines our epitaph and our legacy.

What kind of path are you leaving? Too heavy? Too light? Too erratic? Too crooked? Are you leaving tracks that your sons and daughters and friends—not to mention your wife—can easily follow in this hazard-strewn, unraveling culture of ours?

There will come a time in every man's life when the light fails, the trail dims, hope burns low, and the long winds blow cold. When those dark days come, fortunate are the men—and boys—who find sure, steady tracks to follow, all the way Home.

Let's lock arms and seek that horizon together.

1. If you were to die today, how would you likely be remembered by your friends? By your family? How would you like to be remembered? What will that require on your part? When will you begin?

2. The man in the opening illustration was so focused on what he was chasing, he left a young boy scrambling after him who couldn't keep up and didn't know the way. Is there some way this might be true of you? Have you become so "focused" on something "out there" that you may be leaving your children to scramble behind, searching for tracks...maybe beginning to feel a little lost?

LOCKING ARMS

1. What does it mean to leave "clear tracks to follow"?

2. Did it surprise you that the naval officer would make the following statement? "Even today, this thirty-six-year-old son is still crying because he's still waiting by the roadside...and there's no dad." Why?

3. What kind of tracks did your father leave? Your grandfather? And what was the impact of those tracks?

4. What kind of tracks are you leaving? Will they have impact?

5. In the end, what will matter most about your life?

6. If your family had to come up with just three words to put on your grave stone—three words that would summarize your life—what would you *want* them to be?

Real Men Stand Together

YOUR LOVE TO ME *was more wonderful than the love of women.*" What words are these? Perverted words? Twisted words? The words of some pathetic sexual deviate? No. A war-hardened veteran penned these words after his best buddy fell in battle. They were written by a warrior, with the piercing grief only a soldier mourning for a comrade-in-arms could begin to understand.

Twisted words? No. They are words straight and true—a swift, clean arrow shot from the heart of Scripture. David wrote these words after the death of his friend Jonathan on the bloody slopes of Mount Gilboa. What the son of Jesse expressed without shame in that lament was something that has burned deep in the soul of every man in one way or another for generations beyond memory.

A desire for friendship man to man. A desire for friendship with nothing between. A yearning for friendship so real, so strong, so compelling, it is willing to share everything about itself and make deep and powerful promises.

Down deep at the core, every man needs a man friend.

Down deep at the core, every man needs a brother to lock arms with.

Down deep at the core, every man needs a soul mate.

Men Need Friends Who Are Men

Yes, beyond question, our wives are to be our most intimate companions. We're to be willing to die for our wives and our children instantly, and many of us are ready to do just that. But within the willingness to die for family and home, something inside us longs for someone to die *with*...someone to die *beside*...someone to lock step with. Another man with a heart like our own.

That's what David was saying about Prince Jonathan. Every warrior needs a fellow soldier. Every fighter pilot needs a wing man. David was demonstrating something that even the U.S. Army, in all its relational ineptitude, understands. When you're going to do something that stretches the very fabric of your soul, like get through nine weeks of army Ranger school at Fort Benning, Georgia, you're going to need a buddy. A "Ranger Buddy." Those two words mean a world to me. It was my Ranger Buddy, Lou Francis, who clung to my arm and I to his through sixty-three days of unbelievable physical and mental trauma. Together, we made it through the toughest experience either of us had ever faced to that point in our lives.

Some might argue with me, but I know of no more intense training regimen in the U.S. military. These guys know how to take a young man and stretch him tendon by tendon—physical tendon by physical tendon, emotional tendon by emotional tendon.

I remember well that last, most intense phase of our training, called "Unconventional Warfare." We were in the swamps of western Florida in the dead of winter. I would never have dreamed Florida could be so cold. We were at the end of a several-day patrol, and nearly at the end of ourselves. We'd been without sleep for most of those days, and very nearly without food. Our particular mission required us to proceed to a certain set of coordinates at the corner of our map. Unfortunately, those coordinates happened to be on the other side of the Yellow River.

We had been staggering knee-deep through the numbing water of a cypress swamp for what seemed like eons. The temperature was below freezing, and our bodies were at the ragged edge of our endurance. The "knees" of the cypress trees, invisible under the black waters, savaged our shins and ankles. And the river was still somewhere ahead of us.

When we finally reached the river, it was practically indistinguishable from the water we'd been wading in. The only way we could tell it was a river was by the rapidly moving current and the lack of cypress trees.

Our goal was a piece of higher ground on the other side. We knew we couldn't get our clothes wet or the cold would finish us. So we stripped down to our skimpy briefs and, as we'd been trained, made a little float out of our two ponchos, with our rifles and packs protected. Wading out into the icy water, we were surprised by the strength of the current. Though we were both fair swimmers, we found ourselves being swept further and further downstream. It was fearsome. Reaching back for a burst of strength from some final untapped reserve, both of us began kicking with all our might. The effort was rewarded as we inched toward the slimy bank and finally achieved it.

We crawled out of the water, blue from the cold, trailing bits of river weed and slime. So delighted to be alive. So exultant at having reached our goal. I remember our looking into each other's eyes and then spontaneously throwing our arms around each other. We stood there for a moment on the bleak winter bank of the Yellow River, two dripping, shivering young men in their briefs, laughing and crying and holding on to each other as if we'd never let go.

If we each live to be a hundred, I expect neither of us will ever forget the camaraderie of that moment.

We'd made it. We'd stayed alive. The two of us.

Every man, whether he admits it or not, needs a Ranger Buddy. Every man needs someone with whom he can face adversity and death. Emerson wrote: "We take care of our health. We lay up money. We make our roof tight. We make our clothing sufficient. But who provides wisely that he shall not be wanting in the best property of all, friends—friends strong and true?"

Why Men Don't Have Friends Who Are Men

A professor at Southern Methodist University had this to say after ten years of study on the subject:

To say that men have no intimate friends seems on the surface too harsh, and it raises quick objections from most men. But the data indicates that it is not far from the truth. Even the most intimate of friendships (of which there are few) rarely approach the depth of disclosure a woman commonly has with other women…. men, who neither bare themselves nor bear one another, are buddies in name only.[1]

Oh, we may *want* that friendship. Every man, whether he admits it or not, walks around with a hollow place in his chest, wondering if he is the only one. But there is something within us that keeps us at arm's length. *What is that something that keeps men distant and friendless?*

I saw a man about my age the other day in a crowded parking lot. If one Vietnam vet can spot another, then I knew this man for what he was and what he had endured. I felt an immediate love for him. He was on crutches, and one pant leg was folded and pinned up to the top. Everyone in that busy lot seemed to avert their eyes from this disabled gentleman. It's something we find ourselves doing in that sort of situation, isn't it? One glance tells us something isn't normal. Something isn't right. Something's missing. In the physical sense, this man wasn't "all there."

I think most of us would have to admit that when it comes to open and vulnerable man-to-man friendships, we are walking on one leg. We're really not "all there." Something's missing. Something's pinned up and empty in our souls. We may be "kings" and "warriors," but we seem to have lost something of the tender side. So we're really one-legged men. We simply don't know how to fellowship.

If the most basic definition of "fellowship" is two fellows in one ship, then we don't know what to do with ourselves when we're out at sea. In a fine fresh wind on a starry night when we stand together at the bow looking out into the dark, mysterious depths— on a night that cries out for deep talk and sharing of the soul—we lapse into silence or mutter idly about how many chunks of salt pork it takes to fill a barrel below decks.

Kent Hughes, a thoughtful pastor in the Midwest, makes this observation about our culture:

> There has been an interesting development in suburban architecture. Long gone are the days when homes all had large front porches, with easy access to the front door enabling one to become quickly acquainted with others in the neighborhood.
>
> In the 1990s we have architecture which speaks more directly to our current values. The most prominent part of the house seems to be the two- or three-car garage. Inside are huge bathrooms with skylights and walk-in closets larger than the bedroom I grew up in. Modern architecture employs small living and dining rooms and now smaller kitchens as well, because entertaining is no longer a priority. Today's homes boast smaller yards and an increasing incidence of high fences.
>
> The old adage that "a man's house is his castle" is actually coming true today. His castle's moat is his front lawn, the drawbridge his driveway, and the portcullis his automatic garage door through which he passes with electronic heraldry. Once inside, he removes his armor and attends to house and hearth until daybreak, when he assumes his executive armament and, briefcase in hand, mounts his steed—perhaps a Bronco or a Mustang—presses the button, and rides off to the wars. Today's homes reflect our modern values of individualism, isolation and privatization."[2]

Individualism…isolation…privatization. These are destructive words. Painful words. They have an empty sound to them, don't they? They leave a hollowness in our chest.

Patrick Morley, author of *The Man in the Mirror*, wryly observes that while most men could recruit six pallbearers, "hardly anyone has a friend he can call at 2:00 A.M."[3]

Referring to a recent study in Britain, sociologist Marion Crawford stated: Middle-aged men and women had considerably different definitions of friendship. By an overwhelming margin, women talked about "trust and confidentiality," while men described a friend as "someone I could go out with" or "someone whose company I enjoy." For the most part men's friendships revolve around activities, while women's revolve around sharing.[4]

We're not talking now about a golfing buddy. We're talking about somebody we can be soulish with.

Why are these things true? I have my theories. If we men are comprised of steel and velvet, most of us feel more comfortable with the steel. We find it easier to live out the "provide and protect" functions than the "mentor and friend" functions. It stands to reason that the hard side dominates the tender side. Many of us have underdeveloped tender sides because we've been taught wrongly about manhood. Not deliberately, but wrongly. We need to become more tender. The warrior in us wants to be strong and needs to be strong. But we don't want to admit to any chinks in our armor. We don't want to admit to any vulnerabilities—*the very element that is essential for true friendships*. Oh, the vulnerabilities are *there*, all right. But most of us have learned to carefully hide them. Some might call that "manliness." Others might more accurately label it for what it is: *dishonesty*.

Friendship requires honesty. Friendship requires trust. So it also—no way around it—requires vulnerability. I think that's the bottom line of this no-friends syndrome in us men. And it's spelled P-R-I-D-E.

We all want to think of ourselves as some kind of warrior, as some kind of man's man. Unfortunately though, as much as we love John Wayne, there is a side to the Duke that never emerged. All you ever saw was the steel. You never saw the velvet unless it was for a fleeting moment in *She Wore a Yellow Ribbon*. John Wayne left us with the impression that real men stand alone. And so they do…when it is necessary. But the only reason it seems "necessary" most of the time is our stubborn, unyielding pride.

Real men stand together. We need to start thinking that way. Real men need one another. Real soldiers love each other.

Hal Moore and Joe Galloway capture that love powerfully in the prologue to their great book about the Vietnam War, *We Were Soldiers Once…and Young*:

> Another war story, you say? Not exactly, for on the more important levels this is a love story, told in our own words and by our own actions. We were the children of the 1950s and we went where we were sent because we loved our country….
>
> We went to war because our country asked us to go, because our new president, Lyndon B. Johnson, ordered us to go, but more importantly because we saw it as our duty to go. That is one kind of love.
>
> Another and far more transcendent love came to us unbidden on the battlefields, as it does on every battlefield in every war man has ever fought. We discovered in that depressing, hellish place, where death was our constant companion, that we loved each other. We killed for each other, we died for each other, and we wept for each other. And in time we came to love each other as brothers. In battle our world shrank to the man on our left and the man on our right and the enemy all

around. We held each other's lives in our hands and we learned to share our fears, our hopes, our dreams as readily as we shared what little else good came our way.[5]

It's always been that way. Real soldiers stand together. It was that way in Hal Moore's Ia Drang Valley in 1965, and it was that way long before in the hot sands of Alexander's ancient Near East. Real world conquerors stand arm in arm. Alexander the Great was "great," I suppose, because at one time he owned most of the habitable real estate on the planet. His secret weapon was something called the "Macedonian Phalanx," which was little more than a simple military formation with a straightforward mandate: *"You never go into battle without the man beside you."*

The Macedonian Phalanx was a formation that allowed the man's weak flank to be protected by his buddy. With his shield in his left hand and his sword in the right, a soldier thrusting with his blade could find his right side exposed, vulnerable to the enemy's spear or sword. In the Macedonian formation, the warrior had a trusted man guarding the area where he was most exposed. Although Alexander came along centuries after David, I think the son of Jesse would have called such a companion, "the man of my right hand." Where I am most vulnerable and exposed, that's where I want the man of my right hand.

Dr. Charles Sell writes: "Men who have neglected intimate friendships with other men have far greater difficulty handling the midlife turmoil. These men are also devastated at retirement because their whole basis of significance and identity evaporates, and they're left without a network of friends or support."[6]

Close friendship with a man or a woman is rarely experienced by the American male. Author David Smith asserts: "Men find it hard to accept that they need the fellowship of other men. The simple request, 'Let's have lunch together' is likely to be followed with the response, 'Sure, what's up?'"[7]

Can you imagine women saying that to each other? My wife calls your wife and says, "Let's have lunch." Your wife says, "Great, here's my calendar. Where shall we go?" But a man will say, by implication, "What's going on? What's your problem? Why are you doing this?"

Dr. Smith continues: "The message is clear: The independent man doesn't feel he needs the company of another man. In fact, the image of the independent man is that he has few if any emotional needs. Therefore, men must manufacture nonemotional reasons for being together…"[8]

Most of us think we have to conjure up "practical" reasons or excuses for picking up the phone and calling another man. That's part of the myth that says I have few, if any, emotional needs. If men get together, it's because, in Dr. Smith's words:

A business deal must be discussed or a game must be played. Men often use drinking as an excuse to gather together. Rarely do men plan a meeting together simply because they have a need to enjoy each other's company.

Even when men are frequently together, their social interaction begins and remains at a superficial level. Just how long can conversations about politics and sports be nourishing to the human spirit? The same male employees can have lunch together for years and years and still limit their conversations to sports, politics, and dirty jokes, and comments about the sexual attractiveness of selected female workers in their office or plant.[9]

A Willingness to Go Deeper

Going beyond those surface subjects requires transparency. What transparency says at the bottom of it all is, "I really need you. I'm going to take the risk and be honest enough to tell you who I am."

Someone pointed out a moving little piece from a magazine to me. Because it deals with relationships, I think we Tender Warriors can learn something from it.

The woman who wrote the article states:

One day the doorbell rang and there stood my beloved brother. It was a delightful surprise. His work as an executive of an international petroleum company keeps him out of the country most of the time, so his visits are rare, unexpected and usually really brief.

It seemed as if he'd just arrived when after an hour, he got up to say good-bye. I felt tears sliding down my cheeks. He asked why I was crying. Hesitating, I said, "Because I simply don't want you to go." He gave me a surprised look. He went to the phone and left a message for the pilot of his company's plane.

We had a wonderful forty-eight hours together. But I suffered a nagging feeling that my selfishness had caused him great inconvenience. Because I had told him I needed him.

Some time later my brother received an important award for his contributions to the oil industry. A reporter asked him at the time, "Is this the greatest honor that you've received?"

"No," he said, "my sister gave me my greatest honor the day she cried because she didn't want me to leave. That's the only time in my life anyone ever cried because they didn't want me to leave. It was then that I discovered the most precious gift one human being can ever bestow on another is to let him know he is really needed."[10]

That's transparency. That's the destination toward which we must journey. Yes, sometimes our childhood patterns keep us from progressing on that journey. If children are to be seen and not heard, if boys don't cry, then we tend not to be very candid about our hurts and needs.

A Determination to Practice

Practice, practice, practice sharing your emotions. Find some moment in your week that's been especially emotional for you, and then pick out that friend whose name is turning over in your mind and heart today, and go share your emotions with that friend. Start at whatever level. If you need to prime the pump, start with your wife. Most women would treasure a husband's attempt to climb out of his shell.

I remember when I began trying—really trying—to express some honest emotion to my wife. It was like learning to speak all over again. It took some stuttering and stammering, but I had a growing desire to let her know what was going on inside me. I recall one night in particular. It was a number of years ago, following our middle son's high school basketball awards program.

Blake followed his older brother Kent at Barlow High School. Kent was big and tall and mobile and made a name for himself as a starter on the varsity squad. Blake was smaller and shorter. He didn't have the obvious physical advantages of his brother. It was a little intimidating to think of finding a niche at a high school where guards were a dime a dozen.

But he did make the team. Before the season began, the coach said, "I wish we could start twelve guys. Hey, we'd kill everybody in the league! But the rules say we have to start five. So I want you to know that we're going to start five, and then we're going to have three or four substitutes, role players as we call them. Beyond that, we're going to have three or four practice players. Whether you believe me or not, guys, the starters and the role players and the practice players are all essential to this team."

Blake chose to believe the coach. He ended up being one of the practice players, but he stuck with the program. He practiced hard and stayed ready. Still, he didn't get into the games too much unless they were substantially ahead or substantially behind. So in the course of the season he played a limited number of minutes.

When the awards ceremony came, Linda and I sat together in the high school cafeteria, listening to Coach Johnson announce the awards. Every year, the two most coveted awards were the Most Valuable Player trophy and the Most Inspirational Player trophy. Coach went into the usual long buildup prior to the "inspirational" award, talking about what a certain young man had meant to the team and to his teammates. Finally, he called out the name…"Blake Weber." He may not have had as much playing time, but he spent his energy encouraging others. He had marked his team.

Something happened inside of me that night. I experienced more sensations than I could readily describe. My heart filled with potent waves of emotion. This was the boy I had been so concerned about because he had to walk in the big shoes of his brother. This was my middle guy, surrounded by two brothers with individualistic personalities. This was the kid who, in years past, I was most afraid would struggle with positive self-image. And even though he got into the game sparingly, even though he barely got a chance to really handle the ball, he had such a positive self-image he won the Most Inspirational Player award. I tingled all over.

I remember driving home with Linda that night, opening and closing my mouth a few times before I could get out any words. It wasn't easy for me to talk about something so personally moving, something so deep inside. The old Stu Weber would have kept it bottled and corked on a dusty back shelf of memory. But that night I didn't want to put those feelings in a bottle. I didn't want them gathering dust on a back shelf. So I took the plunge. Staring straight ahead at the road, I finally said, "Lindy, I just want to tell you what's happening inside of me—what happened when his name was called tonight." Bit by bit—and then in a great rush—the pride and gratitude and wonder of it all came out through my lips. *And it felt so good.*

Practice sharing your emotions. Find somebody who seems more relaxed and skilled at it, and watch how they do it. When you open your Bible, spend some time in the psalms with David. This was a true man's man and mighty warrior who knew how to put his emotions into words. He knew how to spill his guts before God. He knew how to cry out his fears and discouragement and hopes and joys. You can see the whole range of feeling in this man's words. Joyful laughter. Shouts of praise. Burning anger. The deep hurt of betrayal. Paralyzing fear. Overwhelming waves of discouragement. Sweet relief. Overflowing gratitude. Love. It's all there. He's all over the emotional, spiritual map. His journey is the spiritual journey of a Tender Warrior, recorded forever in Scripture for warriors like you and me who want to follow in his wake.

Practice with your wife. Practice with the psalms of David before your God. And practice with other men, too.

I have one friend in particular who knows me—my marriage, my heart, my life. And I know him and his. As I'm out driving around on my errands during the course of a week, I often find myself thinking about him, praying for him. (Now when I'm out on my hospital calls or other business and think of my wife, I try to stop and give her a phone call. That was a *gargantuan* step for me to take as I've been struggling to learn to speak her language. It has taken a lot for me to remember to stop, dial her number, and say, "Hey, I was just thinking of you." She always appreciates that.)

I decided to take another massive step. I decided to try that with my friend. I was in Chicago. At O'Hare airport. There were thirty minutes between flights, and I picked up a telephone and called him.

I almost found myself wishing he wouldn't be home. I almost choked and hung up when I heard his voice on the other end. *What in the world am I doing? What in the world is he going to think?* But I didn't choke. I heard myself saying into the mouthpiece, "I have no reason for calling you except to say I've had you in my mind today. I've had you in my heart." That was not easy for me to do. But just a few minutes later, I was on that next flight to who knows where and I was glad I had done it. We had a good conversation. I was encouraged.

Small Steps Pay Off

When my father was in World War II, he made friends with a young man named Joe Carter. They were young draftees, plucked out of a peaceful civilian life and thrown into the same barracks at training camp. For a good chunk of the war, they were together. Serving together. Sweating together. Dreaming together of home. It has been over fifty years since they last saw each other. But every year, without fail, my dad gets a birthday card from Joe Carter in the mail.

It's hard to believe that friendship started when my dad walked across the barracks one afternoon to offer a guy named Joe one of the chocolate chip cookies he'd just received in a package from home. Dad is now in his seventies. And every once in awhile, he will pause and look out the window with a distant stare. Then, with a smile on the corner of his lips, he'll say, "You know…I should grab a train and go see my friend, Joe."

A fifty-year friendship sprang from a single chocolate chip cookie. It's that way sometimes. All it takes is breaking the ice. All it takes is walking across the barracks. Or across the hall. Or across the street. Or across the room to pick up the phone. It takes a willingness to choke back some pride and reach out a hand.

Are you giving yourself to anyone? Are you opening up to anyone? Do any of your fellow soldiers know where the chinks in your armor might be? Are you looking for a soul mate, a Ranger Buddy?

Some dark day when your knees are weak, the current is swift, and the water is cold, you will be glad you did.

Locking Arms

I FIRST LEARNED the word *piton* in the same army Ranger school I described in the last chapter. We did some tension climbing, where we would climb on vertical surfaces with nothing above us to pull us up, and with rope fed through snap links. The "piton" is a little anchor bolt. We would find a crack in the wall face, drive this piton into the rock, put the snap link on it, and pass the safety rope through it. That way, we knew we would never fall below that point. We might fall, because we were doing some unbelievable things; but the piton would catch us. We wouldn't fall any further than the anchor in the rock.

So what is a *piton* of friendship? It's a relationship principle that you can count on. It is an anchor bolt in a relationship that will bear your weight, that will hold you up when you find your fingers are slipping. There are other elements in a friendship, of course, but these are basic anchors. You don't want to fall below these levels.

Four Piton Principles of Friendship

Israel faced desperate days in that oppressive year of 1050 B.C. The young kingdom was in pain. Misery. Humiliation. The nation faced harsh military domination by her neighbors, the Philistines. I use that word "neighbor" in the same sense that Iraq was a "neighbor" to Kuwait before the Gulf War and that Nazi Germany was a "neighbor" to Poland before World War II. The Philistines were a coarse people, a militarily strong people. They had bullied and intimidated Israel for years. Backs were bent low. Heads were down. Men passing each other on the dusty roads couldn't meet each others' eyes. The dominance was so strong, Scripture says, that blacksmiths weren't allowed in the country, because the Philistines didn't want any weaponry made.

Israel was helpless in these days. Down and depressed and demoralized and discouraged. Life in the nation was a concentration camp of despair.

Then there was Prince Jonathan.

This young man, the son of King Saul, was an initiator. Masculine to the core. He saw the castdown eyes, slumped shoulders, and drooping heads. He saw all of that, but he still had some hope in his eyes and some fire in his belly. Prince Jonathan believed in the God of Israel. He believed the things he had been taught from childhood about the God of the universe and the God of his people.

Armed with this faith in the living God—and with one of the few swords available in Israel—this young man thought long and hard about taking the initiative. Breaking the stalemate. Giving the Philistines back something of their own. Jonathan had his weapon, all right. Nobody could take it away. If you can't imagine pickpocketing Jim Bowie's knife or sneaking Jesse James's pearl-handled Colt from its holster, don't bother trying to picture a Philistine militia-man walking away with Prince Jonathan's sword.

Circumstances needed to change. Life needed to be different. God's people ought not live in defeat and humiliation. So Jonathan thought through what he might do.

On a given day, armed with this sense of conviction, he and his armor bearer stepped across a line in the sand.

Now the day came that Jonathan, the son of Saul, said to the young man who was carrying his armor, "Come and let us cross over to the Philistines' garrison that is on yonder side" (1 Samuel 14:1).

The prince made his crossing at a little ravine near Michmash.

And between the passes by which Jonathan sought to cross over to the Philistines' garrison, there was a sharp crag on the one side, and a sharp crag on the other side, and the name of the one was Bozez, and the name of the other Seneh. The one crag rose on the north opposite Michmash, and the other on the south opposite Geba. Then Jonathan said to the young man who was carrying his armor, "Come and let us cross over to the garrison of these uncircumcised; perhaps the LORD will work for us, for the LORD is not restrained to save by many or by few." And his armor bearer said to him, "Do all that is in your heart; turn yourself, and here I am with you according to your desire" (vv. 4-7).

Jonathan's masculine heart of steel and initiative shines through. "Perhaps the LORD will work for us, for the LORD is not restrained to save by many or by few." Arithmetic isn't all that critical when God is on your side. His armor bearer doesn't wait for a direct command. "Go for it. Let's do it. I'm your man, heart and soul."

Look at what follows:

And when both of them revealed themselves to the garrison of the Philistines, the Philistines said, "Behold, Hebrews are coming out of the holes where they have hidden themselves." So the men of the garrison hailed Jonathan and his armor bearer and said, "Come up to us and we will tell you something." And Jonathan said to his armor bearer, "Come up after me, for the LORD has given them into the hands of Israel." Then Jonathan climbed up on his hands and feet, with his armor bearer behind him; and they fell before Jonathan, and his armor bearer put some to death after him. And that first slaughter which Jonathan and his armor bearer made was about twenty men within about half a furrow in an acre of land (vv. 11-14).

Can you read into the neat, clean, white spaces between those lines of biblical text? Can you imagine what was happening here? This was hand-to-hand, face-to-face combat. This was muscles tight, teeth clenched, chests heaving, blood splattering, bones snapping, voices yelling, and swords flying. And they did it. Against ten-to-one odds. In one bloody little half-acre of land, overlooking a dry ravine, fighting hand-to-hand in the hot Middle East sun.

When it was all over, two warriors were standing, and twenty Philistine corpses were strewn like rag dolls across the sand. Can you imagine standing there when it was all over, swords and arms and shields dripping with gore? Can you imagine what they must have experienced together in those moments? Smiles? Joyous eye contact? Hugs? Arms locked together, raised to the One who had enabled them?

Just two men left standing, casting long shadows. Jonathan was victorious. It was a great day for him, his armor bearer, and for God's people.

What followed? As you read on in Scripture, it becomes obvious that Jonathan's courage added some fiber to the Israeli army. They stood up straighter. Lifted their eyes. Squared their shoulders. The heart returned to them. They succeeded in rebelling against the Philistine bully boys.

When all the men of Israel who had hidden themselves in the hill country of

Ephraim heard that the Philistines had fled, even they also pursued them closely in the battle. So the LORD delivered Israel that day, and the battle spread beyond Beth-aven (vv. 22-23).

The army covered some turf that day because one lone man said to his friend, "Would you go with me? Maybe the Lord will work for us. In fact, I'm sure of it. Let's go climb that cliff and strike a blow for the Lord."

Following this mini-rebellion, Israel enjoyed a few breaths of free air. There were some pleasant days in the land. It was better. All too soon, however, King Saul turned back to his old, careless ways, and the nation once again began to slip away from a courageous walk with God. As a result, they lost His blessing, and the Philistine army rushed back in to fill the vacuum.

By the time you flip over to chapter seventeen, there is absolutely no one to face a Philistine champion in single combat. No one. Not even Jonathan. Not even the plucky prince who had crawled hand over hand up that crag and with a cry of joy and faith took on a whole garrison. When Saul asked for volunteers, Jonathan wasn't there to take a step forward. There's no record of him being the one to stand in the gap against a nine-foot loudmouth named Goliath. Why? Scripture doesn't tell us. But I think it's reasonable to speculate that the valiant prince might have been thinking thoughts such as: *Here we go again. Back under these jokers' thumb. Whining in a corner like scared puppies. How many crags do I have to climb? How many garrisons do I have to fight alone? Why do we always end up here? I can't carry this battle on my shoulders. I just can't do this anymore.*

For the moment, perhaps, Jonathan lost heart. The warrior-prince stepped back into the shadows. But God hadn't run out of heroes.

David spoke to the men who were standing by him saying, "What will be done for the man who kills this Philistine, and takes away the reproach from Israel? For who is this uncircumcised Philistine, that he should taunt the armies of the living God?" (1 Samuel 17:26).

Can't you just hear him, this upstart Jewish kid fresh from the sheep pens? "What's going on here? Who is this big goon? Why is he getting away with that stuff? We're God's people, aren't we? Life shouldn't be like this." It sounds like an echo of Jonathan, doesn't it?

David said to the Philistine, "You come to me with a sword, a spear, and a javelin, but I come to you in the name of the LORD of hosts, the God of the armies of Israel, whom you have taunted. This day the LORD will deliver you up into my hands, and I will strike you down and remove your head from you. And I will give the dead bodies of the army of the Philistines this day to the birds of the sky and the wild beasts of the earth, that all the earth may know that there is a God in Israel" (vv. 45-46).

I don't know where Jonathan's voice had gone, but here was a fresh voice, singing the second verse of the prince's own ballad of courageous faith. It was a faith rooted in the very nature of God.

Apparently it fanned some flames in Jonathan's spirit. David's bravery and white-hot love for God evidently served to draw the prince out of the shadows. As the chapters of 1 Samuel continue, you see a warrior's heart begin beating in the prince's chest once again.

David had stood alone. David had stood strong. David had stood faithful. David had faced the odds. David had taken action. And a disillusioned hero named Jonathan found a friend. Someone that marched to the same tune. The warrior's song that apparently had died in the prince's throat found full voice once again. Only this time, it was a duet.

Note what happens as chapter 17 draws to a close.

Now when Saul saw David going out against the Philistine, he said to Abner the commander of the army, "Abner, whose son is this young man?" And Abner said, "By your life, O king, I do not know." And the king said, "You inquire whose son the youth is." So when David returned from killing the Philistine, Abner took him and brought him before Saul with the Philistine's head in his hand. And Saul said to him, "Whose son are you, young man?" And David answered, "I am the son of your servant Jesse the Bethlehemite."

Now it came about when he had finished speaking to Saul, that the soul of Jonathan was knit to the soul of David, and Jonathan loved him as himself (17:55-18:1).

Jonathan had seen the whole thing. And when David spoke to King Saul, his father, the king's son heard his own heart beating in another man's chest. From that moment, the souls of the two men were knit together.

What a strong statement. Their *souls* were knit. How do souls get knit? Through four piton principles of masculine friendship. Let's look at them, one at a time.

1. Shared values.

You may have many friends in the course of your life, but you will never have a *soul mate* who does not walk with your God. It was David and Jonathan's *souls* that were knit together. The soul is that invisible part of us that combines our minds and wills and emotions. Here were two men whose minds believed the same truth, whose wills locked on to the same course, whose emotions burned at the same injustices.

They were committed to the same God. They loved the same kingdom. They marched to the same tune. They were headed in the same direction. They even dreamed about the same things…a day when their people, their families, their friends, their kingdom could actually live in hope before God.

Now these guys didn't necessarily have the same interests. One was a prince; the other was a shepherd. They didn't necessarily have the same skills or talents or bents. *But they had the same values.* That's at the core of all meaningful friendships, particularly man-to-man. At the core level, at the passion level, at the vision level, they were the same. You don't have to have identical interests or the same kinds of hobbies to be friends.

I have lots of friends here on the staff at Good Shepherd Church, but I'm thinking now of one, Steve, who's probably as different from me as any man in our fellowship. Steve is detail oriented. I don't even know how to spell the word. Steve is competent with numbers. I'm on the verbal side of things. Steve has all daughters. I have all sons. Steve is a specialist with incredible skill. I'm an incurable generalist. Steve is an artist; he can spend hours patiently carving a single piece of wood. I can't even sit still long enough to play a game of tic-tac-toe. We don't have any of the same interests or skills or hobbies or pastimes. *But we are soul mates.* At the VALUES level of our lives, we're walking together step for step. How we want to live well with our wives! How we long to see our children make a difference in a world that's yet to come! We're committed to the same kingdom. We're committed to the same body of Christ. We're committed to the same vision of ministry. He was willing to write off his career in order to be with us here at the church. Our friendship doesn't *require* the same interests or hobbies. It doesn't require listening to the same music, reading the same books, or eating at the same pizza parlor. At the core of who we are, there are shared values. And that is enough.

David and Jonathan both wanted to be part of something that mattered. They wanted to change the way things were where they lived. They wanted to be a part of something bigger than themselves. They owned a flaming desire to serve that greater cause. They wanted to sacrifice together. They wanted to leave a heritage that mattered. They spoke with passion of their futures, their children, and their children's children. They wanted to put their mark on a kingdom, and if necessary to die together for it. Because of their shared values, they were willing to stand together for something much larger than themselves.

That's at the core of friendship. It's much bigger than golf or football. It's much wider and deeper than trout fishing or skiing or woodworking or the Elk's Lodge. It's much more elemental than common interest. It's at the core level of values where we decide we want to do something together no matter what it costs us. That shared dream bonds men together. It's the very essence of meaningful male friendship.

I'm thinking of a scene in the musical, *Les Miserables*. It's in the middle of the French Revolution where a bunch of young men are gathered in a pub the night before a battle. They're students, hardly more than teenagers. But they're part of the Great Revolution, and when daylight comes they must man the barricades. They know they will most likely never see another sunset. And that night...in that little pub...that night before they die together for the principles of the Revolution, they become blood comrades. Brothers. Soul mates. And they sing a song called, "Come Drink with Me." Their song says, in effect, "We're in something bigger than we are and we're in it together. We're willing to pay the price, so we are going to enjoy this last evening together."

Let's sing together. Let's go for it together. Let's die together if that's what it takes. Shared values is at the heart of it all.

2. Unselfish love.

You would have to look long and hard through the pages of scripture—or history—to find a more ringing story of selfless love.

> The soul of Jonathan was knit to the soul of David, and Jonathan loved him as himself.... Then Jonathan made a covenant with David because he loved him as himself. And Jonathan stripped himself of the robe that was on him and gave it to David, with his armor, including his sword and his bow and his belt (1 Samuel 18:1, 3-4).

He was saying in effect, "Son of Jesse, I love what I see in your heart. I'm willing to die with you. Everything I have is yours, and I want to be with you. Take it all." Jonathan, in effect, surrendered the very symbols and emblems of his office. He handed them over to a ruddy young warrior out of the hills who dressed in homespun and spoke with a back-country drawl. The two young men were soul mates from that moment. Unselfish love has incredible bonding power.

I'll never forget an incident many years ago when I was in seminary. I found myself carrying a full academic load, holding down three jobs in different parts of the city, and trying to be a husband to Linda and a daddy to two little boys.

We had nothing. We've never been so poor before or since. We subsisted on smelt (tiny migrating fish) friends caught in the rivers and ten-cent packages of green peas from

Safeway when they had once-a-month stock-the-freezer sales.

Life was very stressful and times were lean...but I had a desire in my heart to go hunting. One of my last acts before I got out of the military was to buy a rifle. I'd never had one of my own, so I found a good deal, spent a chunk of my final paycheck, and got my gun—knowing it would probably be a decade before I could again afford to get one. I had a friend who knew how much I longed to go hunting and how I needed a break from my busy schedule. So we agreed to go hunting together.

No, there wasn't time, and no, there wasn't money. But we went.

I had been so busy and stressed out and overwhelmed before we left that I hadn't even had time to get my rifle sighted in. But I figured, hey, sighting the rifle—and even finding some game—that's the irrelevant part of hunting. It was just getting out in the woods and being there with a friend that really mattered. So I told him that I didn't have time to sight my rifle, but that it didn't really matter. After all, I laughed, I probably couldn't hit anything even if it *was* sighted correctly.

"It's okay, Stu," he said quietly. "I'll do it for you."

So he took my rifle. It was an old Savage seven-millimeter Remington Magnum with no scope on it, just some open sights. He took it to sight it in. Then, a few days later, we piled into our rigs with our wives and took off.

We took two campers. My dad loaned me his camper, and my friend and his wife took theirs, and we headed over the Cascade Mountains for eastern Oregon to go deer hunting. We arrived at our camp site at ten o'clock on a chilly night. I can't describe how good it felt to be out of the city. The star-strewn sky, the deep quiet, and the fragrance of pine trees and sage brush were like a tonic. Before we hit the sack that night, our friends invited us over to their camper for a steaming mug of hot chocolate—and maybe an Oreo or two.

As I sat down at the little table, my friend said casually, "Oh, by the way, I have your gun here."

He brought out my gun and handed it to me. And there, mounted on it, was a shiny new scope, worth more than the rifle itself. It was completely sighted in. Ready to go. My heart was taken, not because of the value of the gift, but because of the value of the *expression.* That particular gesture at that particular moment in my life hit me in a way I can't easily describe. We became a little more bonded at that point, because he had unselfishly given to me without any fanfare or any big deal. There was no mention of it. It was just something he had wanted to do for me, and that was the end of it. But it wasn't the end of it. John Holmlund's spontaneous act of unselfish love has warmed my heart through long years. I will never forget the act, or the friend. We're still hunting together more than twenty years later.

I want you to notice something else in this David-Jonathan friendship. Something that *isn't* there. It's conspicuous by its absence. Jonathan stripped himself of his royal robe and gave it to David along with his sword, bow, and belt. What's missing from that picture? What's not there?

Jealousy.

There is none. There is absolutely no competition or comparison between the two men. Jonathan didn't rehearse his inventory of who he was and what he should have. He just yielded his rights and gave generously to his friend. There is no evidence of comparison.

Friends stand by unselfishly, and we draw strength from that.

I have another friend. I don't see him very much anymore, maybe a couple times a year. But over eighteen years ago, he looked me straight in the eyes and made this statement: "Stu, I want you to listen to me a minute. Someday, somewhere, somehow...you're going to need *something* very much. I don't know when. I don't know what. I don't know why. But I *do* know I want you to call me. I will be there."

That's unselfish love. That's a piton principle you can hang your very life on.

3. Deep loyalty.

The plot of this unforgettable saga thickens when Jonathan's father, King Saul, becomes insanely jealous of young David and tries to remove him from the scene.

Now Saul told Jonathan his son and all his servants to put David to death. But Jonathan, Saul's son, greatly delighted in David. So Jonathan told David saying, "Saul my father is seeking to put you to death. Now therefore, please be on guard in the morning and stay in a secret place and hide yourself.... I will speak with my father about you; if I find out anything, then I shall tell you." Then Jonathan spoke well of David to Saul his father, and said to him, "Do not let the king sin against his servant David, since he has not sinned against you, and since his deeds have been very beneficial to you. For he took his life in his hand and struck the Philistine, and the LORD brought about a great deliverance for all Israel; you saw it and rejoiced. Why then will you sin against innocent blood, by putting David to death without a cause?" (1 Samuel 19:1-5).

Jonathan was saying, "You're jealous, Dad. *I'm* the one who should be jealous. I'm the prince, the heir to the throne, and I'm not jealous or intimidated. I'd give my life for this man. Why can't you open your eyes and see that he's on our side?"

Jonathan's loyalty was so deep he was even willing to defend his friend when face-to-face with his father, the king. Loyalty is absolutely essential to a friendship.

Listen to these verses from 1 Samuel 20. Prince Jonathan was speaking to David.

If it please my father to do you harm, may the LORD do so to Jonathan and more also, if I do not make it known to you and send you away, that you may go in safety. And may the LORD be with you as He has been with my father. And if I am still alive, will you not show me the lovingkindness of the LORD, that I may not die? And you shall not cut off your lovingkindness from my house forever, not even when the LORD cuts off every one of the enemies of David from the face of the earth (vv. 13-15).

Could our friendship live through the generations, David? Even when it's going great for you, when the Lord has done for you all that's in His heart to do, will you remember me? Will you remember my kids after I'm gone?"

And Jonathan made David vow again because of his love for him, because he loved him as he loved his own life (v. 17).

Have you ever said something like this to a friend? "My wife and I have talked about it and we would really be honored—if something ever happened to us—if you would raise our children." You need to consider making that a part of your legal will. What a comfort to hear loyal friends say, "If anything would happen to you and your wife, we'd be honored to have your children. We'd be honored to be part of your future. Our friendship will live through the generations. Let's get it in writing."

Loyalty is something you *express*. You say it out loud. You write it down. It isn't just "understood" in some vague sort of way; it is expressed in a vow, in a covenant, in a promise, in a conversation man-to-man. We need to learn to express it: a complete and total loyalty that says, "You are my brother."

After the death of Hollywood great, Jack Benny, fellow entertainer George Burns had these words to say about his long-time friend. "Jack and I had a wonderful friendship for nearly fifty-five years. Jack never walked out on me when I sang a song, and I never walked out on him when he played the violin. We laughed together. We worked together. We ate together. I suppose that for many of those years, we talked every single day."[1]

A man-to-man friendship says, I'll never walk out on you. Barring unrepentant sin against the Lord God, you'll never be able to do anything that will repulse me or break our fellowship.

4. Real transparency.

We spoke of this "piton" briefly in the previous chapter. There can be no soul-level friendship without it. In 1 Samuel 20:3, David spoke his heart again, saying:

Your father knows well that I have found favor in your sight, and he has said, "Do not let Jonathan know this, lest he be grieved." But truly as the LORD lives and as your soul lives, there is hardly a step between me and death.

In verse 9, Jonathan replies, "Far be it from you! For if I should indeed learn that evil has been decided by my father to come upon you, then would I not tell you about it?" Implication? *Of course I would!*

Verse 41 tells us that "David rose from the south side and fell on his face to the ground, and bowed three times. And they kissed each other and wept together, but David more."

I'll never forget when my brother experienced a season of separation from his lovely and loving wife. Today you would never know that they'd been through those kinds of waters, but there were twenty months early in their marriage when they didn't live together. I remember my brother coming and staying with us at our home. I don't even remember how long it was, but it wasn't long enough. I wouldn't trade those months of closeness and sharing for anything. I remember crying together. I remember rubbing our beards together as we cried. I'd never hugged my brother like that before. I'll never forget it. I don't think he will either.

David and Jonathan were not ashamed to embrace and weep together. They were that genuine with one another. They were that unconcerned with their "image." They expressed their emotions with utter and total transparency.

It was Jesus who said, in effect, to his men: "You know, I used to call you all slaves. I used to call you all servants. I'm not going to do that anymore. I'm going to call you friends, because friends know what's going on with each other. And I'm going to include you in the know" (see John 15:15).

What defines our friendship is the telling of ourselves. The revealing of emotions. David Smith, author of *The Friendless American Male*, writes,

Very early in life, little boys receive the cultural message that they're not supposed to show emotions. Expressing feelings is generally a taboo for males. Boys soon learn to dread the words, "Don't be a sissy; Big boys don't cry; Aren't you a little too old to be sitting on your daddy's lap?" Other messages come through loud and clear—Boys have to learn to be men. And to be a man means you conceal your emotions.[2]

Boys do need to learn to be men. But being a man does not mean concealing your emotions. Part of being a man is real transparency. It's also a piton principle of friendship.

John Powell's classic book, *Why Am I Afraid to Tell You Who I Am?* walks us through some of the degrees of transparency that we need to be alert to. When we're communicating with our friends, there are at least five levels of communication. The **cliché level** is little more than elevator talk. It's a quick "How ya doin'?" without really waiting for the answer. It's a "Whaddya think about this weather?" when you really don't care. The degree of transparency in this sort of communication is practically nil. You can have an exchange like this with total strangers. In fact, this kind of empty chatter serves as a protective relational buffer that *keeps* people total strangers.

Then there's the **fact level** of communication, which is sharing what you know. The degree of transparency is a little more real, but it's still the kind of talk that you can engage in with just about anyone. Do you remember "Dragnet," the old television series? The hard-bitten police lieutenant, Joe Friday, was always interrupting some lady's woeful recitation of her miseries with the monotone line, "Just the facts, ma'am." Facts are the hallmark of this level of conversation. And while facts reveal what you know, they do little to reveal who you are. This sort of talk holds people at arm's length. It doesn't let them in.

Next comes the **opinion level** of communication. This is sharing what you *think*. You're starting to let a little bit of yourself out, but you're still keeping people at a "safe" distance. Yes, there are fewer people you can communicate with on this level, but you really can't build a relationship on opinions. Friendship has to go deeper than that.

When you finally get to the **emotional and transparent levels** of communication, you are actually sharing *who you are*. The degree of transparency greatly increases and the number of people with whom you can share is much smaller. The levels of trust and commitment and bonding take a dramatic upward curve on the friendship chart. That kind of sharing makes for much deeper and stronger relationships.

Emotional communication means conveying hopes and fears and dislikes and aspirations and disappointments and sorrows. It's giving away who you are. It's giving away a part of yourself.

Sometimes we're not very good at this sort of thing because of a false concept of manhood and pride which prevents us from sharing our feelings. Or maybe we have a warped view of spirituality that says, *If I was really a good Christian, I wouldn't feel this way.* That's pure bunk, of course. The New Testament brims with exhortations to humble ourselves, speak truthfully, and to encourage one another along this sometimes bumpy road called "the Christian life."

We need to practice sharing our emotions with other men. So it isn't easy. So what? Who ever said that growth *was* easy? Kent Hughes writes:

> Men, if you're married, your wife must be your most intimate friend, but to say "my wife is my best friend" can be a cop-out. You also need Christian male friends who have a same-sex understanding of the serpentine passages of your heart who will not only offer counsel and pray for you, but will also hold you accountable to your commitments and responsibilities when necessary.[3]

I'll never forget the day, maybe twenty years ago, when my friend interrupted me midsentence. There was steel in his eyes as he looked right into mine. His words were,

"Why don't you just DO IT. It's your JOB as his father." It was a confrontive statement, and it stung…for the moment. Nevertheless, because he was my friend, I had given him the right to say it. His words struck deep and strong, and it made a change in my life.

Transparency is very real, very powerful. When you practice it with a true friend, you will find that friend increasingly drawn to you rather than repulsed. The reason we *don't* tell people what we feel is because we're afraid they won't like us. Yet Scripture says that every temptation you face, every sin you struggle with, every liability that curses your life *is common to man.* We all struggle with the same things, to one degree or another. So everything that's killing you is somewhere in the chest of every man you know. The Bible also says that everything you have that's an asset, an encouragement, a positive trait, *is a gift from God.* Those things being true, none of us have anything to brag or boast about. None of us has anything to feel cast down or destroyed about that is not common to man.

So here we have four principles of friendship. Four principles hammered into the rocky face of daily life. Drive them in deep, Tender Warriors. You never know when you might lose your grip. You never know when you might fall. Real friendship will keep you from hitting the bottom.

THE MATERIAL BELOW WAS
EXCERPTED FROM AN
ARTICLE BY STU WEBER IN
LEADERSHIP JOURNAL

What it Takes to Reach Men

Strengthening the Church's Silent Minority

Several years ago, I watched a local television talk show about men who had attended a seminar with Robert Bly, author of *Iron John*. I thought, *Now I'll get to see what the men's movement is all about. These local guys will give it to me straight.*

But I was stuck by how confused the men were. As if in a recovery group, they shared their stories of disappointment and pain.

But they never got beyond them—except to say, "It's been great sharing."

There must be more to being a healthy man, I thought, *than saying how disappointed you are.*

This yearning has caused the male-identity search to spread to the Christian arena. This year more then 250,000 men participated in Promise Keepers weekends in Boulder, Colorado, and other cities. But this is more than a reaction to prevailing secular winds. This Christian men's movement is an artesian well bursting through all the loose places on the surface of our country. It's a gusher not created by human engineering. It's nothing less than the Spirit of God at work.

I've always wondered why the church had such tremendous ministries to women, students, and children but nothing to men. When I connect with other guys, I feel fulfilled, vision-oriented, energetic. As I saw what was happening in our culture, a dream began to take shape: Wouldn't it be great to gather a hundred guys who enjoyed being men? And wouldn't it be great to do it in the local church?

RIGHT TIME, RIGHT PLACE

Not knowing where to begin, I decided to preach a series on the family and to start with men. What began as three messages on what it means to be a man turned out to be eight. I can't explain why, but the topic connected powerfully with our congregation. The feeling on those Sunday mornings was electric. I could sense people leaning forward to listen.

The normal number of requests for sermon tapes (from our homespun tape ministry) was thirty or forty per week. The weeks I spoke on the principles of masculinity, the requests shot up to three hundred (which says more about their hunger than about my preaching). But I couldn't continue preaching about men forever.

As an aside, on the last Sunday, I said, "I'll be here at the church next Saturday morning at 9:00. If you're a man and you're interested in discussing more on what it means to be a man, show up then, and we'll talk some more."

You have to understand what I had just asked of our men. Oregon and Washington are the forty-ninth and fiftieth states in church attendance per capita. This is a put-me-on-my-acreage-and-let-me-be-a-pioneer culture. Saturday mornings are especially sacrosanct in Oregon. I expected maybe ten or twelve guys.

The next Saturday, three hundred men showed up. I was flabbergasted. We stayed till noon, and before everyone left, I said, "We're going to start a men's ministry. You're telling us that much."

PREPARE, PREPARE, PREPARE

Something worthwhile is worth getting ready for. In creating a ministry to men, we did not want a false start. The quickest way to a false start was to say, "Let's get on the bandwagon and get some guys together and have a few donuts and see how long we can last."

Something substantive would take leadership.

But I knew I couldn't lead the ministry. As a pastor, I was too busy already. I began to pray and committed myself to find two or three lay leaders with the vision.

Two guys in their upper thirties, who were best buddies, emerged. One is more an up front person; the other more behind-the-scenes. Both are rock-solid believers, and their friendship has been a salvation in rough water, so they understand the power of male friendship.

Those two lay leaders, a staff pastor who would oversee the ministry, and I attended a Promise Keepers weekend in Boulder, Colorado. The rally and worship with fifty thousand men were breathtaking; the spiritual fireworks were spectacular. The most helpful part, though, was the three-day leadership conference prior to the weekend rally. The training provided us with the vision for our ministry.

During that week, our group kept saying, "This is great, but how would this fit in our church?" We didn't want to copy Promise Keepers, though that organization provided some excellent resource material; we wanted to be Good Shepherd Community Church. God changes history when the little people in the little places do what they should. We wanted to be God's men in little Gresham.

So, we looked a little further and dug a little deeper. We also profited greatly from Cross Trainer in Des Moines, Iowa, a ministry that has effectively brought together men from many denominations.

TAKING THE HIGH GROUND

The fall before our January kickoff, we invited twelve to fifteen men to a series of planning meetings. Some were senior-aged men, some in their middle forties, and some CEO-types, some blue-collar men. They helped us form our purpose and our plans for a kickoff event.

Our culture keeps punching at men. We felt the best way to motivate a man is to point to the high ground and say, "That's what the Lord wants of us, and none of us is there yet. Let's lock arms and lean into the wind and climb that mountain together."

We didn't want to heap guilt on men or pressure them into accountability groups. The key for us was affirmation and acceptance: Let's learn to be men together. Our purpose statement: to point men to the High Ground of God's intentions in their relationship with him, with one another, in their homes, their church, and their world by providing biblical teaching, strong encouragement, motivating challenges, and mutual accountability.

For the kickoff, we landed a well-known speaker for a Friday night and Saturday conference. Men lined up to register ahead of time. We even sold gift certificates to the women in our church, saying, "Guys, this is what we're planning (a bunch of us are coming). By the way—daughters, wives, moms—if you want your guy to be here, pay for it and give the registration certificate as a gift."

Men responded, and a surprisingly large number showed up for the kickoff event held in our church.

PLATOONING

It's okay to go to a battalion meeting, but most combat takes place in the platoons. At the end of our opening weekend, we announced, "We're going to get together every Tuesday morning at 6:15 at the church." In our planning phase, we had decided we needed to funnel the men into smaller groups, but we wanted to offer them freedom to make that decision at their own pace.

We called these Tuesday morning meetings "High Ground" because we live in Oregon where everybody loves to go to the mountains. Here is how we did it last spring:

From 6:15 to 6:30, men arrive and hung out, eating donuts (non-fat, of course) and drinking coffee. From 6:30 to 6:55, an instructor, usually I or another staff member, taught. One morning, for example, I told about one of my best friends who died, while I knelt beside him in the woods, on opening morning of hunting season in Oregon. He left behind a seventeen-year-old son, a thirteen-year-old daughter, and an eight-year-old son. I asked the question, "Now that his life was over, what had he done that really mattered?" In his case, he'd left a powerful legacy. He was committed wholeheartedly both to his family and to God's family.

After the twenty-five minute talk, we dismissed the group, giving the men four options:

Leave. Some men need to get to work; others were not yet comfortable with the intimacy of a smaller group. We'd say, "It's not even 7:00 A.M.; you can still get to work on time. But if you'd like to stay, here are other options, which will take only thirty minutes."

Attend a newcomers' group. This is an informal time when men get oriented to the group, meet leaders, and ask questions.

Attend a "Bull Pen." These are informal groups (ten to fifteen men each) offering the opportunity to discuss the morning's topic. Men can just sit and soak in the conversation or jump into the discussion. Each group has a leader with prepared questions from the morning's talk.

Join a 4-A Team. These groups of two to five men meet once a week (on Tuesday mornings or at another time). This is clearly the next level of commitment, and we want all our men to end up here. We tell them that the highest ground is deep friendship with another man.

The goal is to become accountable with the other members of the 4-A team. The understood rule: confidentiality, which allows men to talk about tough issues.

The next Tuesday after our kick-off weekend, more than a third of those conference attendees showed up bright and early. We met every Tuesday morning until the first of June. (In Oregon, summers are off limits. You don't fight it; you join it.)

LEARNING TO SWIM

Our ministry to men is young; we're just wading into the water. But several principles have helped us.

Model both failure and conviction. Last spring, I told our men one of my big failures with my first-born son:

"I had never been a dad before; my son had never been a son before; we were going to school together. One time he made the mistake of violating the two rules of my home of origin: Don't sass your mom; don't sass your dad. When he did, my hand 'involuntarily' hit him in the chest. I say involuntarily because it happened before I knew it was happening. I knocked him backward over the couch.

"As he fell, I realized what I had done, so I fell with him. As we lay on the ground, I began crying and said, 'Could you possibly forgive me?'"

That story provided a teaching moment for our men. Father failures, leadership failures, husband failures—every man has failed, so they can identify with failure. Men's speakers must be able to say, "Here's what happened to me. I often blow it."

But transparency isn't enough; you have to model open conviction, the commitment to grow beyond the failure and in Christ. Both emphases must be there.

Know the men you're trying to reach. We continually remind our men that they have a choice; we want them to move to the 4-A teams, but they might need to test the waters, and they might not end up staying on the first 4-A Team they choose. Some men's ministries, however, demand high commitment up front. For instance, men won't be allowed to attend unless they bring at least one friend and commit to attending each session for the entire year.

The difference in commitment is the result of a difference, I believe, in culture. A more white-collar congregation might rise to an up front call for high-level commitment; they may not feel threatened by it because, as CEO-types, they've been taking on challenges their entire lives.

But for other congregations, a more open-ended approach, where men are allowed to proceed at their own pace, seems to work better. The point is, each church needs to evaluate its locale in order to create the right program to reach its men.

One myth of men's ministry is that men won't join. They will join, if it's not forced and if the cause is big enough.

Ease men into deeper relationships. We tell the men in our 4-A teams to temper their expectations, that it is not a miracle group. It's a group of guys committed to one another's best interests. It's not a pass-fail test.

At the beginning of each new group we suggest that the men make a list of four questions, personal and specific, they want to be asked each week. Then, they may hand that list to someone in their group the next time they meet.

This helps to short-circuit the awkwardness that can plague the early stages of intimacy. And it allows for those incredibly bonding "Oh, you too? I thought I was the only one" kind of moments.

Speak to their issues. It sounds obvious, but men need to hear about men. We try to speak to the issue of fathering, for example. Recently, to do that, I told our men about my youngest boy:

"My youngest son is the third of three boys. The first two are high-powered; the third is not any less high-powered, but he's the third out of three. By the time you've had a brother who's All-Conference this and another brother who's All-Conference that, there's not much left for you to do.

"As a father, I worried about our caboose. He is the most sensitive of the three. To encourage him, I spent a lot of time with him in the outdoors—camping, hunting, fishing. Anybody who has spent time in the outdoors knows that a pocketknife is essential gear—the man with the best blade gets the job done. So, whenever you're setting up camp, you're always looking for the knife.

"My son Ryan had a pocketknife that became his identity. His older brothers always had to ask him to use the knife as we were setting up camp. That became his status in the tribe. He was the man with the blade.

"My birthday came around one year, and my family was planning a party for me. Earlier in the afternoon, my youngest walked into my office at home where I was studying. At first I didn't hear him; I felt him—I could sense his presence—and I turned around.

"He had chosen this moment because he wanted to give me a birthday present, but not at the birthday party. He wanted it to be just me and him. He handed me a present, and I opened it—it was his knife. As my eyes lifted to his, his eyes looked into mine. This was one of these rare moments when the spirit meets the spirit, with no verbal way to communicate adequately the deep feeling between you."

The story provided the foundation for other men to ask questions about their father and how they're fathering.

Train leaders. C. S. Lewis wrote, "It is painful, being a man, to have to assert the privilege, or the burden, which Christianity lays upon my sex. I am crushingly aware of how inadequate most of us are, on our actual and historical individualities, to fill the place prepared for us."

We believe the leaders of men must be men who are confident of their masculinity. Our leaders must be able to answer the question, "What does it mean to be a man?" If a leader can't answer that, he certainly can't help other men celebrate their masculinity.

For us, the answer to that question lies in the Creation account and other key scriptures. We believe God holds a man responsible for those near and dear to him. A married man is called to give himself up so his wife can be the woman God intended her to be.

In addition, male leaders must be secure enough in the grace of God to share their failures because that's what opens up the hearts of men.

MODELING MASCULINITY

Garrison Keillor says manhood, once an opportunity for achievement, is now an obstacle to be overcome. That's why today, more than ever, men need to know masculinity is to be celebrated. They'll follow anybody who says, "I'm glad you're a man, and I respect you for being one."

A pastor doesn't have to be the athletic, outdoor type to lead men. The real muscle of a man is not on his shoulders or in his biceps. It's in his heart, in his character.

One man I would follow to the ends of the earth, in fact, has always doubted his masculinity. His father never approved of him, and his mother was a perfectionist. But I'd follow that guy anywhere because he's authentic, a man who is committed in his heart to do right by God.

That kind of modeling gives men permission to be men. They want to know it's not only okay to be a man, it's critical to be a man. That's what it takes to reach men.

Chapter 2

1. C. S. Lewis, *The Four Loves* (New York: Harcourt & Brace Jovanovich, 1960), 104-105.

2. Ibid.

Chapter 3

1. *New York Times,* complete source unknown.

2. Ibid.

3. Mortimer B. Zuckerman, "Where Have Our Values Gone?" *U.S. News and World Report,* 8 August 1994, 88.

4. Charles Colson, "The Thomas Hearings and the New Gender Wars," *Christianity Today,* 25 November 1991, 72.

5. Chuck Swindoll, *The Strong Family* (Portland, Ore.: Multnomah Press, 1991), 26.

6. Gordon Dalbey, *Healing the Masculine Soul* (Irving, Tex.: Word, 1988), 9-10.

7. *Psychology Today,* complete source unknown.

8. Natalie Angier, *New York Times,* 17 May 1994, B5.

9. Robert Bly, *Iron John* (New York: Addison-Wesley Publishing Co., Inc., 1990), 146.

Chapter 4

1. C. S. Lewis, *The Four Loves,* 98.

2. As told in Dale Carnegie, *How to Win Friends and Influence People* (New York: Pocket Books, 1981, revised edition), 57.

3. Eilleen Rockefeller Growald and Allan Luks, "Beyond Self," *American Health,* March 1988, 51.

4. Robert Fulghum, *Uh-Oh* (New York: Random House, 1991), 59-61.

Chapter 5

1. "Rangers' Raid: A Valorous Failure," *The Oregonian,* 25 October 1993, A1.

2. "The Ranger Credo," *The Oregonian,* 25 October 1993, A1.

3. John Leo, "The PC Attack on Heroism," *U.S. News and World Report,* 31 October 1994, 36.

Chapter 7

1. Jack Hayford, *A Man's Starting Place* (Van Nuys: Living Way Ministries, 1992), 12.

2. Ibid., 58.

3. Quoted in *Leadership*, Fall 1992, 47.

4. C. Norman Kraus, *The Community of the Spirit* (Grand Rapids: William B. Eerdmans Pub. Co., 1974), 55-56.

5. Note from author: In a sermon years ago, I used this quote from Dr. Robert Webber but neglected to note the source at the time. When I am able to identify it, I will include it in subsequent printings.

6. Note from author: In a sermon years ago, I used this quote from Ed Dayton but neglected to note the source at the time. When I am able to identify it, I will include it in subsequent printings.

Chapter 8

1. The terms; "Acceptance", "Affirmation", "Accountability", and "Authority" were originally used during a pastors seminar entitled "Resolving Personal and Spiritual Conflicts" presented by Dr. Neil T. Anderson of Freedom in Christ Ministries; La Habra, CA. These concepts inspired Denny Deveny (and in turn, me) to further develop and adapt them for "Milestones on the Friendship Highway".

2. Frederick M. Lehman, © 1817. Renewed 1945 by Nazarene Publishing House.

Chapter 11

1. Miles J. Stanford, *The Green Letters* (Grand Rapids: Zondervan, 1975), 13.

Chapter 12

1. Quoted in Mary Farrar, *Choices* (Sisters, Ore.: Multnomah Books, 1994), 57.

2. Ibid., 26-30.

3. Ibid., 52.

4. Ibid.

5. Note from author: Years ago I quoted this statement in a sermon, but (never anticipating a later book) did not record the source. If the reader can provide me the original source (was it Ed Stewart?), I'd

happily include it in any subsequent printings.

6. Quoted from speech by George H. Gallup, Jr., "The Healing of America," Small Groups Conference at Eastern College in St. Davids, Pennsylvania, 2 June 1995.

7. Ibid.

8. Ibid.

9. Gretel Ehrlich, "The Solace of Open Places," as quoted in Joseph F. Trimmer, *Writing with a Purpose*, (Dallas: Houghton Miffin, Co., 1992), 134-135.

10. Will Durant, *The Life of Greece* (New York: Simon and Schuster, 1966), 235-236.

11. Julius Segal, "Conquering Crisis—Lessons from Captivity," *Reader's Digest*, March 1982, 139-140.

Chapter 13

1. Linda Weber, *Mom, You're Incredible!* (Colorado Springs: Focus on the Family Publishing, 1994), 51-53.

Chapter 14

1. Rousas John Rushdoony, "Inheritance, Barbarism, and Dominion," *Chalcedon Report* 16-17.

Appendix A
Real Men Stand Together

1. Michael E. McGill, *The McGill Report on Male Intimacy* (N.Y.: Holt, Rinehart and Winston, 1985), 157-58.

2. As cited in R. Kent Hughes, *Disciplines of a Godly Man* (Wheaton: Crossway Books, 1991), 59.

3. Patrick Morley, *The Man in the Mirror* (Brentwood: Wolgemuth & Hyatt, 1989), 117.

4. As cited in Dr. Ron Jenson, "High Ground Perspectives" (audio tape series), San Diego, Calif., Summer 1992.

5. Harold G. Moore and Joseph L. Galloway, *We Were Soldiers Once...and Young* (New York: Random House, 1992), xiv.

6. Charles Sell as cited by Dr. Ron Jenson, "High Ground Perspectives."

7. David W. Smith, *The Friendless American Male* (Ventura: Regal Books, 1983), 15.

8. Ibid.

9. Ibid.

10. From Stu: "Try as I may, I was unable to locate the original source of this mimeographed handout."

Locking Arms

1. Dr. Ron Jenson, "High Ground Perspectives" (audio tape series), San Diego, Calif., Summer 1992.

2. David W. Smith, *The Friendless American Male* (Ventura: Regal Books, 1983), 14.

3. R. Kent Hughes, *Disciplines of a Godly Man* (Wheaton: Crossway Books, 1991), 61.

For conference or speaking information contact Stu Weber at:

Stu Weber

2229 N.E. Burnside, #212

Gresham, Oregon 97030